ŚABDA

A Study of Bhartṛhari's
Philosophy of Language

ŚABDA

A Study of Bhartṛhari's Philosophy of Language

Tandra Patnaik

DK PRINTWORLD
Publishers of Indian Traditions

Cataloging in Publication Data — DK
Courtesy: D.K. Agencies (P) Ltd. <docinfo@dkagencies.com>

Patnaik, Tandra, author.
Śabda : a study of Bhartṛhari's philosophy of language / Tandra Patnaik.
pages cm
Reprint of: Second revised and enlarged edition, 2007.
Includes bibliographical references and index.
ISBN 9788124604083

1. Bhartṛhari. Vākyapadīya. 2. Sanskrit language – Grammar. 3. Sanskrit language – Semantics. I. Title.

LCC PK541.B483P37 2019 | DDC 491.25 23

ISBN 978-81-246-0408-3
First Published in India in 1994
Second revised and enlarged edition, 2007
Reprinted in 2019

Printed and published by:
D.K. Printworld (P) Ltd.
Regd. Office: 'Vedaśrī', F-395, Sudarshan Park
(Metro Station: ESI Hospital), New Delhi - 110015
Phones: (011) 2545 3975, 2546 6019
e-mail: indology@dkprintworld.com
Website: www.dkprintworld.com

for
Priyadarshi

Four are the definite grades of speech
The learned and wise know them
Three of these are deposited in secret
They indicate no meaning to the common man,
Men speak the fourth grade of speech
Which is phonetically expressed

— ***Ṛgveda*, I.164, 45**

Foreword

THE intellectual climate for interdisciplinary research is almost non-existent in India. Under these circumstances a book on Bhartṛhari — which requires competence in philosophy, grammar as well as Sanskritic studies — is not a mean achievement. Dr Tandra Patnaik deserves special encomium for filling up a major gap in knowledge.

Present-day philosophy gives considerable attention to the distinction between the knowable and the sayable, to what is said and what is meant and to the distinction between the semantics of ordinary day-to-day discourse and the literary discourse. Dr Patnaik has assessed herself to all these questions besides giving a lucid exposition of the *sphoṭa* theory.

In the developmental history of philosophical thought in the West, it was only in the post-Fregean period that philosophy of language was recognized as the starting point of the study of philosophy. As Matilal points out, "The philosophy of language was a part of Indian philosophical activity from the beginning of its history." (Matilal, Bimal Krishna : *The Word and the World*, p. 4.) *Vyākaraṇa* (grammar) is one of the six *vedāṅgas* (auxiliary or preparatory disciplines for the study of Veda). A strong and continuous grammatical tradition exists in India from the days of Pāṇini, although Pāṇini mentions several grammarians prior to him. In the West critical concern with grammar is a recent phenomenon. Whether it is Sir William Jones laying the historical foundation of the study of Indo-European, Bloomfield laying the foundation of American Structuralism, or Chomsky fathering Generative Linguistics, all have acknowledged the contribution of Pāṇini. In the field of aesthetics the Western scholars are anticipated by Indian scholars centuries ago. The theory of Crowe Ransom that poetry is language was anticipated by Rudraṭa's statement *nanu śabḍārtham kāvyam* (poetry is language) and by Kuntaka's identification of word and meaning. The Western scholars were ignorant of the rich Indian philosophical, grammatical and aesthetic traditions. The imposition of colonialism not only led them to propagate Western supremacy but also made us subservient to Western thinking.

In the chapter "The Word and the Meaning" Dr Patnaik discusses words vs. sentence cognition and language, ordinary meaning and what is shown but not said in language. In this presentation she succeeds in suggesting the interconnectedness between the ordinary grammatical meaning and the profound aesthetic meaning.

The present book is a commendable introduction to India's contribution to the study of language and the interconnectedness of approaches to linguistics, philosophy, logic and aesthetics in ancient India. It is a seminal contribution to contemporary concerns of reading ancient texts in linguistics and philosophy. To the extent it is accepted by linguists and philosophers, it would have proved its merit.

Dr D.P. Pattanayak
Former Director
Central Institute of Indian Languages, Mysore

Preface to the Second Edition

Fourteen years back, when this book was published, I was full of apprehensions about the interest the work could generate in the readers' mind. I had some tangible reasons for such uneasiness — Why should a reader be interested in a philosophical viewpoint dating back to fifth century and more importantly, in a philosopher who himself has not been accorded the status of a *philosopher* by his own tradition? I clearly remember that many of my friends and well-wishers in the academic circle had dissuaded me from the misadventure of undertaking Bhartṛharian study when I got seriously involved in the work some time in 1980's. But in the last decade there has been a sudden spurt of interest in the philosophy of language of Bhartṛhari, especially after B.K. Matilal's *The Word and the World* was published. During these fourteen years, since the publication of my book, many National and International seminars have been organized on the philosophy of Bhartṛhari in which philosophers and academicians have taken active interest. With this change of attitude I feel assured that the Bhartṛhari has finally been ensconced more as a Dārśanika than a Vaiyākaraṇika.

I had grounds to feel happy when my publisher Shri Susheel K. Mittal of D.K. Printworld sought my permission for bringing out a second edition of the book. I took this opportunity to revise some of the chapters. All these years, since the publication of my book, I have been studying some new materials on philosophy of language and philosophical psychology. In the course of my reading I have always wondered how Bhartṛhari would have faced the issues raised by these new breed of philosophers. Keeping this in mind I have incorporated some changes as well as some additions in the fifth and sixth chapter of my original book.

In the fifth chapter entitled "Language and Communication," while discussing the views of the modern Western philosophers on the problem speaker's intention and the conditions of its communicability, I decided to add Kent Bach's very insightful theory of "conversational implicature" along with the views of Wittgenstein, Austin, Grice and Searle. The sixth chapter of the original book entitled "Language and Thought" has been totally reformulated keeping in mind the recent discussions on philosophy of mind as well as philosophical psychology. Besides, I thought it necessary to place in the appendix two more chapters that I believed to be relevant for understanding Bhartṛhari's philosophy of language. I have placed them separately as my approach is slightly different here. In these two chapters I have tried to look at Bhartṛhari from within the tradition to bring to light the radicalism of his approach to the issues and concepts that have played an important role in our own version of philosophy of language. Let me cite a case as illustration. In the Indian tradition of philosophy of language, the problem of communication of meaning has been investigated mostly from the hearer's angle. So the concept of *śabdabodha* (the hearer's understanding of language) have been given more emphasis. Bhartṛhari, on the other hand, prefers to approach the problem of the communicability of meaning from the speaker's angle.

I owe a lot to Susheel K. Mittal, the young and enthusiastic man at the helm of D.K. Printworld. He never allows one to be careless and complacent. His flare for perfectionism, accuracy and awareness of various subjects is praiseworthy. I am extremely grateful to him for all that he has done for the wide circulation of the first edition of my book. I also owe my gratitude to all those readers who took interest in my work.

15 December, 2006 **Tandra Patnaik**

Preface to the First Edition

ARISTOTLE defined man as a social animal. But Bhartṛhari would have liked to define man as a "languageing" animal. For he says: "It is the speech which prompts all mankind into activity. Without this power man is nothing more than a log of wood or a piece of stone." (*Vākyapadīya* I.127). In fact, the ways Aristotle and Bhartṛhari define man are complementary. Man cannot live without a society; and hence society is no society without the bond of linguistic communication. Therefore language is the anchor-sheet of man's individual and social existence. This realization has prompted the philosophers, both in the East and the West, to view "language" as an important concept for philosophical speculation. In India, there is a rich tradition of philosophical discussion on the nature of language. But Bhartṛhari's treatise *Vākyapadīya* stands out as an unique attempt at a comprehensive philosophy of language.

The exact period during which Bhartṛhari lived is still not clear. One comes across varied estimations of the period. But on the basis of some standard evidences the time can be fixed somewhere between CE 450 to 500. He belonged to the Grammarian tradition of Pāṇini and Patañjali. But he transcended the limits of grammar and language analysis set by his predecessors to develop a very original philosophy of language.

Unfortunately, in the philosophical circles Bhartṛhari is a much neglected figure. He is sidetracked either as a linguist or a mystic. Such contrasting pair of epithets seem quite incongruous. A linguist cannot afford to indulge in mysticism; nor can a mystic come down to the level of empirical analysis of language. Such distorted versions of Bhartṛhari's philosophical contributions prompted me to attempt an unbiased study of his work. And this made me realize that Bhartṛhari's insightful analysis of the concept of language can stand up to the challenges faced by the modern philosophers. So I decided to present this ancient philosophy of language in modern idiom — often comparing notes with the new ways of handling the issues relating to "language." I strongly feel that all that is a matter of antiquity need not be obsolete. Rather the present is always enriched by the wisdom of the past. As Bhartṛhari himself remarks, "the Goddess of learning does not smile on those who neglect the past." (*anupāsīta-vṛddhāṇāṁ vidyā nāti prasīdati*) [*Vākyapadīya* II.485]. Besides, in philosophy we do not discover new truths with advancement of time, as it happens in case of natural sciences. In this context Jayanta Bhaṭṭa, another ancient Indian philosopher, offers us this crucial wisdom about doing philosphy. He says, "we cannot discover a new truth in philosophy, but we can do something novel by presenting the old truths propounded by ancients in modern terminology." (*kuto vā nūtanaṁ vastu vayaṁ utprekṣitum kṣamāḥ* । *vācovinayasavaicitrāmatraṁ atra vicārayatām.*) ।। [*Nyāya-Mañjarī, Āhnika* 1.8]. It is no wonder, then, that the issues handled by Bhartṛhari still continue to haunt the modern philosophers. The problems are old; maybe the approaches to them are new. Therefore an understanding of Bhartṛhari's philosophy may prove rewarding. Within the limited scope of this book many important dimensions of Bhartṛhari's work have been left out. I sincerely hope the new generation of scholars will take interest in them and come forward to explore them.

My fulfilment of the long cherished dream of publishing this book on Bhartṛhari could be possible because of my association with three outstanding scholars — Prof. G. Misra, Prof. B.K. Matilal and Dr D.P. Pattanayak. My Guru Prof. G. Misra not only taught me how to do philosophy but also the difficult art of facing the challenges of life. I cannot forget the amount of enthusiasm he had shown when I started my work on Bhartṛhari. I learnt the art of presenting the ancient Indian philosophy in contemporary idiom from reading late Prof. B.K. Matilal's works. Though I never had the opportunity of meeting him in person, he had been very prompt in answering my queries on the topic. A decade ago, Dr D.P. Pattanayak, the then Director of Central Institute of Indian Languages, Mysore, suggested to me to study Bhartṛhari. And once I started taking interest in the subject he has been constantly encouraging me to write a book on Bhartṛhari. Like a true mentor he has never allowed me to slacken the pace of my work. I pay my obeisance to these three great personalities. I salute all those great scholars like K.A.S. Iyer, G.N. Sastri, T.R.V. Murti, H. Coward, John Brough, R.C. Pandeya and many others who have kept the interest of the scholars alive in Bhartṛhari studies through their monumental works.

My special thanks to my publishers M/s. D.K. Printworld. Their constant encouragement and constructive suggestions have provided me the necessary boost to complete the work.

Tandra Patnaik

Contents

Abbreviations

Vāk / VP	:	*Vākyapadīya*
PI	:	*Philosophical Investigations*
Tractatus	:	*Tractatus Logico-Philosophicus*

1

Philosophy of Language
Its Scope and Limits

The Linguistic Turn

WHAT is language? What is meaning? How do we communicate our thoughts through words? How does the language function? What is truth? Many such "language"-related questions have largely occupied philosopher's attention for the last few decades. Gilbert Ryle calls this phenomenon "occupational disease"[1] of twentieth-century philosophy. However, it will be too much to say that philosophical activity of the century is largely confined to the narrow boundaries of "language"-related issues. Still there is a trend of philosophy which flourishes and will continue to flourish as long as men continue to meditate on their moral nature and situation. The philosophical reflections found in the writings of Sartre, Heidegger and Nietzsche and, the latest addition to the list is surprisingly enough, Wittgenstein (latest publication *Culture and Value*) belong to this category. What distinguishes the twentieth-century philosophy from what has been done in the name of philosophy since time immemorial is the "linguistic turn" it took in 1930s. The philosophical scene since then is dominated by those figures who prefer to call themselves "linguistic analysts." They claim that their avowed task is philosophical analysis of language. However, there is no unanimity in their practice of going about their job of philosophical analysis of language. So one comes across varied forms of philosophical activities under the titles of

1. Gilbert Ryle, *Collected Papers*, II, London : Hutchinson and Co. Ltd., 1973, p. 150.

"linguistic philosophy," "philosophical logic" and "philosophy of language." It sometimes appears quite difficult to demarcate their exact areas of operation.

Linguistic philosophy, primarily, is the name of a method — a method of solving and de-solving the classical philosophical problems by paying attention to the ways in which certain philosophical concepts are used. Moore's analysis of the statements about the external world, Russell's analysis of definite description, Ryle's analysis of the concept of mind, Ayer's analysis of the concept of perception, etc. are some of the examples of this new way of doing philosophy. Later on, it branched off to a different way of looking at a philosopher's job, i.e. the philosopher as a therapist. He undertakes to cure intellectual disorders created by muddled use of concepts. Wittgenstein says: "The philosopher's treatment of a question is like the treatment of an illness."[2] The "traditional" philosophers get entangled in problems when they allow the concepts to "idle" and get detached from their actual use. So "what **we** do is to bring words back from their metaphysical to their everyday use,"[3] says Wittgenstein summing up the nature of the therapy.

Philosophical logic, on the other hand, is not the name of a method but a special approach to philosophical understanding. Broadly speaking, it "considers the vocabulary of logic. What constitutes a statement, in what 'logical form' consists or implication or entailment or disjunction or modality . . ."[4] It aims at finding out the "logic" of propositions, of truth, of reference, of predication. Wittgenstein of *Tractatus Logico Philosophicus*, Russell, Frege, Strawson, Grice, all the adherents of philosophical logic try to explicate the logical structure of language and the issues related to proposition, truth, reference, etc. in their own

2. L. Wittgenstein, *Philosophical Investigations,* London: Basil and Blackwell, 1978, p. 255.
3. Ibid., p. 116.
4. John Passmore, *Recent Philosophers : A Supplement to Hundred Years of Philosophy*, London: Duckworth, 1985, p. 6.

ways. Russell even goes to the extent of saying that philosophical logic **is** the philosophy. However, in later phases, this approach was extended to unfold the "logic of morality," the "logic of religion," the "logic of justice," etc. The most important example of this specialized version of philosophical logic is R.M. Hare's analysis of the nature of most general moral concepts to demarcate the structure of moral argument and moral assertions.

Philosophy of language is considered to be distinct from philosophical logic in the sense that it does not aim at providing a structural geography of any and every concept. Philosophy of language, as the name suggests, exclusively deals with the basic principles of "language" and the concepts associated with the general forms of language. In a certain sense, it does not appear to be very different from the strict and original version of philosophical logic. According to Searle — one of the chief exponents of philosophy of language, it aims "to give philosophically illuminating description of certain general features of language."[5] Philosophy of language proposes to deal with issues such as meaning, truth, reference, necessity, etc. Searle also clearly indicates that philosophy of language should not be confused with linguistics. According to him "linguistics attempts to describe the actual structures — phonological, syntactical and semantic — of natural human languages."[6] Though philosophy of language draws its data from natural human languages, yet its theories and conclusions are supposed to be true of any **possible** language. Philosophy of language in short, deals with **language**, not **languages**.

However, the development of thoughts during the last two decades shows that the boundaries between linguistic philosophy, philosophical logic, philosophy of language and linguistics are gradually becoming fluid. Linguistic philosophy as a method of conceptual analysis is not opposed to the rest. One can apply the

5. John Searle, *Speech-Acts : An Essay in the Philosophy of Language*, Cambridge : Cambridge University Press, 1969, p. 2.

6. Ibid.

method of linguistic analysis while doing philosophical logic or philosophy of language. But the areas of philosophy of language, linguistics and philosophical logic mostly criss-cross each other. J.J. Passmore while assessing the post-Wittgensteinian developments in his book *Recent Philosophers* observes that, "Philosophical logic fades into philosophy of language and that . . . into linguistics."[7] The present science of linguistics, especially the Chomskian model of understanding it, incorporates within its scope much of what was counted as philosophy of language. Therefore, in the present context with overlapping of boundaries amongst specialized areas of study of language one can broadly say that philosophy of language stands for understanding the structural principles of "how language functions."

The Indian Viewpoint

In case of Indian philosophical developments we notice that the inquisitiveness about "language" as a concept is as old as Indian culture itself. By saying so, I don't claim that in Western thought the concept of language and meaning was not discussed at all prior to the twentieth-century "linguistic turn." Plato made significant contributions to the analysis of "meaning" through his theory of "Ideas." But subsequently it never drew that much of attention. J.F. Staal while writing on "Sanskrit Philosophy of Language" very aptly observes: "at times almost excessive preoccupation with language on the one hand and with philosophy on the other, may indeed be regarded as a characteristic of Indian Civilization."[8] The comment is justified in the sense that *Ṛgveda,* one of the oldest scriptures of India, contains innumerable insightful remarks about the nature of language (*śabda*) and speech (*vāk*). The subsequent scriptures and texts are full of elaborate discussions on the concept of language and its purpose. Of course, the nature of the discussion is largely determined by the cultural

7. Passmore, *Recent Philosophers*, p. 6.
8. Quoted in B.K. Matilal, *The Word and the World*, Delhi: Oxford University Press, 1990, p. 5.

and philosophical tradition of the time. We must be fully aware of the fact that such deliberations occur several centuries back in time. At the same time, the area of discourse and the scope of discussion has many things common with the modern version of the philosophy of language. The varied philosophical systems that flourished in ancient India concentrate on certain common themes, such as the problem of meaning, word-world relationship, speaker-hearer relationship, the formal conditions of language and communicability, etc.

Most of the philosophical systems of India take up the problem of language as a part of their epistemological concern, otherwise known as *pramāṇa śāstra*. As is well known, they draw a clear line of distinction between *jñāna* (roughly translated, it means "cognition") and *pramā* (knowledge). While analysing the concept of *pramā* they categorise different methods or means of knowledge (*pramāṇa*). However, there is no unanimity of views regarding the number of such valid methods of knowledge. Some like Pūrva Mīmāṁsā and Vedānta, admit of six methods — *pratyakṣa* (perception), *anumāna* (inference), *upamāna* (comparison), *arthāpatti* (postulation), *anupalabdhi* (non-apprehension) and *śabda* (verbality); whereas Cārvāka accepts only the method of *pratyakṣa* as valid. So it is obvious that all the schools of thought do not accord independent status to *śabda* as a *pramāṇa*. Nyāya, Mīmāṁsā, Vedānta, Sāṁkhya are such systems which admit the validity of *śabda-pramāṇa* and carry on elaborate discussions on the nature of language and its functions. In this connection it may be noted that though Buddhism does not offer the status of independent *pramāṇa* to *śabda*, a very powerful analysis of the concept of language and meaning is found in Buddhistic literature. The *apoha* theory of meaning, advocated by Buddhist logicians Diṅnāga and Dharmakīrti, is unique and novel in many respects. I intend to refer to this theory in a separate chapter.

Does Śabda-Pramāṇa mean Scriptural Authority?

Śabda-pramāṇa, broadly translated means the linguistic method of obtaining knowledge (both, oral and written); and is distinctively different from the other methods of knowledge. Unlike the methods of perception, inference, etc., facts and sense-objects do not form the basis of such knowledge. As a linguistic means of knowledge its object is language itself. However, the traditional interpretation found in innumerable English books on the subject leaves us with the impression that it means nothing more than knowledge based on some form of "authority." The term *śabda-pramāṇa* is very often translated as "verbal authority," which tends to shift the emphasis from the linguistic aspect to the "authoritative" aspect of the theory. Of course, these interpreters have their own justification because some of the definitions confirm their views. But here it seems to be a case of going by the letter than the spirit of what has been discussed within the scope of *śabda-pramāṇa*. To justify this point we need to examine very briefly what the different schools of Indian philosophy state about *śabda-pramāṇa*.

Gotama, the founder of Nyāya school of thought defines *śabda* as *āptopadeśa śabdaḥ* (*Nyāya-Sūtra*, 1.1.7) — "the assertion or instruction of a trustworthy person is *śabda*." The term *āpta* applies to both "a reliable" human being and God, because Nyāya believes that God is the creator of Vedas (the highest form of scripture). Regarding the qualities of a human *āpta*, Vātsyāyana specifies the following qualities: "He (who) has realized or perceived the *dharma*, he is engaged in making a statement in order to communicate objects or facts as he has perceived them."[9] However, Nyāya offers a higher status to the instructions and assertions of Veda, for they are unquestionably and unconditionally true. Such words concerning *dharma* (moral conduct) are the words of God, hence authentic and uncontradictable. Even regarding the nature of human *āpta*, some interpreters[10] argue that by *āpta* Vātsyāyana means not an ordinary person but a seer-teacher (*ṛṣi*), hence his assertions are beyond doubt. Like Nyāya, Mīmāṁsā talks of two

9. B.K. Matilal, *The Word and the World*, Delhi: Oxford University Press, 1990, p. 6.

10. J.V. Bhattacharya, *Nyāya-Mañjarī of Jayanta Bhaṭṭa*, Delhi : Motilal Banarsidass, 1965 p. 316.

types of linguistic sources — *laukika* (human) and *vaidika* (Vedic or scriptural). But Kumārila, one of its exponents, holds a different view. He accords the status of *śabda-pramāṇa* only to Vedic instructions. Even Prabhākara, another important Mīmāṁsaka, who initially accepts *āpta-vākya* as authentic, later on reduces it to *anumāna* (inference), for the validity of such assertions is inferred from the trustworthiness of the speaker. One noteworthy feature of Mīmāṁsā view of *śabda* is that it accords a special status to the *Karmakāṇḍa* portion of the Vedas which is full of injunctive statements about sacrifices, rites and moral behaviour of man. For them Vedic statements are injunctive, not informative in nature. Sāṁkhya philosophers, on the other hand, hold a slightly different view about *śabda-pramāṇa*. For them Vedic statements are the only statements which are free from all sorts of doubt, hence self-valid. But their self-validity is due to the non-personal authorship of Vedas. The Vedic words have a natural power to denote worldly objects and that power is communicated by *āptas*. "Hence the self-validity of Vedas is tested and lived by the *āptas*."[11] Advaita Vedānta offers primacy to *śabda* as a *pramāṇa* because it is a means of acquiring philosophical knowledge (*pāramārthika tattva-bhedakatā*) and not empirical knowledge (*vyāvahārika*) which is acquired by means of perception, inference, etc. It also offers a higher status to *vedavākyas*. But here *vedavākyas* do not refer to what is contained in *Karmakāṇḍa*, but only the Vedānta portions, which contain statements about the nature of the highest Reality. Śaṅkara while emphasizing the importance of scriptural assertions says: "The means (in fact, knowledge-how) that can be known neither by perception nor by inference is what comes through scriptures. And this constitutes the scripturehood of the scriptures."[12] Here

11. *Sāṁkhya Pravacana Bhāṣya*, V.43, as translated by S. Radhakrishnan, *Indian Philosophy*, vol. 1, London : Goerge Allen and Unwin, 1962, p. 301.

12. Śaṅkara under *Brahma-Sūtra*, 2.1.1.

pratyakṣenānumityā va yastūpāyo no budhyate ।
enam vidhanti vedana tasmād vedasya vedatā ॥

by Śruti or the text of Vedas he specifically refers to *mahāvākyas* (great assertions) like *tat tvam asi* (that thou art), etc. They lead us to the ultimate form of knowledge that frees us from wordly expectations and desires and forms the basis of our knowledge of the ultimate Reality (*Brahma-jñāna*).

From the above way of presentation of the concept of *śabda-pramāṇa* one may gather the impression that the Indian tradition encourages blind and dogmatic acceptance of scriptural assertions. In spite of this, surprisingly enough, we find no clear indication about "authority" as a source of knowledge in the sense the term is understood by medieval Western philosophers. Rather the Veda is called *apauruṣeya* (non-personal and authorless). Therefore, there is plenty of scope for confusion if the terms *śabda-pramāṇa* and *āgama* are translated as verbal "authority" and scriptural "authority" respectively. But it seems, some Indian writers in English have strong fascination for the term "authority." This is because still some "so-called" traditionalists believe that the Vedic statements are to be accepted unquestionably and unconditionally. Hence "authority" is the favoured term.

Daya Krishna rightly remarks "The notion of Vedic authority is . . . a myth."[13] Yet a large number of thinkers do not want the "myth" to be exploded. To silence them we have put some counter questions. By this process we can set the record straight. So let us start with the question about the exact significance of the term "scriptural authority." If it means the unquestioning acceptance of Vedic assertions (without any scope for analysis and interpretation of their true meaning) then the traditionalists have wrongly assessed the Indian tradition. Interpretability is very much a part of it. So within ancient texts and commentaries we notice

13. Daya Krishna, "Three Myths about Indian Philosophy," In *Indian Philosophy : A Counter Perspective*, Delhi : Oxford University Press, 1991, p. 9.

See this book for more arguments against the "myth" of authority and other associated myths that are responsible for a distorted presentation of Indian philosophy.

varied and sometimes contrary interpretations of the same Vedic stanzas and lines. Bhartṛhari in his *Vākyapadīya* offers us the finest examples of such variations in interpretation of meanings. He says: "Based on explanatory comments and similar passages, conflicting views have been set forth by the exponents of Monism and Dualism."[14] In his commentary following the verse he goes on to elaborate the point further: "Because of the diversity of human intellect, diversity of speculations take place." He cites several examples to illustrate his point. I take one such example to prove his point. The famous Upaniṣadic verse — "Two birds, companions, united together, occupy the same tree. Of the two one eats the tasty fig fruit, while the other does not eat, only shines" — has been interpreted in different manners. To the Monist, "By two 'birds' the senses and the inner controller, the intelligence or the soul is meant." The Dualists on the other hand, interprete "two birds" as "the differentiated and the undifferentiated consciousness full of seeds." Those who advocate that Vedic statements signify "authority," and hence its truth and meaning is unquestionable, gloss over such explanations found within the Indian traditional texts. In fact, the idea of interpretability is as old as Indian culture itself. Yāska, one of the ancient etymologists (700 BCE) highlights this aspect when he says that without the interpretation of meaning Vedic statements are like "barren cow and mere illusion" (*adhenumāyā*).[15] The importance of interpretation in Indian tradition is evident from the fact that innumerable philosophical views flourished here, in spite of each claiming to follow the Vedic lineage. Their views varied widely because they offered different inerpretations of Vedic passages or most often focused attention on this or that aspect of Vedas which suited their own metaphysical model. If we come to the specific texts the line of argument may become more clear. *Brahma-Sūtra* is regarded as a part of the Śruti by Vedāntins. But Śaṅkara

14. *Vākyapadīya*, 1.8, tr. K.A.S. Iyer, Poona : Deccan College, 1965.

15. Yāska, *Nirukta*, 1.20. Quoted from *The Cultural Heritage of India*, vol. I, Calcutta: The Ramakrishna Mission, 1982, p. 293.

and Rāmānuja offer quite different versions of the same text.[16] If Vedic statements and Śruti would have been considered to be the embodiment of final truth this freedom of interpretation would not have been there. These facts justify that the choice of the term "authority" is a wrong one or else a myth that the traditionalists want to perpetuate at any cost.

The next question that I want to raise about the identification of *śabda-pramāṇa* with "verbal authority" is still more crucial. If *śabda-pramāṇa* means acquisition of knowledge by blindly accepting what the scriptures say, then why do the Indian philosophers waste so much of time and energy in analysing different dimensions of the concept of "language"? Indian philosophical literature is full of very rich and penetrating discussions about the nature of language, meaning, word-world relationship, speaker-hearer relationship and many more language-related issues. Many logical issues are raised within the scope of such discussions. These philosophers, who exhibit rare analytical acumen in their treatment of the concept of language could not have been so dumb as to advocate dogmatic acceptance of the "authority" of scriptures. The traditionalists may put some quotations in support of their stand. But this does not provide much strength to their argument. There are plenty of statements and definitions found within the same texts, which are enough to challenge their viewpoint. Let me illustrate this with some statements and definitions found in different texts about the nature of *śabda-pramāṇa* and śruti. Sāṁkhya defines Śruti as "knowledge obtained by analysis of meaning" (*vākya janitam vākyārtha jñānam śruti*). Similarly Śaṅkara puts emphasis on the analysis of meaning

16. *Bṛhadāraṇyaka Upaniṣad,* 4.3.12 says that while dreaming the "immortal" freely moves about, leaving its nest. While commenting upon this Śaṅkara says: It is impossible to speak of an animal that sleeps, that it runs and comes back from a place where it sleeps from by thousand and thousand of miles. So this does not stand to reason. It is stated elsewhere in the same text that the dreamer moves inside the body only. So Śaṅkara's conclusion is that Śrutis such as these are to be explained away as merely figurative speech. *Brahma-Sūtra Śāṅkara Bhāṣya,* 3.2.3.

(*vākyārtha vicāraṇā*) even in case of the highest form of knowledge (*Brahma-jñāna*). He says: "Comprehension of *Brahman* is affected by the ascertainment, consequent on discussion, of the meaning of Vedānta statements."[17] This, to a large extent, disproves the traditionalists' argument that *Brahma-jñāna* is a matter of mystical experience only, and has nothing to do with language analysis. Similary, according to Sāṁkhya, Vedic statements are not anybody's assertions, but have a natural power to denote, which are communicated to common man by *āpta*s only. So *āpta*s become the medium for the acquisition of scriptural knowledge. But any and every interpretation offered by *āpta*s are not to be accepted dogmatically. In this context Aniruddha in his *Vṛtti* on Vācaspati's *Tattva-Kaumudī* says: "Huge giants do not drop from heaven simply because an *āpta*, or competent person says so. Only sayings which are **supported by reason** should be accepted by me and others like yourselves."[18] Again, Bhartṛhari very rightly points out that there is always the possibility of doubt in case of verbal authority because the intended meaning may not be correctly grasped by the hearer. There are many such instances[19] where the emphasis is put on understanding of the correct meaning by language analysis and the application of reason. The "so-called"

17. *Brahma-Sūtra Bhāṣya* of Śaṅkara, 1.1.2:
vākyārtha vicāraṇādhyavaṣānanivṛttahi brahmāvagatiḥ ।
nānumānādi pramāṇāntara nivṛtta ॥

18. *nāhy āpta vacanān nabhaso nipatanti mahāsurāḥ* ।
yuktimad vacanam grāhyam mayānaica bhavadvidhaiḥ ॥
Quoted from Radhakrishnan's *Indian Philosophy*, p. 802.

19. "Logical analysis must aid interpretation of scriptures" (*śrutyaivaca sahavatvena tarkasyāpy 'bhyupetatvāt*) Śaṅkara under *Brahma-Sūtra Bhāṣya*, 1.1.2.

Professor G. Misra pioneered the movement of interpreting Advaita Concept of *śabda-pramāṇa* as a method of Logico-Linguistic method. For his interpretation see his *Advaita Philosophy : Its Method, Scope and Limits* (Bhubaneswar : 1976). Also refer to *The Proceedings of Fifth Conference of All Orissa Philosophy Association* (Bhubaneswar, Post-Graduate Department of Philosophy, 1973) for a critical discussion on *śabda-pramāṇa* under the symposium on the topic. In a paper included →

traditionalists only present one side of the story without giving the other side any chance. On their Procrustean bed they chop off everything that does not conform to their interpretation.

Still, the upholders of "authority" of scriptures may be left with some more arguments in their favour. It may be argued that the scriptural assertions imply unquestioning acceptance because they are supposed to be uncontradictable and incorrigible. This type of knowledge is only assured by *śabda-pramāṇa.* This is admitted by most of the schools of classical Indian systems. But such characterizations should not be understood at the surface level only. They have deeper significance. The uncontradictability and incorrigibility of scriptural assertions are due to the nature of these statements. According to Mīmāṁsakas the Vedic statements are injunctive in nature and they do not inform us about facts. They are concerning commands (*vidhi*) and prohibitions (*niṣedha*). Such statements cannot be challenged, because such **prescriptive** rules cannot be negated, once accepted. Similarly, according to Nyāya, Vedic statements are concerning *dharma* (which in broader Indian context means moral principles). Moral principles too are prescriptive by nature, hence uncontradictable. On the other hand, for Vedāntins (especially Advaitins), scriptural statements are non-empirical and philosophical by nature (*pāramārthika tattva*), so they cannot be contradicted by factual knowledge. They make a clear distinction between **factual** (*vyāvahārika*) and **philosophical** (*pāramārthika*) statements. Factual statement can contradict a factual statement, not a non-factual statement. That is why Vācaspati says: "even a thousand scriptures cannot turn the knowledge of pot into the knowledge of cloth."[20] In other words, the ways and

→ in the Proceedings volume, J. Dash makes a very interesting point regarding Śaṅkara's method: "Acharya's method seems to start with authorities and then, in final analysis, to discard them, even as costly lunar model by the Lunarnauts."

20. *na hy āgamaḥ sahasrā nāni ghaṭam pratyitamsate* (*Bhāmatī* Introduction.)

Śaṅkara says: "validity of a statement about observable attributes of an object may be done by help of sense-perception, etc.; statements about objects which cannot be verified by empirical means must be done by language analysis." *Śāṅkara Bhāṣya* on *Bhagavad-Gītā*, 18.66.

means of acquiring factual knowledge are different from the knowledge acquired through linguistic means and scriptures. Scriptural statements have nothing to do with facts. Factual knowledge cannot contradict or correct the non-factual knowledge. So it seems that there is no mystery surrounding the scriptural knowledge. I do not at the same time deny the fact that there are many such verses and statements in philosophical texts of different systems which openly declare loyalty to Vedic words. But beyond this apparent dogmatism there lie mines of ideas which are highly logical and analytical in nature. We cannot afford to neglect them while understanding the concept of *śabda-pramāṇa*.

Bhartṛhari: The New Way of Looking at Language

Let us now take up for consideration a completely new way of handling the concept of language or *śabda*. This is embodied in Bhartṛhari's treatise entitled *Vākyapadīya*. As the title suggests, it should have been on "words" and "sentences"; instead it expounds a full-fledged philosophy of language. This is evident from the outline Bhartṛhari himself offers about the scope of the subject-matter of his treatise. He specifies eight topics coming within the fold of his study. They are : (1) meaning determined through analysis (abstracted meaning), (2) given or stable meaning conveyed through the sentence, (3) linguistic forms that figure in grammatical derivations, (4) linguistic forms that are to be analysed, (5) cause-effect relationship between the intention of the speaker and the utterance, (6) the relationship of capability between the forms of speech and the meaning, (7) the relations that lead to merit, and (8) the relations that bring out communication.[21] All these topics mentioned above do not come exclusively within the ambit of "grammar" (as understood in the ordinary sense). The list of topics clearly indicates that Bhartṛhari's interest is not confined to the rules and forms of language. Rather

21. *Vākyapadīya*, I.24-26. As summarized by A. Aklujkar and K. Potter in *Encyclopaedia of Indian Philosophies*, vol. V (*The Philosophy of Grammarians*), ed. H.G. Coward and K.K. Raja, Delhi, Motilal Banarsidass, 1990, pp. 129-30.

he aims at a depth-analysis of the concepts of language and meaning. We have every reason to believe that Bhartṛhari's *Vākyapadīya* is a comprehensive treatise on philosophy of language.

However, it seems that in ancient India a clear line of distinction was maintained between Dārśanikas (technically speaking, philosophers) and Vaiyākaraṇikas (the grammarians). So Bhartṛhari the grammarian's trespassing into the area of philosophy was neither welcomed by Dārśanikas nor Vaiyākaraṇikas. Somānanda and Utpalācārya, the later grammarians, comment that as a grammarian, Bhartṛhari should have confined himself to the business of explaining the forms of Sanskrit language instead of making an effort to dabble in metaphysics and epistemology.[22] But in spite of such distinction between philosophy and grammar one finds that Bhartṛhari's theories of *śabda-Brahman*, *sphoṭa*, *pratibhā*, etc. are taken up for discussion by almost all the schools of Indian philosophy. Right from Śaṅkara to Diṅnāga, most of the philosophers refer to his theory (either directly mentioning his name or indirectly). Most often they repudiate his views. But if his theory would be lacking in philosophical contents, there would have been no necessity of even repudiating it. Still, it is a fact that Bhartṛhari has not been offered the status he deserved, either by the classical philosophers or by the modern philosophers.

Bhartṛhari in his *magnum opus Vākyapadīya* (a treatise with three *kāṇḍas*) treats the concept of *śabda* as the ultimate concern for his philosophical exploration. He also discusses *śabda* as a *pramāṇa*, like other classical philosophical systems. Since in the last section I have focused on the concept of *śabda* as a *pramāṇa*, it would be relevant for us to understand how Bhartṛhari views the issue, and to assess whether in any way he falls short of the philosophical standards reached by Dārśanikas. Bhartṛhari accepts *pratyakṣa*, *anumāna* and *śabda* as the relevant methods of valid knowledge. But in his opinion all these methods are not foolproof. One can get a glimpse of his analytical acumen from the way he proves the

22. K.A. Subramania Iyer, *Bhartṛhari*, Poona : Deccan College, 1969, p. 70.

unreliability of these methods. He observes that perception is helpful as a means of factual knowledge. But perception as a method has limitations. For, sense perceptions can be deceptive. He argues: "The sky looks like a solid surface and fire-fly like a spark (of fire), (but we know that it is all wrong) for there is no solid surface and no fire in the fire-fly."[23] Similarly *anumāna* is useful as an aid to perception. Yet when we can commit errors in case of perception, what to speak of the inference which is indirect in nature? Similar is the case with *āpta-vākya*s, i.e. verbal knowledge acquired through the assertions of trustworthy persons. Bhartṛhari points out, "What one acquires from other people's words may be coloured by one's background."[24] It can sometimes be sensibly different from what the speaker intended to say. Even Vedic statements can have varying interpretations depending upon the metaphysical position one adopts. So what according to him is the right method of obtaining incorrigible knowledge? Bhartṛhari's answer sounds interesting. He says that "we cannot understand the meaning of the words of *āgama* by merely hearing them, we have to use reasoning to determine the meaning and this does not amount to going against the Vedas.[25] This power of understanding the meaning is due to the inherent power, *pratibhā* (intuition) and *śabda-bhāvanā* (linguistic potency) present within us. He elaborates different ways and phases through which this power can be realized. But for the time being we shall not go into details, because our concern here is not exactly epistemological analysis, but the philosophy of language that Bhartṛhari presents.

It is interesting to note that the term *śabda-pramāṇa* acquires a new dimension in the philosophy of Grammar. Bhartṛhari derives his philosophical inspiration from Patañjali's *Mahābhāṣya*. Patañjali

---

23. *talavad dṛśyate vyoma khadyoto havyavāḍiva* ǀ
naiva cāsti talaṁ vyomni na khadyote hutāśanaḥ ǀǀ — *Vāk.*, II.140

24. *vaktrānyathaiva prakrānto bhinneṣu pratipattṛṣu* ǀ
svapratyayānukāreṇa śabdārthaḥ pravibhajyate ǀǀ — *Vāk.*, II.135

25. *vedaśāstrā virodhī ca tarkaścakṣura paśyatāṁ* ǀ
rūpamātrādi vākyārthaḥ kevalānnāvatiṣṭhate ǀǀ — *Vāk.*, I.136

identifies himself as *śabda-pramāṇaka*. Here the term *śabda-pramāṇaka* cannot be translated as, "the follower of scriptural authority." The term has a broader connotation, as is evident from the contexts in which Patañjali uses the term. He says: *śabda-pramāṇaka vayaṁ yacchabda āha tad asmākam pramāṇam*. With reference to the context[26] the above line should be translated in the following manner — "We are the analysts of language, for us, what the word presents is our only way of knowing." In other words, he claims that as a *śabda-pramāṇaka* his job is to understand facts and objects through linguistic forms only. Commenting on Patañjali's statement Bhartṛhari says : *kim asmākam vastugatena vicāreṇa? arthastvasmākaṁ yaḥ śabdenābhidhīyate.*[27] This means, "what is the use of our reflecting on the nature of things? The object for us is what the word presents." This statement should be taken as the basic presupposition of Bhartṛhari's approach to philosophical exploration. For him the limit of language is the limit of the reality. This novel approach to the subject matter of philosophy results in a unique philosophy of language. This also makes his position different from other grammarians as well as philosophers of India.

Bhartṛhari's way of unfolding "what the words present" is both insightful and philosophically illuminating. He understands the world in terms of words. The nature of objects and existence in the world, according to him, is determined by how we cognize it. How we cognize it, in turn, is determined by word-impregnated concepts. Without the use of linguistic elements concepts cannot be formed. Therefore, as a conclusion, it follows that objects, their cognition and linguistic expressions about the affairs of the world — all of them, are dependent on the one and unitary linguistic principle (*śabda-tattva*). In fact, he studies the concept of language

---

26. *Mahābhāṣya*, pt. II.1.1. What the word says is our authority. And the words say here that "something is — this" (is a stick); "is" is implied. That stick which is agent, when combined with another word, (becomes instrument).

27. Bhartṛhari, *Mahābhāṣya Dīpikā*, Part I, Poona, Bhandarkar Oriental Research Institute, 1967, p. 28.1. 16-18.

at two levels — (1) language viewed as an **act**, and (2) language viewed as a **principle** (*tattva*). At the level of act, language functions as a communicative tool. So he undertakes an elaborate analysis of the elements involved in the act of linguistic communication. Again, at the transcendental level, the concept of "language" serves as a metaphysical principle, through which he attempts to explain the phenomenal world. Thus "language" (*śabda*) acquires the status of the highest Reality, i.e. the *śabda-Brahman*.

Bhartṛhari's concern with *śabda* has many areas common with what has been discussed by classical Indian systems within the scope of *śabda-pramāṇa*. All of them analyse the nature of language and meaning, world-word relationship, the primacy of either the word-meaning or the sentence-meaning, and the different dimensions of meaning. But Bhartṛhari's method of approaching "language" is different from others. Bhartṛhari presents the entire gamut of human understanding by analysing the structural conditions of language. His job is not only confined to the analysis of language but also to work out the boundaries of what we can do and cannot do with language.

Metaphysics and Language

If by "philosophy of language" we mean "offering philosophically illuminating description of general features of language," then most of what the Indian philosophers along with Bhartṛhari discuss comes within its scope. But if by philosophy of language we mean understanding the complex phenomena of how we communicate our thoughts through language, and laying bare the structure of "how language functions"; then Bhartṛhari's way of handling the problem comes closest to this objective. Matilal very rightly observes: "The overall concern with how our language works was not the chief concern of most classical Indian philosophers, except for the grammarians like Bhartṛhari."[28] But it is obvious that Bhartṛhari's concern goes beyond just explicating the structural principles of "how language works." He wants to

28. Matilal, *The Word and the World*, p. 4.

present a comprehensive picture of epistemology, metaphysics and linguistics through his conception of *śabda-tattva*. So in certain respects his aim and objective is different from that of other philosophers of language, past and present. Rather, Bhartṛhari's way of handling philosophy of language in certain respects can be described as a form of **metaphysics** of language because he proposes to connect all dimensions of philosophical activity through the network of linguistic and conceptual forms. In this respect Bhartṛhari's model of metaphysics is akin to what Strawson identifies as the "connective" model of philosophical analysis. It is a matter of interesting co-incidence that Strawson elucidates the model with the analogy of grammar (as opposed to the analogy of "therapy" offered by Wittgenstein). According to him, "just as the grammarian . . . labours to produce a systematic account of the structure of rules which we effortlessly observe in speaking grammatically, so the philosopher labours to produce a systematic account of the general **conceptual structure** of which our daily practice shows us to have a tacit and unconscious mastery."[29] With the introduction of this model Strawson proposes to show the interconnection between the irreducible notions which form the basic structure of our thinking; through which ontology, epistemology and logic can be seen as the three aspects of one unified inquiry. Bhartṛhari's method of analysis as well as the objective of his analysis is closer to the above-mentioned model because he lays bare the structural elements of language of which the language user has tacit understanding but no explicit knowledge. And with these structural elements he develops a unified scheme of philosophical inquiry. But, we can go thus far with our comparison, no further. Strawson's approach to metaphysics is "descriptive" — he understands the basic and irreducible concepts in terms of our actual operation with language and concepts. It does not aim at providing a revised picture of the "structure of our thought about the world," by pushing one concept in favour of the other. Strawson is very much aware of this risk in

29. P.F. Strawson, *Analysis and Metaphysics*, Oxford: Oxford University Press, 1992, p. 5.

case of pursuing the "connective" model of philosophical analysis. He warns: "There is, as it were, a tendency to intellectual imperialism . . ."[30] Philosophers have a tendency to produce a strikingly different world picture dominated by a particular concept, representing a particular attitude and interest. Most of the philosophers would not like to leave their philosophical inquiry half-way without a final conceptual commitment. In case of Bhartṛhari, his philosophical inquiry about the nature of language culminates in the idea of *śabda-Brahman*. It is a form of Monism in which the principle of language is identified with the Reality; otherwise known as Śabdādvaitavāda (Linguistic Monism). Some Modern thinkers, like Matilal, are of opinion that Bhartṛhari was one of the earliest exponents of Advaita (the philosophy of non-dualism) — a form of Monism made popular by Śaṅkara.

One of the unique features of Bhartṛhari's philosophical inquiry is that he starts with the concept of *śabda-Brahman* as the ground of all phenomenal multiplicities and changes and goes on to unravel the structural concepts of language and thought and ends his inquiry with an analysis of the nature of utterances. In this sense his treatise *Vākyapadīya* constituted of three parts, is a complete book in the area of language analysis.

Metaphysics and Mysticism

Before concluding this introductory chapter, I intend to make certain issues clear. First of all, we should not have any qualms about the metaphysical nature of Bhartṛhari's work. It will be a distortion of truth to say that his metaphysics is a superficial part of his philosophical inquiry about language. He was part of a tradition — a tradition in which every form of intellectual activity is directed towards the realization of the ultimate knowledge. Be it poetics, music or grammar — every form of inquiry aims to explain the phenomenal in terms of transcendental. It is not a case of deification of concepts but a search for perfection symbolized in the concept of Reality. So Bhartṛhari's philosophy of Linguistic Monism is the culmination of his intellectual inquiry conforming

30. P.F. Strawson, *Analysis and Metaphysics*, 1992, p. 14.

to the trends of the Indian culture and tradition. But in no sense can it be called "unscientific" and "poetic"[31] as W.T. Stace very crudely remarks about the Indian tradition in general, in his book *A Critical History of Greek Philosophy*. Metaphysics, in the sense of "Speculative" metaphysics, is not so peculiar to Indian tradition alone. . . . The obsession with the concept of "Highest Reality" was very dominant in Western thought, too. Ironically enough, Stace makes such a comment in the **Introduction** of a book in which he discusses the philosophy of Plato, who was famous for his use of poetic metaphors and myths in philosophy. Perhaps he was guided by the dogmatic belief that "Indian thought is usually excluded from the history of philosophy because . . . it lies outside the mainstream of human development."[32] I strongly feel that if one wants to do philosophy or write on philosophy, he should not have a closed mind. By this I also refer to some Indian scholars who try to put Indian philosophical views in the straightjacket of Western thought. Ancient philosophers can be understood in modern idiom, without stripping them of their cultural and traditional wrappings. In this book I have attempted to stick to this way of presentation.

Another strong bias is specifically floated about Bhartṛhari. It is believed that Bhartṛhari is a linguist. Hence philosophers have nothing to do with him. The bias has its roots in ancient distinction between Dārśanikas and Vaiyākaraṇikas. It seems, that modern Indian scholars are still under the spell of a very ancient (but now obsolete) dogma. This is evident from the fact that volumes are written on the nature of language analysis undertaken by the accredited Indian classical philosophical systems, but not on Bhartṛhari. It is left to scholars on Sanskrit to keep the philosophical views of Bhartṛhari alive. I feel that the modern scholars must throw away such a bias in view of the recent developments of thought, when the demarcating line between linguistics and philosophy of language is getting blurred.

31. W.T. Stace, *A Critical History of Greek Philosophy*, Delhi: Macmillan and Co. Ltd., 1982, p. 16.

32. Ibid.

2

Śabdādvaitavāda
The Metaphysics of Language

Śabda-Brahman: Its Implications

BHARTṚHARI starts his philosophical exploration with the concept of *śabda-Brahman*. This, according to him, is the unique and ultimate Reality. The concepts of existence, consciousness and language-in-use, which are associated with our understanding of the empirical world exhibit the elements of plurality. Yet all these concepts are word-generated. So they are bound by a common essence. And this essence is called by Bhartṛhari *śabda-tattva*, the **language-principle.** It is the ultimate principle of unity, hence the ultimate reality, the *Brahman*. It is obvious that Bhartṛhari offers primacy to the concept of "unity" in his metaphysical scheme. Therefore, *śabda-Brahman* signifies supreme unity rather than supreme existence. All along his attempt has been to show how the pluralities of the phenomenal world direct us towards an ultimate form of unity. To understand Bhartṛhari's metaphysics, therefore, we will have to assess how far he has been successful in explaining plurality in terms of unity.

The opening verse of his treatise *Vākyapadīya* epitomizes his metaphysical approach. It says:

> *anādinidhanaṁ brahma śabdatattvaṁ yadakṣaram* ।
> *vivartate 'arthabhāvena prakriyā jagato yataḥ* ॥

Following K.A.S. Iyer we can translate the verse as follows:

> The *Brahman* is without beginning and end, whose essence is the Word, who is the cause of the manifested phonemes, who

> appears as the objects, from whom the creation of the world proceeds.[1]

Literally understood the statement may appear to be a sort of mystical rhapsody. For, how can the objects and the world proceed from the Word? So the entire idea seems uncritical and non-philosophical. But the above verse has a deeper significance which gradually unfolds as Bhartṛhari proceeds with his task in *Vākyapadīya*. Here, I shall make an attempt to unravel the significance of the verse by examining the imports of terms and phrases contained in it. This may provide us enough ground for assessing how much of it is mystical and how much is logical.

The first concept that needs elucidation is *śabda*. Very broadly understood it means sound. If we go for a stricter interpretation then *śabda* means "uttered or written strings of words having a syntax and meaning." In short, it means "language." This is the sense in which the term has been used in case of *śabda-pramāṇa* by other philosophical systems. But for Bhartṛhari *śabda* means something more than "language." It is the name of a complex phenomenon implying an activity as well as a principle. As a type of activity it is something in which all human beings, in fact, all sentient beings are engaged. The Sanskrit term for it is *śabdanā vyāpāra*. B.K. Matilal translates it as "languageing."[2] Again as a principle it stands for the very potency for communicating thoughts through language. It is the linguistic potency, the very power of conceptualization, which is the basis of our consciousness as well as the awareness of the external world. This potency itself is *śabda-tattva*, the **word principle.** The *śabda-tattva*, being the central concept of all forms of phenomenal activity is identified with the *Brahman*. The term *Brahman* in Advaitin and Upaniṣadic context means the "Reality," in a metaphysical sense. But etymologically analysed, *Brahman* means the all-enveloping and all-pervading principle. The term is derived from the root *vṛh*

---

1. K.A.S. Iyer, *Vākyapadīya*, Pt. I.
2. B.K. Matilal, *The Word and the World*, p. 85.

which means "to grow, to expand, to become great." In extended sense therefore it means "all-pervading." In case of Bhartṛhari *śabda* is identified with *Brahman* because he conceives the word-principle as the basic principle of consciousness as well as the awareness of the existence of objects which are characterized by "names" and "forms."

Bhartṛhari further conceives this Reality to be "without beginning and end" (*anādi nidhanam*). According to G.N. Sastri the phrase means a concept to which the qualities and attributes of "time" cannot be applied.[3] His interpretation is justified on the following ground. All our cognitive episodes about our inner states of mind as well as the external world are sequential in nature (*krama*). They are conditioned by temporal arrangement. The word-principle being the ground of all forms of cognitions cannot be understood in terms of time, i.e. in terms of beginning and end. Hence it is without temporal sequence (*akrama*) and "without beginning and end." However, B.K. Matilal draws our attention to another dimension of its meaning. Following Bhartṛhari's arguments about the nature of *śabda* he very rightly points out:

> An absolute beginning of language is untenable. Language is continuous and co-terminus with human or any sentient being.[4]

According to Bhartṛhari speech is not a matter of convention made at a particular moment of time. The potency of the words to express meaning is inherent. There is some kind of natural fitness (*yogyatā*) in words to express meaning as it is the case with different sense-organs which are fit for different sense perceptions.[5] This position of Bhartṛhari is radically different from the Nyāya position. According to the Nyāya philosophers language is a matter of convention, either made by man or by God. Against this, Bhartṛhari as well as other grammarians contend that

---

3. Gourinath Sastri, *A Study in the Dialectics of Sphoṭa*, Delhi: Motilal Banarsidass, 1980, p. x.
4. Matilal, *The Word and the World*, p. 125.
5. *Vākyapadīya*, I.97.

convention itself presupposes the use of language. Bringing in God as the creator of convention is not of much help. Even God has to use some linguistic forms to formulate the convention. Therefore, the inherent potentiality of **Word** to express meaning cannot be placed in time. In this sense *śabda-tattva* is eternal. The particular languages and its usages may be determined by convention, but not the concept of "language" as such. So the use of the terms "eternal" and "without beginning and end" in case of Word-Principle do not lead to the assertion of a mystical entity.

However, regarding the use of the term *akṣara*, there may be some misgivings. *Akṣara* ordinarily means "eternal." When we define some principle as eternal it may give rise to the speculation that we are talking of some entity whose nature is in direct contrast to the momentariness of the worldly objects. According to G.N. Sastri[6] *akṣara* means "all-pervading" as its root "*as*" implies eternity. But K.A.S. Iyer and Sukla[7] prefer to translate the term *akṣara* as phonemes. Iyer very categorically states that though the term *akṣara*, in ordinary sense, means eternal, Bhartṛhari uses the term in technical sense to mean phonemes. According to him Bhartṛhari defines *śabda-tattva* as the cause of manifested phonemes. If the term *akṣara* is interpreted as "phonemes" then it can provide certain effective clues to the understanding of the second half of the verse, — "that which appears as objects, and from whom the creation of the world proceeds." The second half of the verse seems more uncritical and mystical. For how can the **word** appear as objects? But if *śabda* is understood as the cause of phonemes then we may drive ourselves towards a more plausible explanation.

It can very broadly be said that the **word-principle** as the embodiment of linguistic potency manifests itself as phonemes (and ultimately as language-in-use). The language in manifested form is our only way of expressing awareness about the objects as well as the activities of the world. If we withdraw this linguistic

6. Gourinath Sastri, *Dialectics of Sphoṭa*, p. x.

7. S.N. Sukla, *Vākyapadīya Bhāvapradīpa*, Chowkhamba, 1961.

potency then there will be neither consciousness, nor cognition, nor sensation of objects. Without the application of concepts and names, objects and facts are devoid of any identity. However, to understand the true implication of the second half of the verse we need to discuss the justifications Bhartṛhari offers in support of his statement that "the word appears as objects." The justifications are not presented very systematically by Bhartṛhari. Sometimes they are scattered. But that should not deter us from making a critical assessment of them.

First, in his explanatory note following the opening verse, Bhartṛhari defines the objects as *śabdopagrāhī*. It implies that objects of our thought are word-determined. Be it perception, inference or any other method, whenever we cognize objects or external reality, we always do so in terms of "names." Without "names" they are unidentifiable, hence not knowable. And our cognition, according to him are *śabdopagrāhya*, i.e. word-impregnated or intertwined with words. Both the objects and cognition being word-generated, they are conceptually dependent on **word-principle**. Objects cannot be understood without language, which in turn, is the explicit manifestation of the word-principle. Secondly, Bhartṛhari employs the logic of causality, prevalent in ancient Indian tradition, to prove that *śabda-tattva* is the root of worldly manifestations. Bhartṛhari (under the verse 1.120) says:

> Just as other thinkers, while explaining causality, saw that properties of cause continue in the effects; and have declared [it] as the source of everything, either the mass of atom . . . or primordial Matter [*pradhāna/prakṛti*], or the collection of powers rooted in Nescience or something which has no birth nor change (but merely substratum) of appearance, in the same way in the scriptures also, the word in which the power of Enjoyer and Enjoyed are submerged has been declared to be the cause of the world in many ways.

What Bhartṛhari intends to say in the above passage can be stated in simpler terms in the following way. The attributes and qualities of cause or manifestor persist through its effects or manifestations.

On the basis of observation of the nature of effects we can infer the nature of cause. For example, the curd as the effect of milk retains some of the qualities of milk. On the basis of these qualities one can infer that milk is the cause of curd, not water. Similarly on the basis of the observation of "word-loaded" nature of phenomenal concepts we can infer that the cause of the world is of the nature of the **word**. Here, by "others" Bhartṛhari refers to the views of Vaiśeṣika, Sāṁkhya and Upaniṣadic philosophy. On the basis of such a logic of causality Bhartṛhari declares:

> It is the word which sees the object, it is the word which speaks, it is the word which reveals the object which was **lying hidden** and it is on the word that the multiple word rests.[8]

In the above passage, the objects are said to be **lying hidden**. The purpose of such a description can be interpreted in the following way: the objects may exist, but their nature is not known unless and until they are subsumed under some name. This is evident from the following statement, where Bhartṛhari is more explicit:

> Even that exists is as good as non-existent as long as it does not come within the range of verbal usage. Even totally non-existent things like hare's horn or something which appears and disappears in the sky like celestial town (*gandharva nagara*), when brought into mind by words, figures like something endowed with primary Reality, in various usages.[9]

This passage offers us sufficient hints about Bhartṛhari's way of looking at the word-world relationship. The function of the word is to "mean." But to "mean" is not to refer to existent objects. It is not a relation if "Fido" — Fido mould, i.e. here is the word "Fido" and there is the dog Fido. According to Bhartṛhari the words do not directly refer to the objects but to the idea or concept of the object. He is not a Realist in this sense. He rather holds that our activities in relation to the external world may be prompted by

8. *Vākyapadīya*, *Vṛtti* under I.1, tr. Iyer, p. 106.

9. Ibid., *Vṛtti* under I.121, tr. Iyer, p. 109.

language but language does not signify them. Whatever reference is made of objects, it is always done through the "cloak" of words.

Regarding this peculiar stand about the word-object relationship he offers further justifications. He argues that "objects" become distinct and identifiable entities once they are subsumed under a word or name. Otherwise the world of objects is indistinguishable and an unidentifiable "something." In other words, distinction is made between one object and another on the basis of "words" or names assigned to them. This position of Bhartṛhari is in direct contrast to the Nyāya theory of perception of objects. Gotama in *Nyāya-Sūtra*, 1.1.4, considers non-verbalizability (*avyapadeśya*) as one of the characteristics of perceptual knowledge. Elaborating on this point Vātsyāyana adds, our perception need not be always associated with verbalizability. There can be non-linguistic cognition. In support of his contention he offers the example of a mute's or a child's perception. In such cases there is scope for cognition and perception but not verbalization. So verbalization is not an invariable condition of our knowledge of the external world. To such an objection Bhartṛhari's answer would be that "verbalization" and "verbalizability" are not identical concepts. Our perceptual cognition need not always be presented in articulate verbal form. But that does not preclude the possibility of the potency for linguistic expressibility. Even the bare awareness of object is not possible without its being potent with cognitive discriminations (*pratyavamarśa*). When we fail to subsume our awareness of objects under a name, we understand them with the help of words "this" or "that." Therefore, without cognitive discrimination there is no object. The discrimination is possible through conceptualization, and conceptualization is penetrated (*anuviddha*) by words.[10]

All these justifications presented in preceding pages are used by Bhartṛhari to vindicate his metaphysical position that "the words create the objects." His arguments shows no trace of

10. *Vākyapadīya*, I.124-25.

obscurity. It is metaphysically cogent and coherent. He takes the concept of *śabda-tattva* as basic and primary. It rather works like a pair of tinged spectacles. Whichever way one looks it appears to be tinged with linguistic potency. But this cannot be considered to be a defect in metaphysics, rather this is the way of doing metaphysics. The metaphysician has only one tool in his hand, i.e. the **concept**. He puts emphasis on this or that concept as the primary one and accordingly his conceptual scheme takes shape. In case of Bhartṛhari *śabda* is the primary concept. With the help of this he develops a non-dualistic (Advaita) and holistic world-view.

Problems of Linguistic Monism

We must now examine how successfully Bhartṛhari handles the problem of bridging the gap between plurality and unity. This is the greatest challenge for any Monistic philosopher. Bhartṛhari's task seems to be more difficult, for his metaphysical Reality is of the nature of **Word**. So he has the double task of bridging the gap between the **Word** and existence, and between the one and the many.

He explains the empirical level of existence with the help of certain key concepts. They are: (1) consciousness/awareness, (2) concepts, (3) existence of objects, and (4) change. So our first job will be to examine these four concepts from Bhartṛhari's standpoint. In the process, we are likely to notice a peculiar feature of Bhartṛhari's method. At each level of his conceptual exploration he exhibits that differentiation implies unity.

WORD AND CONSCIOUSNESS

Let us start by examining what Bhartṛhari means by consciousness or awareness. We, as conscious beings are aware of the innumerable factual events and objects around us. We are aware of them not because of sense perception, but because we can cognize them as distinct and particular things subsumable under different names and forms. So according to him there can be no cognitive awareness without its being intertwined with words. If we take away this property of "word-loadedness" from cognition then no cognitive awareness is worth its name. In other words, **word** and consciousness are inseparably related. Of course, from such an account it should not be presumed that Bhartṛhari means by consciousness a form of "inner speech." Being conscious does not mean we are constantly in the process of using words. Nor does he attach primacy to language over thought. Bhartṛhari, himself, is aware of the two different ways of interpreting the relationship between the words and consciousness. He states that according to some, there cannot be consciousness without words. Consciousness and words are two distinct phenomena, but words have primacy over consciousness because consciousness is not possible without words. Others, on the other hand, hold that consciousness is just this fact of being the word-potent. The two are identical. Though Bhartṛhari does not clearly mention his preference in the verse, yet from the verse 1.118 it is clear that he accepts the latter view. He says: "what is called awareness (consciousness), i.e. *saṁjñā*, is having the form of speech or words (*vāgrūpatā*). Consciousness in all beings never goes beyond it, that is, it is never different from the fact of having the form of the word." We only become aware of the difference between them when the words are expressed in sequential and articulate manner to express our thought. It should be noted in this connection that he makes a clear distinction between the particular linguistic episodes, i.e. when words and phonemes are in particular sequential order, and the inherent linguistic potency in all conscious beings, which has the latent power to be expressed as particular linguistic statements.

WORD AND CONCEPT

The next problem that needs attention is Bhartṛhari's view of "concepts." It is usually believed that all words do not represent concepts. Only class names like "cow," "horse," "beautiful," "red," etc. are conceptualizable and hence they stand for universals. Concepts are formed on the basis of some common attributes shared by the members of the class. But Bhartṛhari's notion of "concept" is quite different. He believes that all words are universal, so all the words stand for concepts. Following Matilal's interpretation we can say that for Bhartṛhari "words and concepts are merely two sides of a same coin."[11] Therefore in Bhartṛhari's epistemological scheme there cannot be any non-conceptual (*nirvikalpaka*) awareness. For, all forms of awareness imply the presence of words. And all words, in turn, are concepts. Even the terms like "this" or "that" which are ordinarily believed to signify pure particulars (something which cannot be brought under the range of description), are also regarded as universal by Bhartṛhari. The reason for such a non-conventional view is due to his analysis of meaning in term of "sense" rather than "reference." Therefore, he considers "sentences" as the primary units of meaning, not the words. In case of linguistic communication it is the "sense" which is expressed by the speaker and grasped by the hearer. So he does not face any problem in explaining all forms of words in terms of concepts and universals. He does not analyse sentences in terms of "**that**" and "**what**." In such a scheme of analysis, the "**that**" of the subject refers to the pure particular which is qualified by the "**what**" of the quality or universal attributes. For Bhartṛhari words can only refer to the universal of objects.

WORD UNIVERSAL AND OBJECT UNIVERSAL

Still one knotty problem remains. Bhartṛhari talks of two kinds of universals, i.e. the universal of words and the universal objects. How are these two universals connected by Bhartṛhari? To understand this problem we will have to clarify the sense in which he uses the terms "words" and "objects"/"referents." In his analysis of "language-in-use" he makes a distinction between the expressed (*vācya*) and the expressive word (*vācaka*). The *vācaka* expresses the meaning and meaning implies the object meant. But objects meant are never directly grasped by the words. The particulars of the world are never knowable. The words always mean the universal of the objects. Whatever we know of the objects is known through the universalized concepts (*vikalpa*s). For

11. Matilal, *Perception*, Oxford: Clarendon Press, 1986, p. 393.

Bhartṛhari these universals do not exist in the objects. Whatever we know of the objects is through the "cloak" of words. The universal of the words and the universal of things, both are word-generated, hence there is no opposition between them. He transforms the "word-universals" to "thing-universals" to explain the existence of the world.

The Notion of Change and Time

So from our discussion we find that for Bhartṛhari: (1) consciousness and word are identical, (2) concepts and words are identical, and (3) the universal of the objects and the universal of words are identical. In fact, all the diversities of concepts that we have discussed are significant in the empirical level of "use." But at the conceptual level they are non-different, one and the ultimate idea, i.e. the word-principle. The diversity of phenomenal level is accommodated within the principle of the one *śabda-tattva* without any trace of quality or opposition. Now let us take up for examination another important concept, i.e. change. We shall have to deal with this concept at two levels: (i) How does the one Reality transform itself into the phenomenal level of plurality, in other words, the change from the transcendental to phenomenal? and (ii) The nature of change that characterizes the world of particularities.

The first issue regarding the transformation of the transcendental to phenomenal is sought to be solved by the theory of causation. Bhartṛhari himself says in the 1st verse of *Vākyapadīya* that, "from the *śabda-Brahman* the creation proceeds." In the Indian philosophical tradition those who subscribe to the view that "effect is cause transformed," are called *satkāryavādin*s. Hence Bhartṛhari's view comes under the fold of the above theory. But, again the theory has been interpreted in two ways. Those who believe that the effect is the real transformation of the cause, are called *pariṇāmavādin*s. According to them the cause changes its nature to become the effect, whereas the *vivarttavādin*s are of the opinion that the transformation from the cause to the effect is apparent. The nature of the cause remains unchanged, and cause is non-different from the effect. The Advaitins, especially Śaṅkara, is the chief protagonist of the latter theory. There is no unanimity of opinion amongst modern scholars as to the real nature of Bhartṛhari's theory of causation. Bhartṛhari's use of the term *vivarttate* in the introductory verse seems to settle the issue. But the issue cannot be settled on the basis of the use of this term. G.N. Sastri raises a valid objection. He very rightly points out: "It appears to us . . . that Bhartṛhari was not familiar with the difference in connotations of two terms (*pariṇāma* and *vivartta*) which is usual in later philosophical literature."[12] He and Ms. Biardeau[13] feel that Bhartṛhari has not interpreted the transformation of the world from the word in the light of *vivarttavāda* (as the term is understood by the Advaitins). They argue that such interpretations found in the *vṛttis* were incorporated by later grammarians. The basis of their argument is that *Vṛttis* of *Vākyapadīya* was not done by Bhartṛhari but by Harivṛṣabha and Puṇyarāja. These later grammarians belonged to post-Śaṅkarite period. But K.A.S. Iyer[14] and B.K. Matilal[15] are of the opinion that Bhartṛhari offers a *vivarttavādin* interpretation of the nature of transformation.

It seems that the controversy cannot be resolved so easily, for there is no conclusive proof available regarding the real authorship of the *Vṛttis*. So let us look at the problem from another angle. Let us go back to what Bhartṛhari says about his philosophical approach. He claims that as a grammarian he is not interested in what the facts present, but what the language presents. In his metaphysical scheme he seems to translate this basic line of approach at every stage. He looks at every problem and concept through the keyhole of language. So he is not bothered about the physical element of existence and creation. All the ideas associated

12. G.N. Sastri, *The Philosophy of Word and Meaning*, Calcutta: Sanskrit College, 1969, p. 56.
13. M. Biardeau, *Vākyapadīya, Brahmakāṇḍa*, French tr., Introduction.
14. Iyer, *Bhartṛhari*, p. 130.
15. Matilal, *Perception*, p. 195.

with the empirical world, such as "objects," "substancehood," and "particularity" are interpreted by him in terms of **Word**. This provides a strong evidence for the view that Bhartṛhari subscribed to *vivarttavāda*. The world is the apparent manifestation of the Word-Principle. The *śabda-Brahman* does not transform itself to become the world.

Coming to another meaning of change, i.e. the change at the empirical level, we find that Bhartṛhari introduces the concept of time (*kāla*) to explain the problem. In *Vākyapadīya,* I.2, he says: "*śabda-Brahman* though one has many powers and one of them is the power of time (*kālaśakti*)." These powers are actually non-different from the *śabda-Brahman*. It is due to our ignorance, we conceive these powers as different from the ultimate Reality. It is obvious that he introduces the concept of diverse powers of the Reality to explain the diverse ways in which we use language to describe the world. Instead of treating these various categories of linguistic presentation as representing the categories of existing things (*dravya*), as is done by the Vaiśeṣikas, he prefers to call them the attributes of Reality. *Śabda-Brahman* as the causal ground of the phenomenal world must include within its conceptual range the various categories used for thinking and talking about the empirical world.

The concept of Time has been discussed in detail in the third *kāṇḍa* of Bhartṛhari's *Vākyapadīya*, wherein he devotes an entire section to Time (*kāla samuddeśa*). His views on "Time" can be summed up as follows:

> The reality called *Brahman,* is without any sequence and consists of True knowledge and it is not affected by Time. Under the influence of Nescience, it assumes sequence and appears as this or that. Thus, through the interventions of Time the phenomena appear in a temporal sequence to the individual selves coming down from time immemorial. Because all differentiation consists of Nescience, all division of Time, adopted from different points of view, are also the creations of Nescience. Once True knowledge dawns, all differentiation

> disappears and, therefore, this division (of Time) also disappears. Therefore to discuss whether it (division) is right or not, would result in labour only.[16]

Thus Helārāja sums up Bhartṛhari's views on Time. Bhartṛhari also conceives Time as the efficient cause (*nimitta kāraṇa*) and it is attributed with the power of production (*abhyanujña*) and obstruction (*pratibandha*) of particular things of the world.

It sometimes appears that Bhartṛhari indulges in a metaphysics of "Time" rather than offering us an analysis of the concept of "Time" with relation to the word-world relationship. It also sometimes seems to express his mystical leanings. Therefore it directly goes against his avowed claim that his philosophical analysis is based on "what language presents." But if we overlook some of these mystical descriptions we may find a logic behind Bhartṛhari's emphasis on the concept of Time. He introduces this concept to explain another important dimension of the phenomenal world, i.e. the idea of "change." Explaining the idea of multiplicity is not enough for providing a correct analysis of the empirical phenomena. He conceives of the Reality as **one** and **unchangeable**. The phenomenal world being characterized by change owes an explanation in terms of the unchangeable Reality. To explain this issue Bhartṛhari introduces Time. In certain respects Bhartṛhari's description of *kālaśakti* is similar to that of Śaṅkara's conception of *māyā*. Both the concepts signify the power of introducing multiplicity and change at the phenomenal level. Yet there is a difference between the conception of *kāla* and *māyā*. *Māyā* is seen from two angles; in its projective form it is *māyā*, and in its negative form it is *avidyā*. But for Bhartṛhari *kāla* is conceived because of *avidyā*. *Kāla* itself is not *avidyā*. Moreover *kāla* is directly related to his explanation of every diversity at the linguistic level. Our experience, cognitions as well as the awareness of objects are intertwined with words. They are conceivable and communicable in terms of language. And all forms of linguistic expressibility

---

16. As tr. Iyer, *Bhartṛhari*, p. 123.

imply the presentation of the phonemes and syllables in sequential pattern. In case of our linguistic utterances we utter them syllable by syllable. We cannot express the whole meaning at one point of time. So sequence (*krama*) is an important aspect of speech. Similarly, our experiences — be it of external world or inner states of our mind, such as pleasure, pain, etc. — are arranged in time. Otherwise we cannot distinguish one experience from the other. As Bhartṛhari analyses the phenomenal world in terms of *śabda*, for him the sequential presentation of words is very important. So he conceives Time as the **a priori** condition of our thought, knowledge and speech. This aspect of Time proves the difference between Śaṅkara's view of *māyā* and Bhartṛhari's view of *kāla*. Śaṅkara has no compulsion for explaining the phenomena in terms of sequence.

Another important aspect of his emphasis on Time is brought to light by Helārāja in his *Vṛtti*.[17] This to a large extent supports Bhartṛhari's approach to philosophy in terms of *śabdenābhidhīyate*. He says that the main purpose of Bhartṛhari in devoting a whole section of his book to Time is not to define it philosophically but to analyse some problems with regard to the use of verbs in different tenses. One problem already discussed in the *Mahābhāṣya* is — how can the present tense be used in regard to eternal things? Another question that crops up is with regard to the use of two words expressive of two different tenses in the same sentence. Innumerable problems may arise in connection with the use of tense forms. These tense forms cannot be understood without reference to Time. Besides all our linguistic expressions refer either to the past or to the present or to the future. They represent the arrangement of events in Time. Therefore Bhartṛhari conceives Time as the effective cause of the phenomenal world.

---

17. *Vāk*, pt. III. Pt. II. I.25-27.

nāsmābhidarśanavivekaḥ prārabdhvaḥ । *kintu śabda vyavahāra yadaṅgaṁ tatparikṣyaṁ* । *asti ca bhinnakālaḥ śābdo vyavahāro 'bhudasti bhaviṣyatitī* । *tatra yathāyogamvicāritaramaṇīyaḥkālo 'bhyupantavya idarthaḥ* ॥

Helārāja's exposition of this particular dimension of Bhartṛhari's conception of Time, at least, removes our misgivings about the inconsistency committed by him. It confirms that Bhartṛhari's approach to philosophy is Word-oriented, not Existence-oriented. He is concerned with the explanation of the nature of Time as far as it comes within the purview of the linguistic representation of the Reality.

Now we are in a better position to understand the basic tenets of Bhartṛhari's Monism. The *śabda-Brahman* as the Reality is presented here as the ultimate ground of unity. This unity is not forced upon the level of diversity, for the diversities at each level point to unity.

(1) At the level of language-in-use, there is a presupposed unity amongst the form of words, meaning and the referent. As long as language is not manifested and expressed, we cannot differentiate these three elements. They are present within us in the form of an undifferentiated **one**.

(2) At the level of consciousness there is the unity between the universal of the word and the universal of things. Only when the words are used we differentiate between the universal elements in the word and the objects meant.

(3) At the level of cognition the diverse elements of objects of reference, actions and relations are united and cognized in an unitary form. In our statements about cognition there is reference to the objects, qualities, relations, etc. Conceptually they are distinguishable but in the sentence they are united.

All these levels of unity presuppose an ultimate unity by virtue of the fact that they are all word-potent. This common element of word-potency is crystallized in our conception of *śabda-tattva*, the ultimate Reality. This is how Bhartṛhari presents a consistent account of the relation between the one and the many; the unity and the multiplicity.

Bhartṛhari's Monism and its Logical Conclusions

Our discussion on Bhartṛhari's metaphysics of language will not be complete without a review of the logical conclusion that follows from his Monism. Depending upon the nature of the basic concepts each philosophical system leads to the formation of a world-view. Such world-views may be Conceptualistic, Realistic, Phenomenalistic or Nominalistic. Bhartṛhari's Linguistic Monism leads him to Phenomenalistic and Holistic world-view.

Let us first of all examine — what sort of logical picture we can form about the world if it is seen from the platform of "language" ? To get an answer to the question, we have to know how Bhartṛhari presents the concept of language-in-use. According to him language-in-use is a vehicle of communicating the meaning. But the meanings that are expressed by particular sentences or the words cannot be considered to present the **Meaning** as a whole. The diverse ways we express meaning can at best give us a "piece" or a "bit" of the **Meaning-whole**. When we use language for communication we extract a "part" of it on the basis of selecting what we intend to express. This is done by the method of, what Bhartṛhari calls, *apoddhāra*, i.e. "the process of constant and progressive extraction, comparison, analysis and abstraction."[18] The meaning is attached to these abstracted "bits," extracted from the linguistic whole by abstracting letters from the words, words from the sentences, sentences from the discourse, and discourses from the larger discourse and so on. These "bits" of meaning presented by words, sentences and discourses owe their significance to the **Meaning-whole** or the **Real-word**, which Bhartṛhari designates as the *sphoṭa*. The *sphoṭa* is the operative ground of our linguistic communication. This is the unified point which includes the word, the form of the word and the meaning. At the level of *sphoṭa*, all these elements are undifferentiated. Each conscious being shares this unitary *sphoṭa*. Therefore, the speaker can express his thought in unlimited number of ways and mean innumerable objects. Similarly, the hearer can understand the

18. Matilal, *Perception*, p. 393.

speaker because he shares the same store-house of meaning. So each linguistic expression is nothing but only a part of the expressible **Meaning-essence** or **Meaning-whole**.

When we employ the extracted "bits" of meaning, we also refer to the extracted "bits" of the phenomenal world. Corresponding to the "whole" of meaning, there is a "whole" of the objects-meant. The world of objects as such is not knowable. We only know a "bit" of it as is presented by sentences and words. Whatever we know of the objects is limited by concepts — the linguistic constructs (*vikalpa*). The concepts involve the process of selection and elimination. For example, the word *ghaṭa* (pot) as a concept can only mean a part of the object referred to, namely the universal of *ghaṭatva* (potness). But the particular object referred to can be described and meant in innumerable ways. We can as well refer to the pot's redness by the sentence "the pot is red." If one wants to refer to the colour of the pot then he has to use the concept "redness." So the "whole" of the object cannot be grasped by the language. The object can be "meant" differently with reference to different words that express it. In each case we present a selected and limited aspect of it. The "whole of objects-meant" and the "whole of the meaning" are ungraspable by the "bits" of the linguistic units.

Logical Atomism and Holism

In this connection, it will be of interest to examine the Logical Atomism of Russell and Wittgenstein. Of course, the Vaiśeṣika system of India presents an Atomistic world-view. But their metaphysical position is quite different. They are Realists, and they do not look at facts from the standpoint of language. Coming back to Logical Atomism, we note that Wittgenstein (of *Tractatus*) conceives that the language and the reality (world) share the same logical structure. So by analysing the logical structure of language, we can unravel the logical structure of reality. According to Russell and early Wittgenstein, to determine the logic of the language we must analyse it into its simplest and unanalysable form. The simplest form of linguistic statement is the atomic proposition.

These atomic propositions picture the simplest and unanalysable facts, called "the atomic facts." These atomic propositions, according to them, are not further analysable into proposition but to the elements, called the "logical proper names." And these logical proper names refer to the simplest element of reality called "objects." So at the linguistic level, the ultimate unit is the "proper name" which corresponds to the ultimate unit of referents, i.e. "objects." These "objects" are neither objectively nor ontologically determined. They are logical and are assumed in the context of the logical analysis of language. With this interpretation of the relation between word and world, Wittgenstein and Russell successfully overcame the problem of relating physical things to the words. Here, the nature of the reality is determined in terms of the logical analysis of language. We find that both Bhartṛhari and the Logical Atomists analyse the structure of the world in terms of the structure of language. Both analyse language through the method of abstraction. But for Bhartṛhari the whole is real whereas the abstracted and analysed "bits" are unreal and artificial. For the Logical Atomists the abstracted unit is logically real but the whole cannot represent the real. For Bhartṛhari the whole is indivisible whereas for the Logical Atomists the ultimately abstracted "bit" is indivisible and unanalysable. So their logical conclusion is entirely different from Bhartṛhari's. The entire analysis of the Logical Atomists leads to a form of Referential theory of meaning. For the logical proper names must be hooked to the referent — "object." The atomic propositions are a picture of atomic facts. In a sense, logically there are two parallel levels — the level of facts and the level of language, bound by the common logical structure. But in Bhartṛhari's theory the level of referents and the level of language are non-differentiable, as the referents and facts are not analysable except through language.

In Bhartṛhari's metaphysical scheme there is no scope for duality. So the world of objects and the world of words cannot be cognized independent of one another. But Bhartṛhari, at the same time does not deny the existence of empirical world independent of cognition. What he simply means is that the true nature of the existence is beyond the scope of cognition. Cognition being word-potent can frame the picture of the objects as it is presented through words. The objects are known only through the "guise" of words. The real existence (*mukhya sattā*) is unknowable. But it exists, for all our activities prompted by language deal with external realities. Otherwise our activities would not be possible. "Being asked for food we cannot very well present the speaker's 'mental' food."[19] Then why does Bhartṛhari believe that we can only know the objects as represented by words? In answer Bhartṛhari would say "It is extremely difficult to establish by reasoning the nature of objects, because the properties differ according to difference in circumstances, place and time" (I.32.). So the objects are understood so far as they are caught within the network of the universal of words. And we transfer the universal of the words to thing-universals. So objects have a metaphorical existence (*upacāra sattā*). The attributes of words are metaphorically superimposed on objects.

Quine would call such an explication of the relation between the word and the object as a non-critical and primitive way of looking at things. He says: "you and I never confuse physical things with their names, but primitive people do view names as somehow the soul or the essence of the thing."[20] But in case of Bhartṛhari such criticism would not apply, for Bhartṛhari is not confusing names with the essences of things. For him whatever we can know of the objects is how it is presented to us by the words. His position is in this sense Nominalistic, i.e. we know the things as they are represented by the names and words. B.K. Matilal very aptly points out that in the philosophy of Bhartṛhari there is no confusion, but "fusion"[21] between the words or names and the object. So words and the meanings are regarded as non-

19. Matilal, *Word and World*, p. 129.

20. W.V.O. Quine, "Mind and Verbal dispositions," in *Mind and Language*, ed. S. Gutten Plan, p. 50 quotation taken from Matilal's *Perception*, p. 396.

21. Matilal, *Perception*, p. 397.

distinct prior to their manifestation. The manifested form of articulate words illuminate the meanings for the hearer to grasp, and then it becomes superimposed and identified with the things. According to Bhartṛhari's viewpoint there is no fallacy involved in saying "This is a cow" instead of saying "This is the object which we call a member of the cow-class." "This **fusion** of sign and object constitutes an important part of what language actually is."[22] Bhartṛhari would call this "**attributive** identification" or "identification through attribution" or "superimposition" (*adhyavasāya*).[23]

Thus Bhartṛhari offers us a Metaphysics of Word — which is conceived by him to be the principle of ultimate unity. It is such a form of unity which allows the possibility of differentiation and division. But these divisions and differentiations are not logically independent, as they imply unity as their explanatory principle. They have significance only with reference to the empirical and phenomenal. But for those who have achieved the knowledge, the essence of language, the phenomenal divisions of concepts and forms have no real significance. Therefore, according to Bhartṛhari the study of Vyākaraṇa is the doorway to liberation.

---

22. Matilal, *Perception*, p. 397.
23. Ibid.

Helārāja's commentary on *Jāti Samuddeśa*, 6. Quoted from Matilal, *Perception*, p. 397.

3

The Sphoṭa Theory of Language

Language Analysis and Metaphysics

THE concept of *sphoṭa* as the ultimate principle of linguistic communication is unique and novel in many respects. Matilal very rightly points out that "the Indian grammarians' theory of *sphoṭa* has been acclaimed as one of the most important contributions to central problem of general linguistics as well as philosophy of language."[1] However, the worth of such a theory has for a long time remained unnoticed. It is only with the revival of interest in philosophy of language, that the *sphoṭa* theory has come to the limelight. The concept of *sphoṭa* is not originally offered by Bhartṛhari. But it cannot be denied that it was he who used it as the fundamental concept of the study of language. Later grammarians have successfully developed the theory further, but they have done so only on the basis of the ground work provided by Bhartṛhari.

It is unfortunate that some early Indologists like Keith[2] and De[3] have described the concept of *sphoṭa* as a mystical entity. A careful study of Bhartṛhari's analysis does not show much trace of mysticism. Some analogies and epithets used by Bhartṛhari may create such an impression. But such instances are rare. Rather his

1. Matilal, *Word and World*, p. 77.
2. A.B. Keith, *A History of Sanskrit Literature*, Oxford: Oxford University Press, 1928, p. 387.
3. S.K. De, *Studies In the History of Indian Poetics*, London: Luzac and Co., 1925, p. 180.

analysis and explanation through metaphors are clear and straightforward. Under no circumstances can we interpret them as mystical. According to some modern thinkers such wrong ascription of mysticism may be due to his theory of *śabda-tattva Brahman*. If such is the case, then it shows the strong bias of the critics and interpreters against Bhartṛhari. It may be also due to the misconception that any talk about the **Reality** in metaphysical sense is another way of indulging in mysticism. If so, then all the theories of the past in India, as well as in the West, can be bundled off as mysticism. Even the concept of "Absolute" of Hegel and Bradley, the Logical Atomism of Russell, will not be spared from the charge of mysticism. But this is not the case, as is evident from large volumes of critical writings available on all these philosophers and metaphysicians.

Coming back to Bhartṛhari's theory of *sphoṭa*, we may note that this is more a part of his philosophy of language than the metaphysics of language. In spite of some metaphysical underpinnings his philosophy of language is theoretically autonomous. Rather, after going through his philosophical analysis of language-in-use, one may be left with the impression that his concept of *śabda-Brahman* draws its logical support from the former and not vice versa. And the theory of *sphoṭa* is the anchor sheet of his inquiry about "how language functions?" This inquiry utlimately leads him to the conception of Reality in the form of *śabda-tattva*. Passing from language analysis to metaphysics is not a new thing. There are plenty of instances in the history of philosophy where the notion of language implicitly or explicitly has determined the nature of metaphysical theories. The phenomenon of language has always perplexed the critical thinkers of the past. The questions like — What after all is language?, How do we express our thoughts through language?, Whether language can offer us some clue to the understanding of human experience and cognition?, etc. contine to haunt the philosophers. Therefore, we come across many metaphysical theories which are largely determined by one's speculations about the nature of language. Plato, for example, finds a clue to the solution of the riddle of Being and Becoming by looking at the nature of the words that are used in our cognitive episodes. He finds that the words that signify concepts remain unchanged amidst the fluctuations in the level of experienceable facts of the world. Unless the concepts and names are taken to be objective, universal and stable, no thought, no judgements about the nature of the world would be possible. The words and concepts go on conveying the same meaning in spite of the variations and changes in the level of the referred objects. Therefore he offers the status of **Reality** to universal class names. He calls them "Ideas." Aristotle on the other hand looks at the nature of judgements and their linguistic expressions to pinpoint the basic categories through which our mind understands the facts. Out of ten such categories he offers primacy to substance and quality. These two categories are represented by the subject and predicate of judgements. These two primary linguistic elements are turned into the metaphysical principles of "form" and "matter." Russell very rightly observes that Artistotle transforms the simple linguistic fact of subject and predicate into metaphysical Realities. Kant, another gifted and original philosopher of the West, escapes the metaphysical trap of the Platonic and Aristotelian kind. But in his *Critique of Pure Reason*, he analyses the judgemental forms to delienate the structural map of the "knowable." His categories of understanding, which according to him are the a priori conditions of the knowable and experienceable, are in fact drawn from the forms of judgement. But he avoids turning them into transcendental Realities. His metaphysics is different. It is not transcendental metaphysics but, as he claims, the "metaphysics of experience." Strawson analysing it further shows that Kant's is a form of "Descriptive Metaphysics"— which instead of offering a revised conceptual order, draws its principal materials from the actual way of describing the world.

So, we notice that the analysis of linguistic forms and principles have many a times determined the metaphysical stand of a philosopher. Bhartṛhari's way of doing metaphysics is not an exception to the rule. What makes Bhartṛhari a philosopher of a different kind is his deliberate and explicit effort to explicate every concept in terms of linguistic facts. No doubt, he begins his treatiste with the announcement about the ultimate metaphysical Reality, but it is entirely based on the workings of language at the phenomenal level. Like the twentieth-century philosophers of language, his chief concern is to examine "how language functions" at different levels of our conscious activity. "Language" is the only "object" as well as the only "means" of doing philosophy. So we need not always drag in the metaphysical concept of *śabda-tattva* to understand what he has to say about the nature of language and linguistic communication.

At the outset I must mention that the concept of *sphoṭa* is very much a part of his philosophy of language. Though sometimes he uses the terms *śabda* and *sphoṭa* interchangeably, the contexts of his statements make it clear that in such cases *śabda* does not mean *śabda-Brahman*. The concept of *sphoṭa* is presented by him as the ultimate ground of the linguistic communicability. It is the co-ordinating factor amongst the varying aspects of language-in-use.

Sphoṭa : Its Meaning and Implications

It is very difficult to translate the term *sphoṭa* into English. It has been varyingly translated as the "Real-word," "Logos," "Real Language," the "Bearer of meaning," etc. Things will be easier if we explain it etymologically. The term *sphoṭa* is taken from the root *sphuṭ* which means "bursting forth" or which has a tendency to manifest itself. Nāgeśa Bhaṭṭa, a follower of Bhartṛhari, describes *sphoṭa* in two ways — that from which meaning bursts forth, and thus is the meaning-bearer; and the principle which is manifested through phonemes. By no means, Bhartṛhari is the first philosopher to use the term *sphoṭa*. Its etymological history dates back to Pāṇini's reference to the term *sphoṭāyana* in his treatise *Aṣṭādhyāyī*.[4] Haradatta,[5] the follower of Pāṇini, believed that

4. Pāṇini, *Aṣṭādhyāyī*, 6.1.123.

5. Haradatta, *Padamañjarī*, Under Pāṇini's above rule.

Sphoṭāyana was the first propounder of the *sphoṭa* doctrine. Yāska,[6] however, refers to another ancient scholar Auḍumbarāyaṇa, who propounded the philosophy of *sphoṭa*. John Brough[7] is of the opinion that in all probability Auḍumbarāyaṇa was the forerunner of Bhartṛhari's theory of *sphoṭa*. However, it was Patañjali who explicitly discusses about *sphoṭa* in his *Mahābhāṣya*.[8] According to him *sphoṭa* signifies speech/language, and the audible sound (*dhvani*) is its special quality. The audible noise may be variable depending on the speaker's mode of utterance, whereas *sphoṭa* as the unit of speech is not subject to such variations. But Bhartṛhari develops the idea of *sphoṭa* in a completely different way. He ascribes to it an unique philosophical dimension. For him *sphoṭa* is neither a meaning-bearing unit nor a linguistic sign. It is something more than that. The true implication of Bhartṛhari's version of *sphoṭa* theory will be clearer as we proceed with our discussions.

The question that needs some elaboration at this stage of our discussion is — why does Bhartṛhari talk of *sphoṭa* as the primary basis of all sorts of deliberations on the nature of language? To answer this, we must first of all identify all the elements involved in the case of our linguistic expressions. Language-in-use involves a complex network of elementary factors. First, our linguistic utterance involves the use of audible noise through vocal organ. But any and every audible noise is not language. The sounds and syllables uttered have a form of their own, which only make some audible sounds a part of language. Then comes the question of meaning that is expressed through the audible sound patterns. It also involves the ordering of sound forms and words in a particular order. In other words, without the rules of grammar and syntax meaning is not articulately expressible. Again the words and

---

6. Yāska, *Nirukta*, 1.1.

7. John Brough, "Theories of General Linguistics in the Sanskrit Grammarians," in *Transactions of Philosophical Society*, 1951, pp. 27-46 (34).

8. Patañjali under Pāṇini's rule, 1.1.70.

sentences that are uttered, are supposed to have an object of reference, i.e. a "designate." If we probe still further, we notice that linguistic utterances imply the notion of a speaker, who primarily and essentially uses language to express his thought and intention. But the process of linguistic act will be valueless if there is no hearer to understand what the speaker means to say. At least, all these factors mentioned above must be explained to offer a complete account of how language works. For Bhartṛhari language is not simply analysable in terms of phonetics, syntax, grammar and semantics. Language is above all, meant for communication. It is inter-subjective, where both the speaker and the hearer have an active role to play. Therefore, Bhartṛhari takes care to analyse the multiple nuances of language. Not only he explains these varied dimensions of "language" but offers a coherent account of it. Here the concept of *sphoṭa* is needed to provide an anchor-sheet to the complex activity called language. Bhartṛhari begins his discussion on the nature of language by distinguishing two aspects of language. In verse I.44 he says, in any case of meaningful linguistic utterance (expressive word) the experts on language comprehend two elements. One is the root cause of manifestation (*nimitta*), and the other is the applied (*prayujyate*), when manifested, to convey meaning. The latter element is called *sphoṭa* and the former is *nāda/dhvani. Sphoṭa* is the real basis of language, the very linguistic potency, which is manifested by *dhvani. Dhvani* is the audible sound pattern, wihout which the very potency of meaning and its expressibility is impossible. That is why the audible speech, which is presented sequentially syllable by syllable, is called the *nimitta* (cause) of the manifested meaningful expression. The *sphoṭa* is defined as indivisible, partless, sequenceless whole. All the grammatical and syntactical divisions are discernible only when the thought is translated into the audible sound pattern. At this stage, the language becomes applicable, because along with the phonetic elements it also expresses the meaning. The unit of meaning, expressed by the sound pattern, is there in the verbal dispositional ability of the speaker as well as the hearer. In his commentary on the verse I.44 he says:

> In the sequenceless nature of the *vāk* (speech) [which also means *sphoṭa*] both the powers, the power to be articulated in sound (audible form) and the power to convey meaning, lie intermixed.[9]

In spite of the risk of misrepresentation we can interpret the *sphoṭa* and *dhvani* distinction in terms of the distinction between the propositional content and the speech-act. I bring in the term "propositional content" to make it clear that according to Bhartṛhari the same *sphoṭa* can be expressed in different languages, like English, Sanskrit, etc. Yet it will be wrong to say that *sphoṭa* is the "bearer of meaning." *Sphoṭa* implies the total "unit of linguistic potency" — which when expressed is diversified into two elements, sound-word and meaning-word. The entire idea can be expressed clearly with the help of the following diagram.

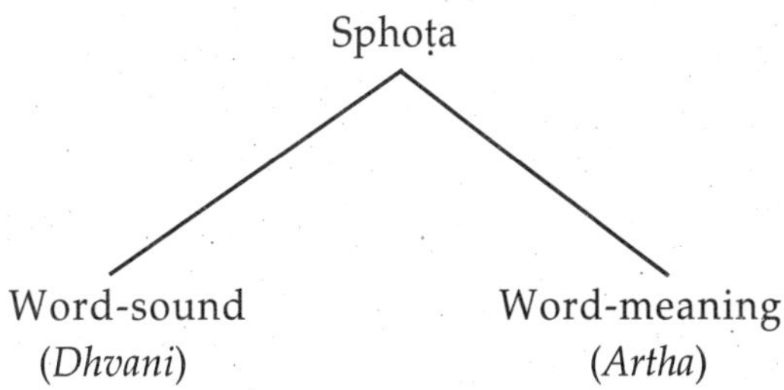

From the above diagram, it follows that the indivisible, changeless *sphoṭa* is a two-sided coin. One of its dimensions is the sound pattern and the other is meaning-bearing unit. It is believed that *sphoṭa* along with expressing the meaning also expresses itself. This is expressed by Bhartṛhari in the following way, under the verse I.46:

> Just as light/fire (*jyoti*) resides in the *araṇi* (churning) stick and (being manifested) becomes the cause for manifesting other

9. Brough, "Theories of General Linguistics," p. 34.

> objects; *śabda* resides likewise in the MIND (*buddhi*, the inner faculty) and being manifested becomes separately the cause for manifesting itself as well as the meaning.[10]

The concept of *sphoṭa* has been explained by Bhartṛhari through many such analogies. They sometimes lead to confusion regarding the exact significance of this term. So we come across varied interpretations of the meaning of the term. There is no unanimity of opinion regarding the exact significance of *sphoṭa* amidst the scholars. John Brough and K. Kunjunni Raja interpret *sphoṭa* as the linguistic sign in its meaning-bearing aspect. According to Joshi[11] and Cardona[12] *sphoṭa* should mean sound unit of the language system. Iyer,[13] however, refutes the latter view and argues that *sphoṭa* should include the meaning-bearing speech unit. I feel that Matilal offers the most balanced and plausible explanation of what Bhartṛhari means by *sphoṭa*. According to him "*sphoṭa* is the real substratum, proper linguistic unit, which is identical also with its meaning. Language is not the vehicle of meaning or the conveyor belt of thought. Thought anchors language, and language anchors the thought. *Śabdanā*, "languageing" is, thinking; and thought vibrates through language. In this way of looking at things, there cannot be any essential difference between a linguistic unit and its meaning or the thought it conveys. *Sphoṭa* refers to this non-differentiated language-principle."[14]

Now let us see why the concept of *sphoṭa* as the "language-principle" is presupposed by Bhartṛhari. He could have done away with such a concept and could have carried on his discussions about language in term of the words and the meanings. What

10. K.K. Raja, *Indian Theories of Meaning*, Madras : Adyar Library, 1969, pp. 97-148.
11. S.D. Joshi, *The Sphoṭa Nirṇaya of Kaunda Bhaṭṭa*, Poona, 1967, p. 40.
12. G. Cardona, *Pāṇini : A Survey of Research*, The Hague: Mouten and Co., 1976, p. 302.
13. K.A.S. Iyer, *Bhartṛhari*, pp. 158-59.
14. Matilal, *Word and World*, p. 85.

exactly is the role of *sphoṭa* in our understanding of the nature of language? To justify Bhartṛhari's need for introduction of the concept of *sphoṭa*, we should still go deeper into the analysis of how language functions. And on the basis of this we can offer justifications for Bhartṛhari's need for assuming the idea of *sphoṭa*.

One of the questions that baffles the philosophers of language is connected with the human ability to formulate and understand unlimited variations in linguistic expressions.

> There are limitless sentences and combinations of sentences of which we know, in advance, the sense, the significance, though we shall only over use, or hear or read, a comparatively insignificant portion of them.

So "we ask: how is it that we have vast and potentially limitless understanding"?[15] Strawson, one of the most eminent philosophers of our times, formulates the problem for the modern philosophy of language in the above manner. It is obvious that this vital issue of the language-speakers' limitless ways of expressing thoughts must have bothered Bhartṛhari and the ancient Indian grammarians too. Though the nature of the problem is the same for both Bhartṛhari and the modern philosophers of language there is a difference in their formulation of the problem. For the modern philosophers of language the problem is how the limitless understanding is generated by the limited rules of vocabulary and syntax? For Bhartṛhari the basic question is: "how does our language function in limitless ways along with the variations in the rules of syntax and vocabulary?" For him the rules of syntax and vocabulary can be varying and they are formulated by the grammarians for the purpose of articulate expression of the sense and meaning. But the power of the words to express meaning in multiple contexts is ultimately rooted in the very dispositional linguistic ability present within each conscious being. The questions of vocabulary and syntax comes only after this linguistic ability is

15. P.F. Strawson, "Meaning and Understanding," in *Analysis and Metaphysics*, p. 98.

manifested in the form of audible noise. *Sphoṭa* is the basic ground of linguistic expressibility itself. It implies the limitless potentiality which is rather expressed in limited and varying rules of syntax and vocabulary. So Bhartṛhari would rather consider what the modern philosophers call the "rules of syntax and vocabulary" a part of our very linguistic potency. They do not precede our understanding of "language" as a concept, rather the rules are the results of our capability to present our thought in a meaningful way. So he says that the real linguistic potency is in our inner faculty of intellect (*buddhi*) — all the differentiations, including the differentiations of the grammar and syntax are due to its presentation in the forms of audible noise (*śabdo 'pi buddhisthitaḥ śrutīṇāṁ kāraṇam pṛthak*).[16] The concept of *sphoṭa* is considered to be non-differentiated. But when expressed in language it not only varies according to the variations in the speaker's way of saying, but also according to the regional usages prevalent in different parts of the world. The rules of grammar and syntax vary from language to language. But such variations do not affect the very basis of "language," as the ultimate ground of words and meanings. Bhartṛhari's solution to the basic problem raised above may not sound very appealing to the modern philosophers of language. But their way of solving the issue has so far been not very satisfactory. Some of them have sought a solution by laying bare structural principles of our limitless linguistic understanding by an appeal to the formal logic. So they take resort to an analysis of truth-conditions, reference, predication, etc. If Bhartṛhari's metaphysical basis is Monistic, then the Western philosophy of language is rooted in the metaphysics of dualism. In other words their way of looking at language is always determined by the fundamental distinction between the particulars and the concepts, the reference and predication, the "that" of the subject and the "what" of the predicate. So the Western philosophy of language is inextricably related with the problem of "truth" and truth-conditionality. The concepts of "reference" and "predication" are

16. *Vākyapadīya*, I.46.

epistemological. But when these two concepts form the very basis and structural ground of all sorts of analysis of linguistic principles, then automatically they are raised to the status of the metaphysical principles. At the same time we must take care to notice that the modern version of the metaphysics of language is a form of descriptive metaphysics, for it abstracts the ultimate principles of language from the very nature of the general pattern of discourse. But Bhartṛhari's is revisionary metaphysics, because his world-view as well as the general view of language is largely influenced by his conceptual preference for the "non-difference" and "unity."

Let us now come back to the issue we had taken up earlier, i.e. what is the role of *sphoṭa* in explaining the nature of language? I have already stated the importance of the concept of *sphoṭa* in explaining the puzzle about the limitless ways of linguistic understanding. Now, we will pay attention to another, equally perplexing problem of philosophy of language. We all know that language is a means of communication. In case of linguistic communication the speaker is the person who expresses what he intends to say and the hearer is the person who is supposed to understand what the speaker means to say. Unless the hearer grasps the "meaning conveyed" by the speaker, the communication fails. But the moot question is — how does the speaker transfer the meaning to the hearer? The obvious answer to this question seems to be that it is because both, the speaker and the hearer, share the same linguistic convention. But the problem raised here is not that simple that it can be solved by as simple an answer. Bhartṛhari, at least, would not accept the answer offered as good enough. Following him we can reformulate the problem again. How do we explain the case of the gaps in communication in spite of the speaker and the hearer "sharing" the common linguistic rules? The hearer may be attentive and may hear carefully the utterances made by the speaker, yet there are times when he fails to grasp what the speaker means. How such gaps in linguistic communication arise? Bhartṛhari would say that such an issue is unanswerable as long as we think that the meaning is directly transferred from one person to another. To put it in a somewhat modern way, the meanings are not objects that can be transferred from one place to another place as we load the contents of one car into another car. The ability to express in speech-form, as well as the ability to discern meaning, both, are the two dimensions of the linguistic potency possessed by all conscious beings. This potency is otherwise known as *śabda* or *sphoṭa*. The fundamental idea is that both, the expressive word and the meaning expressed, are present in the consciousness of the speaker and the hearer. In other words the hearer and the speaker share the same *sphoṭa* (which by no means is equivalent to a set of the rules of syntax and convention of a language). When the speaker desires to say something he grasps the unit of meaning first and then expresses it in a sequential form of utterance, syllable by syllable. The hearer on the other hand, grasps the sequential and audible words first and these words evoke his "linguistic potency" and through it he understands what the speaker intends to say. This awakening of the hearer's *sphoṭa* causes the comprehension by the hearer of the sentence uttered. Thus the process of communicability can be seen from two standpoints, the speaker's and the hearer's. From the speaker's standpoint prior to the utterance of a meaningful statement the idea of what he intends to say is within him in non-sequential and undifferentiated form. It is this potency which makes it possible for him to express his intention in the form of utterance. So from the speaker's standpoint the linguistic potency or the principle of language is the cause (*nimitta*) of the uttered sounds. But from the hearer's standpoint the utterance by the speaker allows the hearer to refer to his potency to understand meaning (*pratyayaka*). In this sense the spoken words are the cause of understanding of the meaning. Therefore in the process of linguistic communication both the speaker and the hearer have to use their potential linguistic power, which, as we have seen, implies both — the power to use audible word forms and the power to convey meaning. And this is what is meant by the "sharing of the same *sphoṭa*" by the speaker and the hearer. To express it in Bhartṛhari's way: "The potency of language is like a peafowl's egg. All the colours of a fully grown peafowl is potentially there in the egg. These colours are manifested when the peafowl comes out of the egg. Similarly the *sphoṭa* or *śabda* is the potential stage in which the linguistic forms along with its power to mean is already present in all "languageing" being.[17] This is Bhartṛhari's explanation regarding the problem of transferability of meaning from the speaker to the hearer.

So far we were discussing how Bhartṛhari's concept of *sphoṭa* can be useful in solving some crucial problems of the philosophy of language. Now we will go further to examine the various implications of this concept. But before we do so, we must clear one confusion that arises from Bhartṛhari's explanations about the nature of *sphoṭa*. Sometimes it appears from his statements that when we express our thoughts in language, the *sphoṭa* itself is manifested in the forms of units of meaning. In verse I.48 he says:

> Since *nāda* (sound) arises in sequence, *sphoṭa* which has neither a former nor a latter stage and which is sequenceless (*akrama*) is apprehended (through *nāda*) and appears to be having sequence as well as parts.

Then in the next verse he says:

> (Thus properties of *nāda* are transferred to *sphoṭa*) the reflected image (of the moon for example) although it resides in a separate location, seems to share the operation (the movement of the waves in the water) of objects in a separate location; *sphoṭa* being manifested in the *nāda* in the same way.

The above passage implies that he not only means by *sphoṭa* the unitary and undifferentiated ground of word and meaning, but also the unit of meaning conveyed by the speaker to mean particular episodes, events, or things. But all along he mentions that these expressed units of meaning are impermanent and unreal (like the movement of moon in the flowing water). Besides, in the previous chapter we have seen that according to him the "language" as a principle implies the **whole** which is expressed for communicative

17. *Vākyapadīya*, *Vṛtti* under 1-58, tr. Iyer.

purposes in "bits" and "parts." So we may solve this apparent confusion by making a distinction between the meaning of *sphoṭa* as the very potency for linguistic expressibility and understanding, which is there in human inner faculty (*buddhi*) or the intellect; and the meaning of *sphoṭa* as the unit of meaning expressed by each meaningful utterance. If we accept that the true significance of the term is only the latter one, then there will be innumerable *sphoṭa*s, not one. This will be very much inconsistent with Bhartṛhari's entire philosophical outlook. So in all probability he used the term *sphoṭa* or *śabda* in extended sense when he talks of *sphoṭa* in the context of **words** and **sentences**. He used the term *sphoṭa* in extended sense to signify **any** unit of meaning. This is obvious from the fact that he also talks of *varṇa* (phoneme) *sphoṭa*, *pada* (word) *sphoṭa* and *vākya* (sentence) *sphoṭa*. At the same time in the second *kāṇḍa* of *Vākyapadīya* he offers a series of justifications to show that it is the **sentence**, not the word and phoneme, which is the primary unit of meaning. He rather says that for grammatical and practical purposes we make an artificial division amongst phonemes, words and so on. For a proper understanding of the nature of language, he shows that we can abstract phonemes from words, words from sentences, sentences from passages and passages from still bigger passages and so on. This method of analysis is known as *apoddhāra*. Still some snags seem to remain in his theory. Why does he insist so much on the primacy of *vākya-sphoṭa*? Does he mean by *sphoṭa* the "sense" conveyed by the sentence on different occasions as the fundamental basis of his language analysis? It is obvious that he offers primacy to the "meaning" expressed by a sentence and calls them *sphoṭa* because he in such cases refers to "language-in-use," not "language-in-principle." At the level of linguistic usage the primary unit of meaning can only be located in sentences, not in words. As he is more interested in "sense" than "reference" sentences for him represent the primary linguistic unit. But while talking of the structural element of language as a whole, he introduces the notion of *sphoṭa* as the potential ground for the whole range of elements associated with the linguistic communication. It is made clear in his commentary on verse I.56:

> The external (audible) word employed in verbal usage, is merged in the mind after suppressing all assumptions of differentiation, without, however, abandoning the residual force of differentiation, as in the case of the yolk of the pea-hen. Just as one single word can merge, so can passages consisting of as many as ten parts. The word, thus merged, with all differentiation suppressed, again assumes differentiation and sequences, when through speaker's desire to say something, the inner word (*sphoṭa*) is awakened and **it becomes the sentence or the word**, each with its division. It is this merging and emerging of word which is looked upon as its activity.

This passage clearly shows that though at places Bhartṛhari talks of *sphoṭa* being manifested in particular sentences or words, and though he talks of *varṇa-sphoṭa, pada-sphoṭa* and *vākya-sphoṭa*, the term has a different significance when he talks of *sphoṭa* as the ultimate ground of linguistic manifestations.

Bhartṛhari on Speaker's Communication of Meaning

We have already noted that Bhartṛhari's concept of *sphoṭa* can serve as the logical ground for the communication between the speaker and the hearer. We must now focus our attention to the process of communication, as it is conceived by Bhartṛhari. We know quite well that for linguistic communication to be possible the speaker must express his intention and the hearer must understand what the speaker intends to mean. We have also seen that the process of communication cannot be understood if we keep our investigation only limited to the area of uttered speech. We have to go beyond the level of utterance to explain how language is comprehended.

Bhartṛhari conceives of three stages of linguistic expressibility — the *paśyantī, madhyamā* and *vaikharī*. *Paśyantī* is the latent stage of language. At this stage the distinction between the word-forms and meanings are not there. Following Matilal[18] I will prefer to translate the *paśyantī* as non-verbal stage. *Madhyamā* is the

18. Matilal, *Word and World*, p. 88.

intermediate stage, where despite the identity of thought and language their distinction along with the distinctive elements of words and meanings are discernible. This stage is the "pre-verbal" stage. And *vaikharī* is the "verbal" stage, i.e. when the language is presented in audible form along with the elements of accent, pitch, meaning, etc. This is how the speaker's potential linguistic ability works when he intends to say something. But how does the hearer comprehend it? We have seen that according to Bhartṛhari the spoken words do not directly transfer the meaning to the hearer. It only awakens the hearer's linguistic potency, which in turn leads him to the comprehension of meaning. Such an explanation of hearer's linguistic comprehension may seem very peculiar. Why this round-about way, when the hearer can directly draw the meaning from the speaker's utterance? This is because, Bhartṛhari and other Indian philosophers take very seriously the sequential nature of the utterance. The utterance is expressed syllable by syllable, part by part but ultimately it conveys a unitary meaning. So their problem is: how does the hearer comprehend and the speaker convey the unitary meaning out of the particularized series of sound-patterns ? And this shows why Bhartṛhari does not believe that meaning of a linguistic expression can be directly conveyed to the hearer through the merging and emerging sequences of phonetic elements.

Now let us see how Bhartṛhari handles this problem of sequential syllables and non-sequential and unitary sense or meaning of the uttered words. Bhartṛhari's problem is to show at what stage of utterance the meaning as a unit is conveyed. Let us analyse his problem with an example. If X utters the word "Kamala" — he has to express it vocally as "Ka" "ma" "la." Here, there are three sound units, which taken together implies "Kamala" as a meaningful element. Bhartṛhari believes that each letter serves as a medium of manifestation of the unit of meaning "cow." Now, if the unity of meaning in this series of three letters "Ka" "ma" "la" is manifested from the beginning by the first sound-unit then there is unnecessary repetition and redundancy. If it is the last sound-unit which is responsible for cognition of the unitary meaning, then the preceding sound-units are superfluous. Besides, by the time somebody utters the last sound-unit the preceding sound-units are no more heard. Bhartṛhari avoids the problem of repetitiveness, by postulating that each sound-unit results in a distinctive property (*viśeṣa*) in the level of awareness or comprehension. So the first syllablle "Ka" expresses the whole unit of meaning but in an indistinct way. It becomes progressively clear with the utterance of successive sound-units till the last sound-unit is uttered.[19] By the time the last sound-unit is uttered, the preceding sound-units have disappeared. But the memory impressions of the preceding sound-units are retained. So these memory-impressions along with the hearing of the last syllable gives the hearer the total unit of meaning. However, Bhartṛhari's account of the comprehension of meaning-units may seem to be unsatisfactory. If the whole meaning of the word "Kamala" is expressed by each individual syllable "Ka" "ma" "la," then one can comprehend "Kamala" from the utterance of each syllable. But the hearer perceives each individual syllable separately. And the unit of total meaning is not identical with individual syllables. Bhartṛhari answers this objection with the help of Vaiśeṣika theory of numbers. He says, just as the cognition, of lower numbers "one" or "two" is a means for cognizing the higher numbers, like "three," similarly the comprehension of the units of meaning (be it of the word or sentence), is conditioned by the cognition of the constituent sound-units. According to the Vaiśeṣika theory of numbers, each number is distinct from another number. And all numbers higher than the preceding numbers are produced by a sort of "connective-comparative" cognition, which is called *apekṣā buddhi*.[20] This is the notion through which many unities are brought under one number or another. When two things are cognized, one cognizes them as "this is one and that is one." This gives rise to the cognition of "two" or duality. And in this process each succeeding number is cognized. According to this theory, cognition

19. *Vākyapadīya*, I.83-84.

20. Ibid., p. 92; also *Vāk*. I.87, and *Vṛtti* under the verse.

of the previous number is the condition for cognizing the succeeding numbers. Applying the same logic of the comprehension of numbers Bhartṛhari argues that understanding and awareness of the distinct sound elements is the means for cognition of the combined unity of the meaning. If the speaker wants to convey the meaning to the hearer he has to take recourse to the unavoidable and essential condition of presenting his thought through sequential elements of sound-units (*nāda*). One has to take cognizance of this peculiar characteristic of language. Bhartṛhari also compares the hearer's understanding of language with the process of painting. The painter while painting, say, a landscape perceives his object of painting in parts, then he visualizes the whole and then while painting on a canvas he paints it part by part. Similarly, the hearer cognizes the speaker's words part by part and then grasps the whole meaning; and again, while responding to the speaker's statements, he expresses his thought part by part.

Hearer's Understanding and Pratibhā

Bhartṛhari, we now see, has offered his own explanation about the hearer's comprehension of the unitary meaning from the sequential presentation of the speaker's thought and intention. Still, one feels that the entire issue of hearer's comprehension of language is not resolved. The issue I raised some time back regarding the gap in communication between the speaker and the hearer remains unresolved. We know of many instances, where the hearer in spite of listening to the whole statement fails to comprehend what it means.[21] The above explanation about the comprehension of meaning from sequential speech-pattern does not include this issue. But Bhartṛhari is not oblivious of the problem. He believes that the hearer does not comprehend the meaning directly from the speaker's utterance. So Bhartṛhari introduces another concept, called *pratibhā* to explain the problem

21. *Ṛgveda*, 10-71 offers a very insightful remark about the nature of language. The verse says: "Many who look do not see, many who listen do not hear it. It reveals itself like a loving and well-adorned wife to her husband."

of linguistic communication. *Pratibhā* very broadly signifies the *intuitive* linguistic disposition.

Pratibhā is a concept which cannot be defined. Bhartṛhari explains it in the following way:

> This *pratibhā* cannot be in any way explained to others in terms of "it is this," its existence can be ratified only in the individual's experience of it, and the experiencer himself cannot describe it.[22]

This concept is very unique in the sense that in no other system except Yoga is such a concept brought in to explain the nature of linguistic meaning. Bhartṛhari and other Sphoṭavādins take help of this concept to explain the hearer's understanding of meaning. The gap in communication arises when the hearer lacks this intuition.

We have noticed that the meaning is always expressed through the sequential *nāda*. The "sense" or the meaning of a statement, however, is an indivisible and integral unit. This can be grasped in an instantaneous flash or intuition. So the hearer understands the meaning as if in a flash. Puṇyarāja while interpreting the verse II.2. of *Vākyapadīya* says that the sentence-meaning is not built up gradually on the basis of word-meanings, it is grasped through instantaneous flash of insight. This understanding does not have parts and it is grasped by the mind. This is neither spatial nor particular, nor dependent on peculiarities of particular language. It is the instinctive power of the mind. *Pratibhā* can be experienced but cannot be expressed, because it is the very basis of understanding and linguistic experience. In this sense it is the a priori condition of linguistic understanding.

Bhartṛhari, of course, uses the term in a very wide and comprehensive sense, so as to include the instinctive nature of the animal as well as the special intuitive power of the *yogīs*. He believes that even the birds and animals have this instinctive power to express themselves, though their communicative process is not

22. *Vāk*, III.146.

as articulate as men's. Such an interpretation may lead us to the controversial question, whether animal language is possible or not ? But this is not our concern here. What we must concentrate on is: does *pratibhā* "as a concept" have any significance? It may be very easy on our part to dismiss this idea as a sort of mystical explanation, having nothing to do with philosophy of language. There are also plenty of grounds available for doing so. Bhartṛhari himself says that this concept cannot be stated in the form of a definition. It cannot be even described by the individual who experiences it. Besides, Bhartṛhari says that our instantaneous intuition of linguistic understanding draws its support from the knowledge of words acquired through previous birth (*saṁskāra*). So let us now see how much of his theory is mystical and how much of it conforms to the structural conditions of linguistic understanding.

I shall start by taking the issue of *saṁskāra*, i.e. the linguistic disposition acquired from the previous birth. This notion is no doubt unscientific. What Bhartṛhari intended to prove is that our linguistic ability is not totally dependent on learning the rules of language, i.e. convention and syntax. The human ability to express himself is innate (in the sense, that it is a part of the human nature). The rules of language and convention make it articulate. Without this, what one intends to say may not be properly conveyed. But man's ability to apply these rules in unlimited number of ways is not dependent on such rules themselves. This phenomenon has always perplexed the philosophers and it continues to do so. Bhartṛhari finds an answer to this perplexing issue with the help of the traditional belief of his time. In Indian cultural tradition, especially the orthodox tradition, the belief in immortality of soul as well as in rebirth were uniformly accepted. So we cannot exactly blame him for referring to previous birth. Nobody can deny the fact that the philosophical understanding of every age is determined by the progress of knowledge made during the time. As Galileo could not have talked in terms of neutrons and protons, similarly the ancient linguists could not have talked in terms of "disposition," "linguistic zone" of brain, etc.

Wittgenstein on Understanding

Now we come to the issue of "intuitive" knowledge or "instantaneous flash of understanding." Most of the modern scholars of philosophy will shrink to use the term "intuition." It is generally believed that if we are talking of cognition, knowledge, or language, then we must talk either in terms of "experience" or in terms of the "rules of logic" and "syntax." The knowledge derived from experience is verifiable, hence meaningful. The knowledge derived from the "rules of logic" are meaningful because they do not inform but offer us rules of inference. So the term "intuition" is considered to be unscientific, uncritical, primitive and sometimes mystical. Yet it is a matter of experience, especially in case of our understanding that we do take help of intuition. Sometimes even after several attempts, meanings of certain passages, certain discourses remain vague to us. And then in a sudden flash of intuition we grasp the meaning. In science, in mathematics, in poetics the role of "intuitive" knowledge is already acclaimed. Bhartṛhari, however, talks of intuitive knowledge in all cases of grasping the meaning because he finds the riddle of sequential nature of understanding quite perplexing. This riddle does not figure at all in modern philosophy of language. But no philosopher of language can deny their puzzlements about the human ability to understand unlimited ways of linguistic usage. No philosopher can give a proper explanation of what constitutes the linguistic disposition, except postulating that there is such a power or disposition to use language or understand language in unlimited number of ways. If we take these facts into consideration then it seems there is nothing mystical about Bhartṛhari's postulation of *pratibhā* as the intuitive faculty of operating with language. Before winding up our discussion on Bhartṛhari's notion of *sphoṭa* and communicative meaning I want to draw the reader's attention to a very interesting yet radically different interpretation of the concept of "intuitive" understanding. This is offered by Wittgenstein. We have seen that Bhartṛhari introduces the notion of intuitive flash or *pratibhā* to explain a hearer's understanding. This problem also bothers Wittgenstein. In his book *Philosophical*

Investigations, he emphasizes the communicative role of language. Therefore the idea of a hearer's understanding does not escape his notice, during his post-*Tractatus* phase. He says:

> It seems there are **certain definite** mental processes bound up with the workings of language, processes through which alone language can function. I mean the processes of understanding and meaning. The signs of our language seem dead without these mental processes: and it might seem that the only function of sign is to induce such processes, and that these are the things we ought really to be interested in.[23]

But this interest in mental processes seems to go against his anti-mentalistic stand of *Philosophical Investigations*. Here, he takes resort to a form of linguistic behaviourism which allows no scope for understanding the mental processes. He dismisses the role of any such intermediary step between the actual level of utterance and the hearer's understanding. There is no need to think, he says, that the hearer must be engaged in a mental act before he responds to the speaker's utterance. This intermediary step of mental states is considered to be a "grammatical fiction." In short, there are no such mental states occurring privately in the speaker's or hearer's mind. Neither "meaning," nor "understanding" is the name of any such mental process. We say such things as, "Since he understood what I said, he did the right thing"; or "Because he understood the principles involved, he was able to solve the problem." Embodied in these and other ways of talking is the picture of a person's (processes of) "understanding" as mental cause of his overt behaviour, as a mental reservoir from which action flows. This is a sort of picture-thinking and the manifestation of a "general disease of thinking" (*Blue and Brown Book*, p. 143).

He offers many examples of the cases when we clearly believe that intuitive flash is at work.[24] When 'X' is given a sequence of

---

23. L. Wittgenstein, *The Blue and Brown Book*, Oxford: Basil and Blackwell, p. 3. See also *Philosophical Investigations*, Section 358.

24. Wittgenstein, *PI*, Sections 210-14, 138, 139, 151, 155, 179, 180.

numbers and asked to continue the series, he may be said to have an intuitive understanding about how to proceed. Again everyone has the experience of understanding certain things "in a flash." He discusses such examples and makes an effort to show that there are no such mental states. But, what then is "understanding"? Wittgenstein would refuse to answer such a question. For, "meaning," "understanding" and other such words are not definable, as they have no common essence. "Once we have an overall view of the variety of situations in which the terms "meaning" and "understanding" are used, and of the various criteria of their use, there is nothing more to know about what meaning and understanding are. To know their use, Wittgenstein would say, is to know their meaning."[25] He at the same time admits that words get their life by being used in communication. The speaker must mean something by his utterance and the hearer must understand what he means. But the terms "intention" and "understanding" signify nothing more than observing how and when such words are used. He is not willing to budge an inch beyond the level of utterance, even though he admits that language implies communication.

In case of Bhartṛhari, we have noticed, there is no such hesitation about explaining the questions of the speaker's "intention" and hearer's "understanding" in terms of pre-linguistic mental states. He does not want to reduce the entire phenomena of language-in-use to the process of verbalization. It is very difficult to say which one is the correct account of meaning and language. It all depends on how they (Bhartṛhari and Wittgenstein) look at the concept of "language" itself.

---

25. George Pitcher, *The Philosophy of Wittgenstein*, Delhi: Prentice Hall of India Pvt. Ltd., 1977, p. 275.

4

The Word and the Meaning

Nature of the Relationship

WE all know that human beings take recourse to language to mean something. That "something" may be an event, an object, an emotion, a command or a question, etc. But without the use of words these varied sorts of phenomena included within the word "meaning" are not expressible. Most often common men as well as philosophers forget about the importance of words and concentrate on meaning. But to have a comprehensive knowledge about how language functions one must probe into the nature of relation between the word and meaning. For, this is the very basis of exploring the nature and function of language. However, at the outset, I must make it clear that the term "word" is not used here in a literal sense. By "word" I mean the linguistic expression as a whole.

While discussing Bhartṛhari's theory of *sphoṭa* we have seen that the concept symbolizes an identity between two diverse linguistic elements, viz. the forms of words and the meaning. We have also noted that forms of words do not imply just the phonetic act of producing audible sounds, but sounds with a particular form and order. In this chapter our primary concern is to investigate how Bhartṛhari relates these diverse elements, viz. words and meaning. It should be kept in mind that the words themselves are not meanings, but they express the meaning. In Bhartṛhari's language the form of word is the conveyor or the expression, i.e. *vācaka*, and that which is conveyed or expressed is the meaning, i.e. *vācya*. When the speaker intends to say something, he has to take care of these two aspects of language. He has to express in appropriate form of words and the exact meaning that he wants to convey. Before translating his thought into audible form both the elements, i.e. the form of words and meaning are present in potential form in his *buddhi* (the inner faculty or consciousness). Though these two elements stem from the same source, i.e. the *sphoṭa*, at the pre-verbal stage they are differentiated and distinguished. This is what Bhartṛhari means when he says that the first differentiation of linguistic potency occurs in the realm of *buddhi*.[1] Such differentiation is needed when the speaker becomes conscious that he has to communicate a particular thought or idea. But the words have not yet become audible nor the meaning is conveyed. The particular *vācya* (the contents of meaning) and *vācaka* (the word-forms) are grasped by the speaker before he starts making utterances.[2] The hearer also grasps these two elements before deciphering what the speaker intends by his utterance. We often tend to neglect the role of the *vācaka*. But one may notice that when the word-forms are not properly grasped by the hearer, he is likely to ask: "what did you say?"[3] So both the *vācya* and *vācaka* play equally prominent roles in linguistic communication. Bhartṛhari, in a broad sense, calls the *vācya* as *artha* (meaning) and the *vācaka* as *śabda* (words).[4] He also views the *vācaka* as *śruti-śakti* (the power of being heard) and *vācya* as

1. *Vāk.*, I.86.

   Also *Vṛtti* under I.170, II.19, II.31.

2. "Just as the mind of the speaker first turns towards the word, in the same way, the attention of the hearer is also first directed towards them." — *Vāk.*, I.53.

   "The word is examined in the mind, is then fixed to a specific meaning, and then through the instrumentality of word-sounds is produced (through their causes)."

3. *Vāk.*, I.57.

4. *Vāk.*, I.50.

   ātmarūpaṁ yathā jñāne jñeyarūpaṁ ca dṛśyate ।
   artharūpaṁ tathā śabde svarūpaṁ ca prakāśate ॥

artha-śakti (the power of being meaningful).[5] He also designates them as *prakāśatvam* (illuminator) and *prakāśyatvam* (illuminated).[6]

Bhartṛhari also points out another peculiar feature of language. In other forms of cognition, say, perception — the instrument of perception is not itself perceivable. We see things with eyes, but our eye itself is not visible. In case of cognition by linguistic means the instrument of such cognition, i.e. the word, itself is cognizable. In fact, we cannot cognize linguistic facts without cognizing the medium of cognition (words) first.[7] Therefore linguistic cognition is a special type of cognition. Our language is endowed with two powers, the power of revealing the meaning (*grāhaka*) and that of revealing itself (*grāhakatva*).[8]

Thus far we have seen that Bhartṛhari offers equal significance to word and meaning. Now Bhartṛhari's problem is to explain how these two distinct linguistic elements are related. In the third part of *Vākyapadīya* he devotes one whole section to investigate and explain the concept of "relationship" with specific reference to word and meaning. He envisages this relationship as twofold in nature. The word and meaning are bound by the relationship of inherent and natural fitness (*yogyatā*) and also by the relationship of causality (*kārya-kāraṇa bhāva*).[9] Sometimes he also uses the latter relation to explain the link between the form of words and the speaker's intention. To explicate the nature of relationship in greater detail, he identifies three elements in case of an utterance. They are: (1) the own form of words, (2) the meaning (in certain sense it also includes the object meant), and (3) the speaker's intention.[10] He views the relationship between the phonetic act of utterance and the form of words as the most intimate one

---

5. *Vāk.*, I. See Iyer's translation, p. 102.1.4.
6. *Vāk.*, II.32.
7. *Vāk.*, I.50.
8. *Vāk.*, I.56
9. *Vāk.*, III.3.1.2.
10. Ibid.

(*antaraṅga*).[11] This is called intimate because the hearer along with hearing the audible sounds also comes in contact with the forms of words. This is the initial means of grasping the word-forms. While the relation between the word-forms and meaning is called *vācya-vācaka bhāva*, the relation between the word and the intention of the speaker is called *kārya-kāraṇa bhāva*. Sometimes Bhartṛhari also applies *kārya-kāraṇa bhāva* to explain the relation between the word and meaning. The relationship is called *vācya-vācaka bhāva*, because the word is the conveyor and the meaning is what is conveyed. From another standpoint it is the word which causes the grasping of meaning in the hearer. So it is also described in terms of causality (*kārya-kāraṇa bhāva*).[12]

Both these dimensions of word-meaning relationship stem from a natural fitness (*yogyatā*) of words to express meaning. This power of conveying the meaning is inherent in the words. It is "natural" because it is not created at a particular moment of time by anybody.[13] It is not a case of human decision to use words for expressing meaning. Human beings cannot and have not created this relation. Man only knows that he uses words to express meaning. And he learns to use particular words to express particular meaning by watching the elders.[14] It is a matter of convention when it comes to the level of particular linguistic usage. The convention (*saṁketa* or *samaya*) can be made in two ways. Some words are used to express certain meanings since time immemorial, but certain words can be specifically coined from time to time for use in special and technical sciences.

However, when it comes to the relationship between the word and its expressive power the relationship is to be considered as "eternal" (*nitya*).[15] There should not be any misgivings about the

11. *Vāk.*, III.3.1.2.

12. Iyer, *Bhartṛhari*, p. 204.

13. *Vāk.*, III.3.2.

14. Iyer, *Bhartṛhari*, p. 205.

15. *Vāk.* Quoted in *Śabda Śakti Parikṣā* :

→

use of the word "eternal." Bhartṛhari himself makes it clear. He says that the term "eternal" can have two meanings. Something which has no beginning or end, something unchangeable is called "eternal." But it is eternal in absolute sense (*kūṭastha nityatā*). Bhartṛhari's conception of *śabda-Brahman* conforms to this sort of use. Again "eternity" may be used in the sense of "continuity." In this sense it is applied in case of word-meaning relationship. The words that are used as sound-token in particular linguistic utterances disappear once they are uttered. Yet we recognize such words along with their meaning in a thousand cases of utterances with all variations in accent and pitch. Again, the words continue to express the same meaning, though they are used in different contexts. The word "jar" means a particular "jar" though it can be used to refer to different individual jars. Such continuity and uniformity of meaning amidst variations and changes is also a form of "eternity," according to Bhartṛhari. He calls this *pravāhanityatā*,[16] i.e. the continuity amidst the stream of change. In this sense, *yogyatā*, the inherent fitness of words, to express meaning is eternal. The linguistic communication is made possible only on the basis of such continuity of relation between the word and meaning.

We can express the relation between the word and meaning through two types of statements. Either we say "this expressive power belongs to that (words)" or we can state it as "it (word) is that (expressive power)."[17] In the first way of putting things, a distinction is made between the word and meaning. In the latter case the identity between the word and meaning is emphasized. The former way of looking at the relationship is helpful in case of grammar and lexicography. But Bhartṛhari prefers the latter way

---

→ *ājānikas cādhunikaḥ saṅketo dvividho mataḥ nitya ājānikas tatra ya śaktir iti gīyate,*
kadācitkastvādhunikaḥ śāstrakārādibhiḥ kṛtaḥ
(Refer K.K. Raja, *Indian Theories*, p. 23)

16. Iyer, *Bhartṛhari*, pp. 207-8.

17. Ibid., p. 206.

of describing the relationship, i.e. the relation of identity. It is more appropriate for understanding the communicative role of meaning, in case of language-in-use.

Bhartṛhari also views the word-meaning relationship in terms of causality (*kārya-kāraṇa bhāva*). In this connection we must examine his notion of *saṁjñā* and *saṁjñin*.[18] It is sometimes translated as "name" and "named." It is usually believed that word as *saṁjñā* is used to signify some object or event external to our mind. When we use the word "jar" it is supposed to stand for the object "jar." In this sense, word and the object meant have a relation of "designate and designated." But Bhartṛhari does not understand the relation between *saṁjñā* and *saṁjñin* in this sense. For him, both belong to the realm of language. No doubt, we use words to designate objects. But all "objects" meant are not externally existent. There are words like "wheel of fire," "barren woman's son," etc. which has no corresponding external object. Similarly, in case of negative statement "the tree does not exist" there cannot be an external event corresponding to "non-existence." We may add to the list many such forms of expression, which do not designate any external event. So the object-named does not necessarily imply existent objects. Such cases lend support to Bhartṛhari's theory that *saṁjñā* does not directly mean "objects," but concepts or "thought-objects."[19] Both belong to the level of linguistic cognition. Understood in this sense, the relation between the word and meaning can be viewed as causal. It is the word which brings to the mind of the hearer the "idea of the object." Again in case of the speaker the "idea of the object" causes the use as well as the choice of appropriate words.

---

18. *Vāk.*, I.68-69.

19. Iyer, *Bhartṛhari*, p. 211.

    Vāk., III.3.61-71.

    Linguistic usage does not proceed with this transcending Reality as its basis. Its basis is rather what is **thought** to exist, what is conceptually constructed (as summarized in *Encyclopaedia of Indian Philosophies*, vol. 5, p 159).

If the words do not refer to objects and meaning is not referential then what do the words "mean"? We usually believe that the words always mean a particular object or fact. Since in Bhartṛhari's scheme of analysis there is scope for direct reference, we are left with words without anything being "named" or "meant." But we have seen that according to Bhartṛhari words mean concepts or "thought-objects." They are linguistic entities, not objective entities. Such entities are bound to be universal. But what about the utterances where we use words to mean a particular? When I say "this rose is red," I do not mean by "rose" the universal class of "rose" but a particular rose. Bhartṛhari's answer to this problem is that a word can denote individuals indirectly. This is done on the basis of a universal which belongs to the word itself. He would say the particular "rose" is referred to on the basis of our knowledge of the universal character of "rose-ness." Bhartṛhari sorts out two opposing views regarding the issue of meaning and referent. One is ascribed to *vyādi* and the other to *vyājapāyana*. *Vyādi* regards the individuals as the proper referent, while the latter regards universals as constituting the referent. In other words one regards individuals as the object-meant and the other offers this status to the universals. Helārāja, the commentator on Bhartṛhari's third part of *Vākyapadīya,* adds a third view.[20] According to this view the individual characterized or qualified by the universal constitutes the meaning of a word. However Bhartṛhari asserts that all words first of all mean or designate the universal and this is superimposed on the particular of the objective world. If we accept this view, then a subtle philosophical question may be raised. What is this "universal" that we mean by words? Does the universal belong to the realm of existence or to the realm of words? It is believed by some philosophers that the universal is not simply a mental or linguistic category. It is real and existent in the objects of the world. The rose is called "rose" because it shares the essence of "roseness" existing objectively. But Bhartṛhari does not subscribe to such a

20. *Vāk.,* I.68-69.

view. For him the universals are linguistic constructs (*vikalpa*) and universals are primarily "word-universals" transformed into "thing-universals" for facilitating our utterances about the world and things.[21]

So far we have been discussing the first two elements of a linguistic utterance, i.e. word and the meaning. Now let us do a brief scanning of the third element, i.e. the "speaker's intention." Full credit must be given to Bhartṛhari for bringing the "speaker's intention" within the scope of philosophy of language. In Indian philosophy there are elaborate discussions on the concept of "intended meaning" or "contextual meaning." Therefore some interpreters claim that analysis of "intention" has been a part of philosophical discussions on language in most of the philosophical traditions. Here, I beg to differ from such an interpretation. Such an interpretation is based on the translation of the word *tātparya* as "intention." Some Indian philosophical schools conceive that a sentence in order to be comprehended as a meaningful unit must be characterized by four factors. They are *ākāṅkṣā* (syntactic expectancy), *yogyatā* (logical consistency), *sannidhi* (phonetic contiguity), and *tātparya* (the contextual factors). The last element, i.e. *tātparya* was a later addition made by Nyāya School. As an example of *tātparya*, most often, the case of *saindhava* is stated. The word *saindhava* has two meanings, viz. salt and horse. If somebody says "bring *saindhava*," how is the hearer going to comprehend the meaning? If the statement is uttered while eating, the context demands that *saindhava* should mean "salt" not horse. So *tātparya* is connected with the hearer's comprehension of the intended meaning. But while uttering the sentence the speaker also expresses his intention. There is definitely a difference between the **speaker's intention** in saying something, and the hearer's **comprehension** of the speaker's intention. *Tātparya* stands for the contextual meaning to be comprehended by the hearer.

---

21. *Vāk.*, III.1.6.

svājātiḥ prathamam śabdaiḥ sarvair ebābhidhīyate ।
tato 'rthajātirūpeṣū tadadhyāropa kalpanā ॥

Bhartṛhari also provides a very insightful account of *tātparya*. But this should not be confused with the speaker's intention. For he uses a different word to signify it. It is called the *abhiprāya* of the *vaktā*.[22] In the Western philosophy of language, Grice, Austin and Searle have highlighted on the factor of the speaker's intention. Rather they have over-emphasized it, for their analysis of meaning is more or less speaker-oriented. On the other hand, the classical Indian thinkers placed more emphasis on the hearer's comprehension. But in Bhartṛhari's account of language, a balance is achieved between these two ways of looking at the problem of meaning.

According to Bhartṛhari there is a relationship between the words and the speaker's intention. It is a relationship of causality. It is the speaker's intention to communicate, which initiates his speech. In other words, he expresses himself through spoken words because he has the urge to communicate. So intention of the speaker is the cause of uttered words. On the other hand, the utterances arouse in the hearer the need to understand what the speaker intends. Therefore, there is a relationship of cause and effect between the elements of word-forms and the speaker's intention. In this sense, the intention of the speaker is a part of the network of factors that help us to understand the notion of linguistic communicability.

What does the Word Mean? Some Western Theories

So far we have been concentrating primarily on Bhartṛhari's notion of word-meaning relationship. Now for a while, let us shift our attention to another way of dealing with the issue. An in-depth probe into the Western philosophy of language reveals that their basic concern is not understanding the exact nature of relationship between the word and the meaning. Rather there is a clear attempt

---

22. *Vāk.*, III.3.1-2.

sarva parsad punaridam śāstramiti ye vahysyārthasya śabdavacatvam nechanti tanmatopa saṁgrahārtha vākyābhiprāya rūdhasaiva śabdārthatve tatra kārya kāraṇa saṁbandhamaha ।

to unravel what the words should mean in order to be significant. In other words, their primary concern is locating a criterion for meaning. We cannot avoid examination of this issue, as it forms a part of understanding the nature of language. Besides, our discussions on the topic may provide us with some insight for a better assessment of Bhartṛhari's views.

In the Western philosophy, the problem of meaning has been discussed from two different angles. There are some philosophers who have preferred to handle the concept of meaning in an abstract way. "Meaning" as a concept is isolated from the level of its concrete realm of use. On the other hand, others have explored the significance of the concept "meaning" from the functional standpoint, i.e. the level of actual linguistic transaction. Those who consider the former method as more suitable, treat the term "meaning" as an abstract concept. It is something like geometrical concepts, such as, "triangle" or "circle." In case of abstract concepts a suitable definition is fixed and then any idea suiting the definition is included within the concept. For example, we define the geometrical concept "triangle" as a three-sided bound figure, whose sum of angles is equal to 180. Any figure that conforms to the "essences" of triangle is called a "triangle." Similarly, some philosophers conceive that we can lay down the defining characteristic of "meaning" and anything that conforms to it is called "meaningful." In other words, it is believed that we can fix the criterion of meaning by determining its essential characteristics. Wittgenstein in his later philosophy branded such approach to the problem of meaning as "essentialistic" approach. It is a model-oriented approach, characterized by a craving for the unity of essence. The other approach, popularized by later Wittgenstein, handles the concept of meaning as the part of a function. It is the function of communicating with language. So this group of thinkers analyse "meaning" at the level of its operation in the varied contexts of human life.

(A) ESSENTIALISM

The Essentialistic approach is backed by a typical craving of philosophers for unity and precision. They want to explain the particularities and temporalities of the universe with some neat conceptual framework. In case of meaning too, the craving for unity is expressed through their search for some uniform "essence," i.e. an "essence" that can serve as the principle of unity for the diversities of our linguistic expressions. These philosophers explain the concept of meaning with two basic presuppositions: (1) "meaning" like other concepts is a class-name, which can be defined through the identification of some common characteristics, (2) the "essence" of meaning must be epistemologically independent of the level of practice, i.e. the actual employment of meaningful utterances. For the sake of brevity let us put such theories under two groups.

(i) The Referential Model.
(Meaning defined in terms of referents).

(ii) The Ideational Model.
(Meaning defined in terms of ideas, psychological or logical ideas).

(i) *Referential Theories*

The Referential theorists envisage that meaning of a word consists of what it refers to. This way of defining meaning is based on a desire to understand how our language is connected with the things of the world. The temptation to connect language with the world stems from the fact that often we use the word to "mean" or to ask question about the "referents." Taken at its surface value, the theory represents the common man's attitude to the problem of meaning. We learn language by being pointed out. Moreover, the forms of our language are such that it leaves us with an impression that for every word there must be a physical counterpart. Therefore, the words must stand for something objective, i.e. a thing, a quality, an event or a person. In our language even the mental states are described in physical terms. We talk of big heart, narrow mind, stretching of imagination, etc. whereas, in fact, only the physical objects can be big or small, stretched or turned. This dominance of physicalism, to some extent, lends support to the view that meaning can be attached to the referents alone. It is a sort of entitative view of language, i.e. meanings stand for entities. St. Augustine, in his theory of meaning states that "meaning" means what it stands for, i.e. an objective referent. But it was J.S. Mill who largely influenced the subsequent Referential theorists. According to him the smallest unit of meaningful expression is a word. And the words function as names. As the names stand for a place or person similarly all words must stand for something denotative. We understand the meaning of the word "Fido" because it stands for Fido the dog. But all words are not proper names like "Fido." Elucidating further, Mill argues that the words are names, but not proper names. The term "name" has a broader implication for Mill. It includes not only complex words and descriptive phrases but also adjectives. In short, any word that can stand as the subject or predicate of a proposition is a name. This denotationistic and Referential model offered by Mill strongly influenced some of the subsequent philosophers. Meinong was one of them. For him, meaningful words must have referents. And if the referents are not traceable in the world of existence, then they should be hooked to some "subsistent" entities.

However, a new logical dimension to the Referential model was added by Russell and Early Wittgenstein. Russell with his Theory of Description shows that words cannot stand for objects, in the sense Mill means it. Even the definite descriptive phrases, which are supposed to be the most suitable candidate for being called meaningful on the ground of their referring to the singular object, do not always stand for objects. So Russell thinks that we need a logical analysis of language to explain the role of referents. Russell and Wittgenstein introduced a new method of explaining meaning by the analysing proposition into its simplest form. These simple or atomic propositions are not further analysable into propositions but to simple elements called "logical proper names." The concatenation of such names are propositions. The logical proper names correspond to the simplest elements of Reality called "objects." So it seems that Russell and Wittgenstein stick to the Referential model, but they only replace "ordinary names" by "logical proper names." Such a logical explanation overcomes the problem of relating language with physical facts. Both, the language and the facts are explained in terms of a common logical structure. The referents are neither physical nor ontologically determined. But in all sorts of Referential theory we note a sort of gap. In case of Mill it is the gap between words and objects. In case of Russell and Wittgenstein it is the gap between the logical picture of language and the ordinary language. The logical analysis offered by Russell is neat and rigorous, whereas the ordinary language is too diversified to be bound by such a neat logical picture. Russell was so much enamoured of the precision of his logical analysis that he conceived of replacing ordinary language by an "Ideal Language." Only in case of such ideal language can there be a fixed structural relationship between the language and the reality. But the problem of closing the gap between the logical picture of Referential theory and the actual nature of ordinary language that we use, cannot be solved by dismissing the validity of ordinary language. If the problem of meaning is to be analysed then we must take into account the concrete level of language-in-use. Neither the facts nor the language can be so pinpointed and so adjusted to have the one-to-one relationship between them. It is, however, Wittgenstein who frees himself from this entitative bias in the course of his book *Tractatus* itself. He shows that it is not the words but propositions which have meaning. Our sentences are no list of names or words, but a relationship of words which project a possible form. The realm of facts and the realm of language share a common logical structure. The propositions are meaningful when they picture the reality by projecting this common logical structure. But the problem continues to exist. If we accept Wittgenstein's proposal then meaningfulness can be ascribed only to the descriptive statements. Unfortunately, all our meaningful utterances are not descriptive in nature. There are many meaningful utterances which express command, instructions, emotions or simple rules of day-to-day conduct. If we stick to the Referential model then a large chunk of what we call meaningful propositions would be out of the bounds of meaningfulness.

Another radical form of Referential Theory surfaced during the 1930s. This theory was advocated by the Logical Positivists. They claim to be influenced by some of the remarks made by Wittgenstein in *Tractatus*. But it seems that they were more influenced by the methods of natural science. In their well-known "verifiability criterion of meaning," they suggest that a statement in order to be meaningful must be verifiable, or else the statements must be concerning the rules of logic/mathematics or other a priori sciences. Excluding these two forms of statements, other forms of statements are nonsensical in nature. I claimed that they were influenced by the methods of natural science, because it was believed that these two types of statements were used in science. But the Logical Positivists subsequently realized that all the statements of science are not verifiable in nature. Moreover, the laws of science are stated in the form of universal propositions. But universal statements are not verifiable. So the Logical Positivists went on modifying their criterion and at last almost abandoned the criterion of verifiability. But it cannot be denied that the Positivistic theory of meaning is a form of Referential theory. And all forms of Referential theory narrows down the scope of meaning to the function of referring to the facts.

(ii) *Ideational Theories*

The Ideational theorists, on the other hand, believe that words do not stand for objective referents, but ideas. The ideas may be psychological or logical in nature. The British empiricist Locke advocated that meaning can be identified with psychical entities. For him, the primary unit of our language is a word, and the primary unit of our thought is an idea. The words must stand for ideas. As Locke says :

> The use, then, of words is to be a sensible mark of ideas; and the ideas they stand for are their proper and immediate signification.[23]

23. John Locke, *Essay Concerning Human Understanding*, Book III, Ch. 2, Section I.

Hume is also a co-traveller of Locke, in this respect. He reduces thought in its ultimate analysis, to image. Words are associated with images; and this is the basis of determining the meaning. So the essence of meaning is identified with the accompanying mental states, that a word calls for. These ideas directly or indirectly refer to the sense-impressions or sense-datum that we get from the perceptual world. But this model fails as a theory of meaning. First of all, there are many words which are not accompanied by mental images. Moreover, ideas and images are private and particular. So they lack the desired universality, which must be shared by others to make the linguistic communication possible. Rather Plato's theory scores over this psychological account of meaning. Plato is bothered about the element of inter-personal nature of language. So he locates the objects of meaning in "ideas." Such ideas are not psychological states but universal class essence. I have discussed Plato's theory in my previous chapter. So without going into details, we can say that such a logically promising theory somehow gets muddled by his acceptance of ontological status for the "ideas."

The logical explanation of meaning, in terms of ideas, comes from Bradley. He categorically states, "the idea **is** the meaning."[24] But such ideas are purely logical in nature. According to him ideas are pure, abstract and universal. The logical condition of our judgements reveal that everything has two aspects, the substantive part and the predicative part. Bradley calls the substantive part as **that** of a judgement which stands for the subject. The predicative part is called **what**, i.e. the content of a judgement. According to him, our judgement is an act by which we attach **what** (ideal content) to **that** (reality), which is beyond the act. So there is no brute fact to which we can jump with our judgements. The substantive part is purely logical in nature. It is neither meaningful nor meaningless. So meaning is adjectival in nature, it is the "what" of the proposition, which adds meaningfulness to the subject part. But the predicative and adjectival content is a part of the "meaning-

24. F.H. Bradley, *Principles of Logic-I*, London: Oxford University Press, 1922, p. 6.

whole" or the "ideal-content." The ideal-content is purely universal and abstract in nature, and "wandering adjective,"[25] which we cut loose from conceptual net and apply it to contexts which mind has fixed. The ideal content or meaning is the one and the whole, a complex totality of qualities and relations. It is we, the language speakers, who introduce division and distinction, and call these products separate ideas with relation between them. So every judgement is a part of this whole, it is not just a relation between two particular ideas, i.e. subject and predicate.

Here, we note that Bradley's analysis is completely different from the other theories of meaning we have discussed so far. Other theories, be it Referential or Ideational, analyse meaning in terms of words, not sentences. Moreover, such theories concentrate on particular statements and the conditions of their meaningfulness. Bradley's theory of meaning represents more or less a metaphysics of meaning. And in certain respects it is very similar to that of Bhartṛhari's theory of Śabdādvaitavāda. Like Bhartṛhari, he believes that the "meaning-whole" or "language-whole" cannot be expressed as such. What we present through our language are "bits" or "pieces" of the "meaning-whole" by selecting and fixing a particular part of it. Our language does not refer to facts directly. The brute realm of facts are not graspable by the "bits" of language. However, there is a big difference between Bradley's and Bhartṛhari's metaphysics. For Bhartṛhari, the Absolute metaphysical principle is of the nature of language, *śabda*. But Bradley's Absolutism is not an Absolutism of language. Besides Bhartṛhari does not analyse language in terms of "that" and "what." If there is such linguistic distinction between "that" and "what," Bhartṛhari would rather say that both belong to the "ideal content" or the "meaning-whole."

(B) NON-ESSENTIALISM

Let us now revert back to our discussion on the theories of meaning. We have seen that the essentialistic approach is based

---

25. F.H. Bradley, *Principles of Logic-I*, London: Oxford University Press, 1922, p. 10.

on determining an essence for meaning. Wittgenstein, in his book *Philosophical Investigations*, took to task his own Essentialistic interpretation of meaning in *Tractatus*, his early work. In total opposition to what he said earlier in *Tractatus* he declares that meaning does not represent an essence. It is rather futile to fix a definition for meaning, because it is not the name of an entitative concept, but a function. It is the function of "use." So to understand the true nature of meaning, we must see it "at work." With this new way of handling the problem of meaning in his book *Philosophical Investigations* he brings to our notice three main aspects of philosophy of language: (i) Language is an **act**. It is the act of communication. So we must take into consideration the role of speaker, hearer and the context of speech, (ii) Meaning is a question of workability and applicability in diverse human situations; and (iii) the true nature of language cannot be unravelled in terms of strict structural rules and ideal language. We have to keep ourselves at the level of ordinary language and watch its diverse forms of use.

We need not discuss all the aspects of Wittgenstein's philosophy of language. But it will suffice to say that Wittgenstein's later philosophy marked the beginning of a new way of doing philosophy. Wittgenstein in his *Tractatus* concentrates on the structural and semantical aspects of language. But now he shifts his attention to the functional and pragmatic aspect of language. His dictum "Don't ask for the meaning, ask for use" — brings into prominence the communicative dimension of language. If we notice the phenomenon of language at work, we find that language has multiple facets. It can be used to mean varied sorts of activities. As Wittgenstein points out, we can use language to report facts, to play, to pray, to tell stories and to do many more things. So he discards his early view. He says that the relation between the word and meaning is not like:

> Here the word, there the meaning. The money and the cow you buy with it. (But contrast: money, and its use).
>
> — *PI* 120

By highlighting the functional aspect of language he successfully shows that our language does have multiple functions and forms. Meaning can be determined in various ways depending on what activity is intended to be performed by its use and the context of its use. He compares language with a tool box. As the tool box contain varied sorts of tools, and each of them are meant for specific functions, similarly language performs varied sorts of function. The rule of one "language-game" cannot be applied to another form of game. We cannot decide the meaningfulness of a factual statement with the criterion that is meant for understanding a moral statement. There are multiple forms of language, and multiple ways of deciphering their meanings. In short, for him "diversity" is the keyword not "unity."

This new way of approaching the problem of meaning brought in its wake many new theories, each highlighting one or the other aspect of communicative role of meaning and language. Most prominent amongst them are Grice's and Austin's theory. Grice in a small paper entitled "Meaning," brought into focus the role of the speaker and the importance of "intention" in the communication of meaning. Austin in his book *How to Do Things With Words* showed the different levels of **acts** in the performance of a communication. He very explicitly showed the distinction between the "meaning" which is the propositional content of the utterance, and the "force" which reflects the speaker's intention in uttering a statement. Searle developed Austin's theory of speech-acts to elicit the basic structural conditions involved in speaker's utterances as well as in hearer's understanding. Davidson, on the other hand, focused on the semantical aspect of communicative meaning by adopting a modified version of Tarski's semantical notion of truth. And we expect many more theories of language and meaning to emerge in future.

Another new trend in philosophy also emerged from Wittgenstein's emphasis on diversity and non-essentialism. Wittgenstein in his *Philosophical Investigations* advocates that language is not only communicative but it represents the forms of life. Human life and experience is multi-dimensional, and accordingly language too has multiple facets. So the criterion of meaningfulness cannot be put into the straightjacket of an uniform definition. Each form of language has its own rules of acquiring meaningfulness. The logic of understanding one form of language cannot be applied to understanding the significance of another form of language. When I say "This table is red" and "X is good" — both are meaningful statements. But the former is a descriptive statement and the latter is an evaluative statement. I can discern the meaning of the former statement on the basis of its reporting a state of affairs. But in case of the latter statement no such facts are stated. I cannot verify the "goodness" of a man in the sense I verify the "redness" of a table. This sort of analysis gave rise to specialized branches of philosophy such as, philosophy of religion, philosophy of morality, etc. In such specialized studies philosophers take up for analysis the specific nature of language used in, say, statements of ethics, or religion, etc.; and the nature and meaning of such statements are delineated. Holistic understanding of language, as a result, is replaced by fragmented and piecemeal analysis.

Bhartṛhari on Different Layers of Meaning

Keeping in our mind these new trends of handling the issues of language and meaning, let us assess Bhartṛhari's position. To the question "what does a word mean?" — Bhartṛhari's answer would be, "that which is communicated by the speaker to the hearer." Here Bhartṛhari's way of looking at meaning cannot come within the fold of essentialistic theories of meaning. Nor is it non-essentialistic in Wittgensteinian sense. No doubt, he would admit that language is not necessarily descriptive. It is clear from the examples he uses in his treatise that he admits of varied forms of linguistic usage. Once he admits the communicative role of language, the varieties of meaning communicated are automatically taken for granted. But this does not result in fragmented view of communicated meaning. But how does the hearer discern different forms of meaning communicated? Does he confuse the reporting of facts with the subtle emotions expressed in poetry? In Bhartṛhari's scheme there is no scope for such confusion, nor is there any necessity for the hearer to have the knowledge of the structure of different forms of language. The task of discerning the meaning is left to the inherent linguistic intuition called *pratibhā*. So variety of forms of linguistic utterances do not figure very prominently in Bhartṛhari's philosophy. He treats language as a "whole," which is expressible in multiple number of ways.

(A) PRIMARY AND METAPHORICAL MEANING

One of the most remarkable features of Indian way of looking at language is that all the systems of thought conceive language as communicative. The other important feature is understanding the concept of meaning from the hearer's standpoint. Therefore, the problems they encounter is of a different nature. They undertake to examine the different shades of meaning which the hearer encounters, such as literal meaning, intended meaning, contextual meaning, metaphorical meaning, suggestive meaning, etc. They also undertake to examine certain common linguistic features such as the use of homonyms, synonyms and ambiguous words. And also they offer clues for discerning the meaning of ambiguous words.

It is a fact that our ordinary language is very flexible and fluid. To bound it by the strict rules of one word-one meaning relation will stifle its naturalness. We can do many things with words, we can turn and twist a word to mean different ideas. Therefore in all natural languages we come across the problem of varied shades of meaning. Bhartṛhari takes up the peculiarities of language-in-use with all sincerity and tries to solve the problems arising out of the peculiarities of linguistic usage. First we have the problem of metaphorical transfer of words. This is most often based on similarity or contiguity, and shifts in meaning. In such cases, a distinction must be made between the primary meaning and the secondary meaning, otherwise the force of the metaphor will be lost. But how do we make the distinction between the primary and metaphorical meaning? In Indian philosophical literature we come across varied interpretation of metaphorical meaning of words. In his *Vākyapadīya*, Part II, Bhartṛhari discusses different popular views available on the topic.[26] But it should be kept in mind that for him the primary unit of meaning is a sentence, not a word. And he also believes that the meaning is not necessarily grasped from the knowledge of individual words used in a sentence. Still he does not mind discussing the question of the distinction between the primary and metaphorical meaning of words. Some of the popular views stated by him are as follows:

(i) According to those who hold that a word can have more than one meaning, the distinction between primary and secondary meaning is based on the relative frequency of the usage. The meaning with which a word is frequently and generally used is the primary meaning.

(ii) There are others, who hold that a word can have only one sense, who believe that the word having the primary sense and the word having the secondary sense are actually different words, though they sound alike.

(iii) Another theory attributed to *vyādi*, is that the primary meaning of a word is that which is well known; and which only depends on its form. But the secondary meaning is established with effort, with the help of some context.

(iv) According to yet another view, words refer to the qualities. That object which possesses these qualities to a greater extent is called the primary meaning and the other is called the secondary meaning. Bhartṛhari does not support this view, because this is not the pattern followed in our actual usage.

(v) Another view regarding this distinction, is totally different. According to it, the metaphorical or secondary usage is based on similarity. "Devadatta is a lion" means that Devadatta possesses those qualities similar to that of a lion.

---

26. *Vāk.*, II.265-67, 274, 275, 276, 280.

Though Bhartṛhari takes care to present these popular views, his stand regarding the issue is totally different. According to him the metaphorical meaning, or any other form of intended meaning can be deciphered only in the context of a sentence, and the particular situation in which the sentence is uttered. Thus when a mother says "the tiger eats children who cry" — any sensible hearer will understand that the intended sense is to induce some fear in the child so that he will stop crying. Again in cases like ironical statements, the meaning of the individual words taken together gives a different sense than the sense intended in the context. Therefore Bhartṛhari argues that words as such cannot have metaphorical meaning. It is only the sentence and the context of utterance which can determine whether the sentence expresses the literal meaning or metaphorical meaning.

(B) LITERAL SENSE AND CONTEXTUAL MEANING

As Bhartṛhari emphasizes the role of sentence as the primary conveyor of meaning, he offers a detailed account of deciphering the intended meaning by the hearer. We have noted earlier that some Indian philosophers take *tātparya* as one of the conditions of sentence-meaning. *Tātparya* literally means significance, but in the context of sentence it implies the significance derived from the contextual factors. In a linguistic communication the speaker expresses his intention (*abhiprāya*), but unless the hearer grasps the intended meaning, the communication fails. It is well known that our natural language is full of ambiguous words. So the hearer has no way but to refer to contextual factors to understand the sense of an utterance. Bhartṛhari was one of the earliest philosophers to recognize this peculiarity of natural language. The speaker can use the words to express the literal sense and also to express some intended sense. Therefore Bhartṛhari gives an account of how meanings can be rendered precise with the help of contextual factors, as well as syntactical factors. Briefly they may be stated as follows:[27]

---

27. *Vāk.*, II.317 f.

(i) *Association* — The word *hari* may be used to mean various things. It is the name of God Viṣṇu, it may also mean a monkey. But the term *hari* used in association with *hari* "with conch and discus" would make it clear that by *Hari* lord Viṣṇu is meant.

(ii) *Dissociation* — The word *dhenu* may mean a cow or a mare. But the sentence "*dhenu* without calf" is unambiguous, because the phrase "without calf" implies a dissociation which makes it clear that we are talking of a cow which is now without the calf.

(iii) *Mutual association* — When somebody says "Rāma and Lakṣmaṇa went to forest," we decipher that "Rāma" means the brother of Lakṣmaṇa, not Balarāma (the brother of Kṛṣṇa) or Paraśurāma. Here the meaning of Rāma is recognised on the basis of mutual association of Rāma with Lakṣmaṇa.

(iv) *Hostility or opposition* — *Chāyā* means "beauty" or "shade." But in the compound phrase *chāyā* and *āloka* (light) the meaning of *chāyā* obviously implies "shade." This is because of the opposition of meaning between the light and shade.

According to Matilal all these four factors can be called the general determination of meaning through association. It is mostly a case of psychological association.[28]

(v) *Purpose* — *Sthānu* means a pillar or Lord Śiva. In the sentence "worship *sthānu*" the purpose of the speaker is obviously served when the term is understood in the latter sense.

(vi) *Context or situation* — "Bring me *saindhava*," at the time of eating should mean "salt," and at the time of going out should mean a "horse." Here the contexts determine the intended meaning of *saindhava*.

---

28. Matilal, *Word and World*, p. 25.

(vii) *Indicatory sign* — Some sign may be present in a larger context. In the context of a passage containing a ritual, when it is stated "**wet** pebbles are placed on the altar," it means wetting the pebbles with clarified butter. The pebbles as such can be soaked in any liquid, but in the larger context of a ritual the sentence means soaking in clarified butter. We have to understand it as an indicatory sign.

(viii) *Proximity with another word* — This is also a case of association. But it is not a case of psychological association. In such cases, physical proximity or syntactical connection is meant. The sentence "God, the destroyer of cities" refers to Lord Śiva. Here the proximity or association of "God" restricts the meaning to Śiva, otherwise "kings" can also be meant by "destroyer of cities" (enemy cities).

(ix) *Capacity* — In the sentence "The cuckoo is intoxicated by *madhu*," *madhu* should mean, here, the spring season, not honey. The former sense of *madhu* (spring) has the capacity to intoxicate (in poetic sense) a cuckoo.

(x) *Propriety* — In the sentence "May your beloved's *mukha* protect you," *mukha* means "favour," not "face," since the former meaning will be proper in this context.

(xi) *Place* — In the sentence "There stands the master," "the master" should mean the king not the God. The meaning of "the master" is determined by the use of "there" (the place).

(xii) *Time* — The sentence "*citrabhānu* shines," should mean "the sun shines" if uttered during the day, and "the fire or light shines," if uttered during the night.

(xiii) *Gender and (n) accent* — In some cases grammatical devices can resolve ambiguity. The word *mitra* in masculine gender means the sun, but in neuter gender means a friend. In the compound word *indra-śatru*, when the first syllable is accented it means "one whose killer is Indra." When the last syllable is accented it means "the killer of Indra."

The above list is not exhaustive, nor is mutually exclusive. Moreover, the contextual factors are determined by keeping the peculiarities of Sanskrit language in mind. But it is obvious that Bhartṛhari takes into account the grammatical factors, syntactical factors, psychological factors, contextual factors (both verbal and non-verbal), for determination of the intended meaning. All languages share some of these features. But psychological and contextual factors definitely play a crucial role in the identification of intended meaning. However, prior to offering this exhaustive list, Bhartṛhari gives a limited yet more broad-based list of contextual factors. He says that the meaning of an expression is not to be determined merely by its form but by contextual factors also. They are — syntactical relation, purpose, situation, propriety, place and time.[29] These factors are more universal in nature and not related to a specific language (in this case, Sanskrit). If we go by the spirit of what Bhartṛhari says about the problem of word-meaning relation and communicability of language, it becomes clear that he deals with the problems in a comprehensive manner.

Bhartṛhari and Wittgenstein on Diversities of Meaning

I will like to conclude this chapter with an interesting point that emerges from our discussion here. Both later Wittgenstein and Bhartṛhari start with the presumption that language is communicative, and language can be used to express varied sorts of meanings. Despite this, their analysis of language results in radically different conclusions. Bhartṛhari's analysis ends up with a holistic view of language, on the other hand, Wittgenstein's analysis ends with a diversified account of language. This difference may be ascribed to their inherent purpose in taking up the problem of language. Bhartṛhari was a grammarian-philosopher, so his avowed task was to examine everything in terms of "what

29. *Vāk.*, II.316.

vākyāt prakaraṇāt arthād aucityād deśakālataḥ ।
śabdārthaḥ pravibhajyante na rūpād eva kevalāt ॥

language presents." Wittgenstein, on the other hand, was more or less perturbed by the confusions and muddleheadedness created by the philosophers being "duped" by linguistic elements. In his *Philosophical Investigations* he investigates the nature of language to use it as a therapy. This is clear from the following passage:

> Of course what confuses us is the uniform appearance of words when we hear them spoken or meet in script or print. For their **application** is not presented to us so clearly. Especially not, when we are doing philosophy. — *PI*, Sect. II

The language that we ordinarily speak, often leads us to form a picture of reality. And these pictures entrap us in some form of generalized world-view. Therefore, he conceives that the task of the philosopher is not to be trapped by the structural and grammatical analogies presented by language :

> Philosophy is a battle against the bewitchment of our intelligence by means of language. — *PI*, Sect. 109

> Philosophy . . . is a fight against the fascination which forms of expression exert upon us. — *Blue and Brown Book*, p. 27

Wittgenstein perhaps would have said that the forms of language "duped" Bhartṛhari too. The picture of "word" as all-pervasive phenomenon held him captive. So the ultimate aims of Bhartṛhari and Wittgenstein in handling the concept of language and meaning are radically opposite.

5

Language and Communication

Formalism versus Communication-Intention Theory

BHARTṚHARI conceives language not as a string of dead and sterile syllables but as an act. Language gets its life by being used by the humanity in their exchange of thought and expression. In short, language is communicative in nature. In the context of modern philosophers' interest in communicative role of language, let us examine how they formulate and solve this problem of communication; and how Bhartṛhari looks at the issue.

The philosophical discussions on the problem of language and meaning during the last four decades are dominated by two distinctive strands of thought. On the one hand the Formalists like Frege, early Wittgenstein, and Chomsky projected language as a rule-governed activity; on the other hand the Communication-intention theorists like later Wittgenstein, Grice, Austin and others highlighted the functionalistic and communicative dimension of language. Both the schools agreed that the language was a rule-governed activity but the point of their difference was regarding what should be the primary basis of meaning. For the Formalists **linguistic meaning** is primary, whereas for the latter, the **communicative meaning** is primary. In other words, the Communication theorists argue that the fundamental concept of meaning should be understood in terms of "speaker's **meaning something by** an audience-directed utterance on a particular occasion." As a result they contest the Formalists' thesis that the rules of syntax and convention are all that is to be explicated if one has to understand the concept of language. They rather insist that the rules and conventions are explicable in terms of the communication-intention. Grice even goes to the extent of arguing that it is possible to expound the concept of communicative meaning without presupposing the notion of linguistic meaning. He shows that a system of convention can be modified to adjust to the needs of intention to communicate, which we can scarcely imagine to exist before the system existed. And these modifications in turn can create the possibility of thought which would not have been possible without presupposing these modifications. This proves that language is not just a reproductive activity on the part of the speaker, it is creative too. There is always a scope for modifications and enlargements in the area of linguistic meaning, which ultimately makes language a living affair. There is always an interplay between the rules and conventions on the one hand, and the intention to communicate on the other. As Strawson succinctly puts it, "Primitive communication-intentions and successes give rise to the emergence of a limited conventional meaning-system, which makes possible its own enrichment and development which in turn makes possible the enlargement of thought and communication needs to a point at which there is once more pressure on existing resources of language which is in turn responsive to such pressure. And of course there is an element of mystery in this; but so there is in human intellectual and social creativity any way."[1] The Communication-intention thesis definitely unfolds a very important dimension of language by exploring beyond the limits of the linguistic meaning. One may not agree with Grice on the point that communication-intention itself is sufficient to explain the conception of meaning without any reference to the rules of convention and syntax. But at the same time, nobody can deny that a close relation between the communicative needs and rules of convention should be presumed if one has to conceive language as a living social affair. Still it seems that the presumption about this relationship is not adequate

1. P.F. Strawson, "Meaning and Truth," in *Logico-Linguistic Papers*, London: Methuen and Co., 1974, p. 175.

enough if one intends to investigate the nature of language and its capacity to convey meaning. It becomes mandatory for him to examine the nature of the relationship between the communicative intention and the rules of syntax and convention. The element of creativity that is a part of linguistic expression, which Strawson prefers to leave aside by calling it "an element of mystery," should be explored further to have a comprehensive idea about the true basis of the communicative role of language. Besides, there are certain baffling questions about linguistic communicability which needs considerable attention, viz. Is linguistic communication possible just because the speaker expresses his intention to communicate through the uttered speech? If so, then why in certain cases, the hearer, in spite of listening to the complete utterance by the speaker, fails to grasp the meaning? Again how in certain cases, even before the speaker has completed his utterance, the hearer grasps the meaning? These questions make one uncomfortable about accepting the communication-intention theory of meaning without probing further into some of the basic concepts of communication. For any thinker who advocates the theory of communicative meaning, explication of three primary ideas becomes mandatory, viz. (i) the speaker, (ii) the hearer, and (iii) the common bridge of inter-subjectivity. The **speaker** is the one, who not only utters certain strings of words, but also **intends** to communicate his thought or belief to somebody. Moreover, he not only intends to communicate but through his speech-act, he intends "to secure an uptake" (if I may be allowed to borrow the phrase from Austin) from the hearer. The **hearer** is the person who **understands** what the speaker intends to communicate through his utterance. He follows it up either by speaking his reactions, or by acting in accordance with the speaker's intention. But the most crucial concept in case of communicative interpretation of meaning is providing a ground for the inter-subjectivity. In other words, one has to explain how the meaning is transferred from the speaker to the hearer? The obvious answer to such a question seems to be: because the speaker and the hearer belong to the same linguistic community, they share the same rules and conventions of the "language-in-use." This answer seems so obvious that it prompts David Lewis to remark, "It is a platitude — something only a philosopher would dream of denying — that there are conventions in language."[2] But the philosopher is like a devil, who often loves to tread the area where the angel dreads to step. And he does it with success and sufficient justifications. So philosophers of language analyse the concept of "convention" and examine whether it can serve as a solid bridge for communication between the speaker and the hearer. Before I take up how the Communication-intention theorists handle the issues, I deem it fit to discuss Bhartṛhari's views on the notion of language, meaning and communicability.

Bhartṛhari on Language

Bhartṛhari handles the problems of meaning and language in a more comprehensive manner without assuming any gulf between the two ways of looking at things. He shows that there is an inter-play between the need for communication and the rules of syntax and convention. But obviously his theory seems to be more favourably inclined towards communication-intention theory of meaning. He would agree with these theorists in ascertaining that the intention to communicate is conceptually prior to the rules of convention. For convention itself cannot be the basis of language. The rules of convention presupposes the use of meaningful communication in some form or other.[3] Rather, according to Bhartṛhari the uttered level of speech, which requisitions use of rules, is not the whole language. It is like the tip of the ice-berg. Though the level of utterance is a very important phase of linguistic expressibility, it is not the whole of it. Even when the uttered speech is not at work, our linguistic competency does not slumber,

---

2. David Lewis, "Languages and Language," in *Language Mind and Knowledge*, ed. Keith Gunderson, Minneapolis: University of Minnesota Press, 1975, p. 7.
3. This interpretation is offered by T.R.V. Murty in "Some Comments on the Philosophy of Language in the Indian Context," *Journal of Indian Philosophy*, 2. 1974, p. 326.

for this is the very basis of our thought, consciousness, as well as knowledge of the world. Anything that exists is as good as non-existent unless and until it is named and linguistically conceived. So the phonetic level of speech is nothing but externalization of the very speech-potentiality present within us. Our phonetic expressions are not simply sounds caused by air and the vocal organ. It is the manifestation of *śabda-tattva* or linguistic potency or linguistic principle. This potency is manifested through *prāṇa* (breath) and *buddhi* (intellect).[4] So when a speaker intends to say something he thinks of the appropriate words to express his thought through verbal means. What remains at the level of thought finds expression in the form of utterances with the help of vocal organ and articulation.

Bhartṛhari analyses language from three angles —

1. *Śabda* (broadly translated it means "language") as a *tattva* or the metaphysical principle.
2. *Śabda* as a matter of *loka-vyavahāra,* i.e. as it is used.
3. *Śabda* as a matter of *śāstra-vyavahāra,* as an object of analytical and grammatical study.

Here, my focus would be on the second dimension, i.e. *loka-vyavahāra*. He uses the term *vyavahāra* very often to mean "the use of words to communicate one's thought, verbal usage or exchange of ideas."[5] Thus, it is obvious that, for Bhartṛhari, language is primarily communicative in nature. It is not only an act itself, but also the source of all activities in the world.[6] As an act, it involves the speaker's expression of his intention through the utterance

4. *Vāk.*, I, p. 179, 1.2.f in K.A.S. Iyer's translation of *Vākyapadīya*, I, Poona: Bhandarkar Oriental Research Institute.
5. K.A.S. Iyer, *The Vākyapadīya of Bhartṛhari,* ch. I, Poona: Deccan College, 1965, *Vṛtti* on I.1; Iyer's notes. Here, he draws support from Helārāja's commentary.
6. Bhartṛhari, *The Vākyapadīya of Bhartṛhari,* Kāṇḍa II, tr. K.A. Subramania Iyer, Delhi: Motilal Banarsidass, 1977, II.399-400. For language as the source of all human activities, see I.127.

act and the hearer's ability to grasp what is being expressed along with the intention of the speaker.

One of the interesting features of Bhartṛhari's account of language is his detailed analysis of the elements involved, from the speaker's angle. This approach is somehow different from the general trend of doing philosophy of language in the classical Indian tradition. Language, as a mode of communication can be explicated from two angles — the speaker's and the hearer's. Some of the important schools like Nyāya and Mīmāṁsā prefer the hearer's standpoint. But Bhartṛhari prefers the other angle. By this, I do not mean that he was totally oblivious of the hearer's standpoint. He pays attention to this aspect too.

Structural and Functional Components of Utterance

The utterance act, according to Bhartṛhari, involves a network of constitutive factors. From his writings it is clear that he identifies four such factors — (1) sound pattern (*dhvani/nāda*), which is primarily phonetic in nature; (2) form of the words (*vācaka*), which refers to the syntactic pattern of utterance; (3) then meaning (*vācya*), which is the semantic element; and (4) intention of the speaker (*vivakṣā*), the pragmatic element.

1. *Dhvani/nāda* — *Dhvani* occurs due to the presence of our vocal organ. The phonetic element is characterized by accent, pitch, and intonation that vary from speaker to speaker.
2. *Vācaka* — It consists of the phonemes and words presented in a particular order. It is that to which the hearer pays attention when the speaker intends to communicate something. Thus, it is the conveyer of meaning. Its role is crucial, as Bhartṛhari points out, "both the speaker and the hearer have to think of words first before thinking of the meaning." (1.53).
3. *Vācya* — It is the content of the speech — the meaning. *Vācya* is that which is conveyed and manifested through the *vācaka*. The relationship between the *vācya* and *vācaka*

is very intimate, because words have a natural fitness (*yogyatā*) to express the meaning.

4. Intention of the speaker is the fourth constitutive factor. As Bhartṛhari points out, "the uttered level of speech is possible because the speaker intends to communicate" (III.1). The relationship between speech and intention is described as *kārya-kāraṇa bhāva*, a relationship of cause and effect. Bhartṛhari explains that it is the intention of the speaker which necessitates the use of particular forms of words, so it is the relationship of *kārya* (cause). "When the speaker seeks to superimpose linguistic forms on to his intended meaning, the language appears to change its nature into something else (meaning) and projects it as sounds from the vocal organ" (I.47-48). Thus, when the speaker intends to communicate he uses the expressive word or words (*vācaka*) that are appropriate to the intentions. The intention of the speaker is the cause of the utterance; on the other hand, it is the utterance which arouses in the hearer the need to understand what the speaker intends to say. So there is a relation of cause and effect between the intention of the speaker and the language used for the communication of meaning. Bhartṛhari, while elaborating the principle of the use of meaning (*artha-pravṛtti*), very emphatically expresses the importance of the intention of the speaker. He points out, "the basis for the expression of a meaning is that what the speaker intends to communicate, not whether the object meant has external existence as object or not" (*vṛtti* on I.13).

It should be noted in this context that Bhartṛhari is the only Indian thinker who systematically explains the role of intention in linguistic communication. Nyāya, Mīmāṁsā and others admit the importance of intention. But it is in connection with the hearers' understanding of the import of what the speakers utter. Thus, they talk of *tātparya* as one of the conditions of sentence-meaning which is needed in connection with disambiguation of certain words. Many interpreters translate *tātparya* as the intention but in the true sense of the term, it means the import of a sentence that has to be deciphered by the hearer based on contextual factors. But, on the other hand, Bhartṛhari uses the term *vivakṣā* to refer to the intention of the speaker. Etymologically, *vivakṣā* means the desire to speak on the part of the speaker, i.e. *vaktur icchā*. However, it is not just the desire to speak, it also implies the desire to express a particular intention through the act of utterance. It is evident from the following explanatory notes on I.13 — "Desire to communicate depends upon the existence of suitable words which the desire to communicate brings into the mind of the speaker. It is like applying the right sense-organ when one wants to cognise anything directly." Thus, it is clear that *vivakṣā* implies the intention of the speaker. Sometimes, he also uses the word *abhisandhi* to mean the speaker's intention.

Once the intention of the speaker is accepted as an integral part of the communicative act, certain corollaries have to be assumed. Bhartṛhari's interpretation of utterance in terms of *vivakṣā*, thus, leads to the following corollaries:

(a) What the speaker communicates is the "sense," not the meaning. It is not a case that here is the word, there is the meaning. The sense can only be conveyed by a sentence. Thus, it is the sentence, not the words that should be the primary unit of meaning. We notice that Bhartṛhari propounds a strict form of sentence-holism known as *akhaṇḍa-pakṣa* as opposed to the *khaṇḍa-pakṣa* theory of Mīmāṁsā, which insist on the primacy of word-meaning. For Mīmāṁsā, the meanings of the component words determine the sentence-meaning, whereas for Bhartṛhari word-meaning has no independence, it is always the sense conveyed by the sentence. What the hearer ultimately grasps is the sense of what is being conveyed.

(b) Bhartṛhari's insistence on the primacy of "sense" expressed through a sentence allows him to explicate variations in the "force," for the same sentence can be used with different "force." The scope for varied interpretation of the sense conveyed becomes possible because of his acknowledgement of the role of the speaker's intention. He clearly states, "Meaning of words seems to be created by the intention of the speaker" (III.4.570).

(c) Not only does the speaker express his intention but he also has a desire to "secure an uptake." Sometimes he can do this with metaphorical use, sometimes by maintaining a gap between "what is said" and "what is meant."

Thus the ultimate thesis regarding the workings of natural language, according to Bhartṛhari can be summed up as follows: Speaking language is indulging in a communicative act by which the speaker not only expresses what he intends to say, but also secures an uptake from the hearer through the hearer's recognition of what the speaker intends to communicate.

Language as Function: Grice, Austin, Searle and Bach

In the backdrop of this ancient theory of communication-intention, let us have a cursory look at the modern theories expounded by Grice, Austin, Searle and Kent Bach.

How the structure of language represents the world has been the major concern of the philosophers of language for quite a long time. The major thrust of such theories are the discovery of the structural rules of language in terms of which any significant utterance could be judged as true or false. In their case, thus, statements are regarded as the paradigmatic use of language. We all know how the scenario changed with later Wittgenstein's dictum, "Don't ask for the meaning, ask for the use." But it is

Grice, who in his small paper entitled "Meaning"[7] brings to our notice the depth of the communicative role of meaning. Meaning by an utterance, according to him, is as good as somebody intending to produce an effect on the hearer. Moreover, for him, there cannot be a language *simple citer*, there must be a speaker claiming to utter it. On the other hand, Austin[8] successfully drew our attention to the fact that language is not only meant for communication, it also is a network of acts — locutionary, illocutionary and perlocutionary. However, unlike Wittgenstein, he does not conflate meaning to use. Rather, he very carefully maintains a distinction between the "meaning" and "force," which largely determines how the utterance is used. Suppose, for example, a person of a locality says to a stranger: "This is not a good place" — here the speaker is not only making statement about the place (locutionary act/meaning), but also warning one about the dangers involved (illocutionary act/force), and he wants to "secure an uptake" from the hearer, i.e. he should leave the place (perlocutionary act). However, the problem with Austin is, he not only segregates "meaning" from "force" but explicates "force" in terms of institutionalized conventions. "Force" is not exactly the "intention" as we understand the term today. Strawson[9] very rightly points out this weakness in Austin's theory. He argues that in most cases illocutionary acts succeed not by conformity to conventions, but by recognition of the intention. Intention plays a very important role in the three levels of speech-act. In saying "This is not a good place" the utterer intends to warn the stranger and also wishes that the hearer recognizes his intention that the speaker wants him to leave the place. In this case, the utterer does not have to say "I warn that this is not a good place." What is being conveyed is more than what is being

7. H.P. Grice, "Meaning," *Philosophical Review*, LXVI, 1957.
8. J.L. Austin, *How to do Things with Words*, London: Oxford University Press, 1962.
9. P.F. Strawson, "Intention and convention in Speech-acts," *Philosophical Review*, LXXIII, 1964, pp. 439-66.

said. Understanding of an utterance is not just decoding it, nor is meaningful utterance a matter of encoding by the speaker. The other weakness in Grice's as well as in Austin's theory is a total neglect of the hearer's role. No theory of communication-intention can be successful without the explication of how the hearer understands not only what is being said, but also what the hearer intends. Searle's[10] account of speech-acts is more explicit about the hearer's role. But like Austin he, too, proposes to express illocutionary acts in terms of the constitutive rules (conventions) for using "force-indicating" devices, such as performative verbs and sentential moods. However, the same sorts of illocutionary acts can be performed without such devices. One need not use the performative, as in "I demand, you be quiet" or the imperative mood, "Be quiet." Kent Bach rightly observes that a theory, which relies on rules for using such devices, is not equipped to explain illocutionary forces of utterances, lacking such devices. No such difficulty arises for a theory according to which most illocutionary acts are performed not with an intention to conform to convention but with a communicative intention.

Kent Bach[11] while developing the theory of communicative intention in speech-acts brings to our notice some of the peculiarities associated with natural language like the presence of ambiguous words and context-sensitive expressions like indexicals. But important are the following peculiarities:

1. indirect speech-act, wherein we perform speech-acts by way of performing another;
2. non-literal speech-act, where the sense communicated largely depends on the type of words used; and
3. implicit speech-act wherein it is not spelt out what is meant.

---

10. J. Searle, *Speech-Acts: An Essay in Philosophy of Language*, Cambridge: Cambridge University Press, 1969.
11. Kent Bach, "Conversational Implicature," *Mind and Language*, 1994, 9: 124-62.

In case of indirection, single utterance is the performance of one illocutionary act by way of performing another illocutionary act. For example, "I am thirsty," although it has the force of a statement, may actually be a form of request to give a glass of water. In case of non-literal speech-acts we do not mean what the words state. In such cases, illocutionary forces cannot be predicated just from the meaning of words. Here, he mostly refers to the figurative use of language. Sometimes it can be both indirect and non-literal, like "I love the sound of your voice." Here the speaker tells non-literally that she cannot stand the sound of his voice but thereby also implies that he should stop singing. Implicit speech-acts are those where the words used do not express the full meaning, but are either in need of expansion or in need of completion. For example, if one's spouse says "I will be home late" it actually means she will be home late that night. Here the sentence needs expansion by way of adding the word "tonight." In other cases, such as "Jack is ready and Jill is late," the sentence does not express a complete proposition; for it does not express completely what is that for which Jack is claimed to be ready and Jill is late. In such cases what one means is the completion of what one says.

According to Bach

> Non-literality and indirection are the two main ways in which the semantic content of a sentence can fail to determine the full force and content of the illocutionary act being performed in using the sentence.[12]

The problem of indirection has been covered by Grice[13] in connection with what he called "conversational implicature."

However, there can be cases of implicit speech-acts, which can be explained only in terms of completion and expansion. Bach

---

12. Kent Bach, "Speech-Acts," *Routledge Encyclopedia of Philosophy.*
13. H.P. Grice, *Studies in the Way of Words,* Cambridge, Mass.: Harvard University Press, 1989.

calls them "Impliciture." In such cases, a part of what is meant is communicated not explicitly but implicitly.

Both, in case of the "implicature" as well as the "impliciture" there is a tendency to go beyond what is explicitly stated, but this is done in two different ways:

> An implicature is completely separate from what is said and inferred from it (more precisely, from saying it). What is said is one proposition and what is communicated in addition to that is a conceptually independent proposition, a proposition with perhaps no constituents in common with what is said. In contrast, implicitures are built up from the explicit content of the utterance by conceptual strengthening . . . which yields what would have been made fully explicit if the appropriate lexical material had been included in the utterance.[14]

Implicatures are *implied* by what is being said; whereas implicitures are *implicit* in what is said.

Bhartṛhari on "What is Said" and "What is Meant"

Let us now make an assessment of how Bhartṛhari would have handled such cases of communication acts where there is a gap between what is "said," and what is "communicated." It seems obvious from the detailed study of his *Vākyapadīya* that he was aware of the possibilities of both the "implied meaning" and the "implicit meaning." He very clearly states, "sometimes what is said is not what is meant" (I.136). Supposing, for example, when a fellow traveller says to his companion, "we must go and look at the sun," the meaning conveyed by the speaker is not that of looking at the sun, but the hearer must realize how late it is in the day (II.327). In the above example, the implied meaning is: "it is getting late, we must hurry up." Thus, the implied meaning is conceptually independent of what is said by the speaker. He also exemplifies the cases where the speech-act is both indirect and non-literal. He points out,

---

14. Kent Bach, "Conversational Implicature," *Mind and Language*, 1994.

> From a sentence, the chief meaning of which is praise or blame, a different meaning is to be understood than the one obtained from the individual words. — II.247

These are the cases of ironic statements, where what is meant is a condemnation; and what is said is of the nature of a praise. Thus, Bhartṛhari is very much aware of what Bach and Grice call "implicature."

Now coming to the problem of "impliciture" we notice that Bach includes two categories of semantically under-determinate expressions under this class. One of them refers to the syntactic incompleteness and the other to the semantic incompleteness. The former needs "completion" and the latter needs semantic "enrichment." Again, we notice that Bhartṛhari is very much aware of such peculiarities of the natural language and they find a place in his discussion. However, I would like to take up the question of semantic completeness first. The other issue, that of syntactic completeness, is a matter of serious debate in Indian philosophy of language. Therefore, it needs a little more deliberation. Let us look at the following example. A boy is told: "save the butter from the crows." Here the word "crow" needs expansion; thus the word "crows" includes any destructive agent in general, who may spoil the butter. So, Bhartṛhari elaborates,

> when a boy is told: "save the butter from the crows"; he does not refrain from protecting it from dogs, etc. knowing that the order refers to the destructive agents in general. — II.312

It is a case where the intended meaning is not independent of what is stated but is implicitly present. An averagely intelligent hearer is supposed to grasp the implicit meaning.

Coming to the question of syntactic incompleteness we must notice that the issue gets considerable attention in Indian philosophy of language. The Indian version of this phenomenon is known as *ākāṅkṣā*. Very broadly, the term can be translated as "mutual expectancy" or "mutual interdependence" of the constituents of a sentence. Mīmāṁsā and Nyāya uphold the *khaṇḍa-*

pakṣa theory as opposed to Bhartṛhari's *akhaṇḍa-pakṣa* (sentence-holism) theory. According to the former, word-meanings are autonomous; thus a concatenation of word-meanings ultimately build up the sentence-meaning. So according to Nyāya and Mīmāṁsā, the constituent word-meanings must be mutually interdependent. In other words, the syntactic completeness is a condition of the sentence-meaning. This in fact is ingrained in the very definition of a sentence. Jaimini, in his *Mīmāṁsā-Sūtra*, defines a sentence (*vākya*) in the following way: "a group of words serving a single purpose forms a sentence when on analysis words are found to have mutual expectancy" (II.1.46). This definition, actually, contains two conditions — (i) it must serve a single purpose; and (ii) on analysis the constituent words are found to be in need of one another. The second condition is known as *ākāṅkṣā*. Both Mīmāṁsā and Nyāya insist on the fulfilment of the condition of *ākāṅkṣā* in any case of sentence-meaning. *Ākāṅkṣā* implies the need for syntactic completeness. The hearer, in order to grasp the meaning conveyed to him, expects the sentence to be syntactically complete. But Bhartṛhari would beg to differ with Mīmāṁsā and Nyāya on this count. For him, what is important in the conveyance of meaning through a sentence is the singleness of purpose. Bhartṛhari follows Patañjali's definition of a sentence. According to him unity of purpose of meaning (*ekārthībhāva*) and mutual interconnectedness (*vyāpekṣa*) are mutually exclusive. Acceptance of mutual interconnectedness of words would mean that words are supposed to retain their individual meanings in a sentence. This may lead to certain problems. Therefore, the unity of the purpose should be the only criterion of sentence-meaning. Bhartṛhari's *akhaṇḍa-pakṣa* theory is a logical development of Patañjali's notion of *ekārthībhāva*. So Bhartṛhari insists on the completeness of the "sense" conveyed, not the syntactic completeness. Thus, even a single word like, "door" can be said to communicate a complete sense to the hearer. If it is winter, the intended meaning is "close the door," and if it is summer the intended meaning is "open the door" (II.430). For him though syntax is very important in linguistic communication we do not always strictly stick to the rules of syntax. So, it is the speaker who decides how to present the facts.

> With whatever use a meaning/object-meant is sought to be conveyed by the speaker, the meaning is established like that (in that context), because meaning has several capacities. — II.314

Again, Bhartṛhari says,

> where there is a bare statement of fact and its implications are understood from its expressive power (*śruteḥ*) without the use of words to express them, then also the sentence is complete.
>
> — II.446

Bhartṛhari's position seems to be one-sided. Is he not over-emphasizing the role of the speaker at the cost of the hearer? After all, linguistic communication is a matter of co-ordination between the speaker and the hearer. Without some such conditions of deciphering what actually is intended by the speaker, language cannot serve as an adequate means of communication. But, Bhartṛhari spells out in detail the contextual factors which help the hearer to understand the implicit as well as the implied meaning. He says, "the meanings of words are determined according to sentence, situation, purpose, propriety, place and time, and not according to mere external forms." Śaṅkuka in his *Bṛhaddevatā* originally gave this list of contextual conditions. Bhartṛhari, however, gives another extended list of twelve conditions which covers a wide range of contexts. It should be noted here that it is Bhartṛhari who is quoted by others while explaining the importance of contextual factors in understanding the import of a sentence.

But the question that can be raised is: even if contextual factors play a role, what exactly is the process through which the hearer understands the implicit meaning (especially, syntactically incomplete sentences)? Bach suggests,

> completion and expansion are both the processes whereby the hearer supplies the missing portions of what is otherwise being

> expressed explicitly. With completion a propositional radical is filled in, and with expansion a complete but a skeletal proposition is fleshed out.[15]

Here the process is nothing more than the process of inference, whereby the hearer mentally computes the missing semantical and syntactical elements. Mīmāṁsā also holds a similar position. This process of inference is called *śrutārthapatti*. But Bhartṛhari rejects this proposal by arguing,

> whatever meaning is understood, whenever certain word is uttered, that meaning belongs to that word (and to that word only). There is not more correct definition of meaning than this.
> — II.333

In other words, Bhartṛhari insists on hearer's understanding of the meaning, only on the basis of what is being said. Kent Bach also realizes that mental computation of missing lexical constituents is not the solution to the problem of "implicatures." Therefore, he admits that "what is said" forms the basis of what is understood by the hearer. It is, "what is said," that provides a default value for the hearer's understanding. However, Bhartṛhari's solution is different. He would say that there is no question of inference. The hearer always "grasps" the meaning instantaneously. However, how does the hearer know, how and when a word is used, with what meaning? Bhartṛhari's answer would be

> Human reasoning is the power of words. . . .. It is the word which is the instructor. Speakers follow the power of words and act when urged by a desire to speak based on the availability of the right word. When the hearer follows the fixed power of words to understand a meaning through reasoning, based on meaning, context, indication, interconnection, etc. people look upon the capacity of words as the reasoning of the hearer. — I.137

The above lines are very crucial, as they expose the crux of Bhartṛhari's philosophy of language. To understand the full

15. Kent Bach, "Conversational Implicature," *Mind and Language*, 1994.

implications of this remark we have to keep in mind the basic tenets of his philosophy of language.

(i) For Bhartṛhari the nature of linguistic communicability cannot be adequately explained if we just confine ourselves to the level of utterance only. It will be too simplistic to say that the meaning is conveyed because the speaker utters syntactically a perfect string of words; because the hearer follows the same rule of syntax, he will understand the meaning just by listening to the utterances. For Bhartṛhari, utterance level is just a part of the *linguistic expressibility*. It points to a deeper level, i.e. the level of thought.

(ii) The level of thought, according to Bhartṛhari, is word-determined. No thought, no consciousness, no cognition is possible without being intertwined with the word. In other words, man is a "languageing being." As a conscious being, he is endowed with the linguistic potency (*śabda-bhāvanā*). In case of the speaker, it is this potency, which urges him to express his thought by means of the utterances; in case of the hearer, it is this linguistic potency that allows him to understand the sense expressed intuitively. The hearer's ability to intuit the meaning, i.e. *pratibhā* is, in a sense, another name for the *śabda-bhāvanā* (I.122).

(iii) Bhartṛhari, while analysing the semantics and pragmatics of natural language has made it absolutely clear that it can be very flexible. There is always a possibility of a gap between what is "said" and what is "meant." Thus the problem of explaining how the speaker does transfer the meaning to the hearer is very crucial. Definitely transference of meaning is not like loading the contents of a car into another. Nor is the process clearly determined by the rules of syntax. For Bhartṛhari, it is always the "sense," which is communicated, not the isolated meanings of the constituent words that the speaker uses. So there has to be a common ground for the transmission of the sense. Bhartṛhari locates it in the concept of *śabda* or *sphoṭa*. Of course, *sphoṭa* has been seen by many philosophers as a mysterious entity. However, a dispassionate analysis can help us to realize that there is nothing mysterious about it. *Sphoṭa*, etymologically speaking, is derived from the word *sphuṭ*, which means bursting forth. Following Nāgeśa Bhaṭṭa, we can interpret it as that from which meaning bursts forth or the principle which is expressible through utterances. It is the indivisible unit of meaning which is connected with the verbal dispositional ability of the speaker, as well as the hearer. It is indivisible, because before the utterances are made, all the distinction between the form of words and meaning remains in unmanifested and in indivisible form. In case of the hearer, it is this unit of meaning which is referred to when the utterances are heard as distinguished from the meaning. Besides, the utterances are uttered and also heard sequentially, syllable by syllable. Once a syllable is uttered, it is replaced by another. (This is another peculiarity of linguistic communication, to which Western philosophers, virtually, pay no attention.) The hearer does not compute the series of syllables and infer the meaning. Thus, for the communication of a unitary "sense" an undifferentiated, sequenceless principle is assumed. This is *sphoṭa* or *śabda*. So for Bhartṛhari linguistic communicability is to be understood in terms of *sphoṭa/śabda* (i.e. the non-differentiated language-principle) and *śabda-bhāvanā* (the linguistic potency). These two principles help him to sort out the problem of the communication of the implied, implicit, as well as, the explicit meaning. So, when Bhartṛhari says, "it is the **word** which is the instructor" — the term **word** should be understood as *śabda* or *sphoṭa*. This is the very basis of the human power of using language for communication.

One may find Bhartṛhari's notions of *sphoṭa, śabda* or *śabda-bhāvanā* unacceptable. But the problem as to how communication succeeds continues to remain unsolved. Kent Bach waives off the problem by saying, that "to describe the general character of communication is not to explain how it succeeds." But can we close our eyes to this issue? The speech-act theorists, and very broadly speaking the communication-intention theorists, in their process of highlighting on the speech-acts (also speaker's intention), pay scanty attention to the hearer's role. When it comes to the hearer's understanding, they work with the basic idea that —

> communication essentially involves an audience-directed reflexive intention, so that whether or not the utterance can plausibly be taken at face-value, the hearer must rely on the presupposition that the speaker intends what he is communicating to be recognized (partly on the basis of that intention).[16]

Thus, communication is a kind of "co-ordination-game." But can such a game be played without locating a basic co-ordinating principle? This remains unexplored as far as speech-act/communication-intention theorists are concerned.

16. Kent Bach, "Conversational Implicature," *Mind and Language*, 1994.

6

Thought and Language

Nature of the Problem

IN the previous chapter we have discussed about the issue of communicability in our understanding of language. Now I intend to focus on another important issue that has puzzled the philosophers through centuries. The issue is concerning the relation between thought and language. It is usually believed that language serves as a vehicle of thought. In other words the relationship is one-way relationship, i.e. from thought to language. But is it so? Don't we think in terms of language? So it seems that it may be a two-dimensional relationship, as Strawson puts it ". . . it is surely right to say that . . . speech and writing express thought; that sentences are only in so far as they have power to do this. But if language in this way depends on thought, we must also surely feel the force of the idea that we do not just have one way dependence; that, at the level of complexity, the availability in our language of a sentence for expressing a thought, in general, is a condition of our possibility of thinking of thought."[1] Thus we note that we cannot just dismiss the question of the complex relation between thought and language as understanding its complexities offers us an insight about the richness and the depth of the concept of language. Thus we note that this complicated issue has received serious attention in the philosophical literature in recent times. In this chapter I intend to place Bhartṛhari's views in the backdrop of this crucial problem of the modern philosophy of language as well as philosophical psychology. Bhartṛhari's

1. P.F. Strawson, *Analysis and Metaphysics*, p. 96.

Vākyapadīya can be claimed to be one of the oldest treatises meticulously dealing with this issue. I shall discuss his views on the topic from two angles — (i) Thought and language as components of linguistic communication, and (ii) Thought and language as conceptual entities and their relative priority. On the first issue Bhartṛhari conceives a two-dimensional relation between language and thought. And on the second issue, he prefers to prioritize language over thought, dismissing thereby the popular and common sensical theory that language is just a vehicle of thought. Let me take these two issues one by one.

Bhartṛhari on Thought and Language : The Communicative Perspective

So far from our discussion it has been made explicit that not only Bhartṛhari but Indian tradition as such, accepts the communicative dimension of language. Accordingly five stages are conceived in an ideal communicative situation. They are: (i) what is in the mind of the speaker who makes the utterance, (ii) what the speaker intends his hearer to understand, (iii) what the utterance actually conveys, (iv) what the hearer understands as the meaning of the utterance, and finally, (v) what is in the mind of the hearer on hearing the utterance. In case of an ideal linguistic communication these five aspects must coincide. Since the first and the fifth elements of linguistic communication are little intangible the other three aspects have received more attention. But Bhartṛhari seems to pay attention to all these five elements of linguistic communication, therefore, he prefers to discuss in detail the relationship that may exist between the level of thought (both for the speaker and the hearer) and the level of verbalization.

We have noted in the previous chapter that the act of linguistic communication involves the speaker's expression of his intention through the utterance-act, and the hearer's ability to grasp what is being expressed along with the intention of the speaker. To understand the exact relation between these two phenomena, i.e. thought and language, we must concentrate on the significant distinction Bhartṛhari introduces between *sphoṭa* and *nāda* in verse

144 of the first Canto of *Vākyapadīya*. He states: "In case of expressive words (as opposed to the meaningless sounds) one has to distinguish between two elements — one is the root cause of manifestation (*nimitta*), and the other is the applied (*prayujyate*), when manifested to convey meaning." In other words, every linguistic communication has two aspects: (1) the element that causes manifestation, that makes the implicit potency explicit through the (sentential) utterances, and (2) the element which, being actualized, conveys the meaning to the hearer. The former is called *nāda/dhvani* and the latter *sphoṭa.* Pandit Suryanarayana Sukla (1961)[2] interprets this verse both from the speaker's angle as well as the hearer's angle. Viewed from the speaker's side, *sphoṭa* is the causal ground (*nimitta*) for the audible sound, which conveys the meaning (*artha*). But from the hearer's point of view, it is just the opposite. The audible sequence of sounds is the causal ground (*nimitta*) of the *sphoṭa,* which in turn, conveys the meaning. K.A.S. Iyer (1969), on the other hand, thinks that the verse should be interpreted from the hearer's angle. It should imply that the sequential stretch of sounds that is heard by the hearer is the cause of the manifestation of the indivisible *sphoṭa*, which is within him and which, when manifested, conveys the meaning.[3] All these interpretations of this rather enigmatic verse make at least one thing clear. It intends to offer us a hint about how Bhartṛhari is going to explicate the idea of the communication of meaning. It is suggested that there are spoken words conveying some unitary sense that can be communicated by the speaker and understood by the hearer because there is something commonly shared by both. So the process of linguistic communication necessarily involves three basic elements — (i) the speaker, (ii) the hearer, and (iii) the common ground for inter-subjectivity. For, in

---

2. Suryanarayana Sukla, *The Vākyapadīya: A Treatise on the Philosophy of Sanskrit Grammar (Brahma Kāṇḍa), With Bhābapradīpa Sanskrit Commentary and Notes*, Varanasi: Chowkhamba Sanskrit Series Office, 1961.

3. K.K. Raja, *The Indian Theories of Meaning*, Adyar Library, 1969, p. 153.

Bhartṛhari's opinion communication is not a process of directly transferring the contents of thought from the speaker to the hearer. The competence to express the thought and grasp the meaning exists as an inherent power within human beings. It is a property inter-subjectively available. So the expressive word (that the speaker intends to communicate) is made explicit through a "stretch of sounds" (I use this term following Matilal[4]), because it helps us to clarify that, according to Bhartṛhari, sentences, not the words, are the primary units of communicative meaning; this is *nāda/ dhvani*. This audible stretch of sounds that is presented sequentially, syllable by syllable, is the cause (*nimitta*) of the manifestation of the meaning to be communicated. The hearer too grasps the stretch of sounds along with their multiplicity and sequentiality. But unless the hearer understands the stretch of sounds as representing a unitary and sequenceless meaning, linguistic communication is not achieved. This sequenceless meaning-unit (potentially present in both the speaker and the hearer) is the *sphoṭa*. As Bhartṛhari clarifies, "Since *nāda* (sound pattern) arises in sequence, *sphoṭa* which has neither former nor latter stage and which is sequenceless (*akrama)* is apprehended through *nāda* and appears to be having sequence as well as parts." (*VP* I.48). Thus, the meaning-unit or (*sphoṭa*) is a partless, indivisible whole. In contrast, the discernible elements like grammatical and syntactical divisions are very much prominent when the meaning the speaker intends to communicate is presented through the stretch of sounds. If utterance represents the speech, and the meaning intended to be expressed, is taken to be the non-verbal element present in the mind of the speaker, then it is obvious that Bhartṛhari maintains a duality between speech and thought. Both the elements are autonomous, yet not autonomous to the extent of excluding each other. But he would claim that in the ultimate sense these two elements are indistinguishable, as is evident from his explanatory note on the verse I.144, where he clarifies: "In the

4. Jonardon Ganeri (ed.), *Collected Essays of Bimal Krishna Matilal*, Oxford University Press (Indian Edition), 2002, p. 334.

sequenceless nature of the *vāk* (speech) [which also means *sphoṭa*] both the powers, the power to be articulated in sound (audible form) and the power to convey meaning lie intermixed." It is clear from this statement that Bhartṛhari does not identify *sphoṭa* with the *artha* or meaning. Though the same *sphoṭa* can be expressed in different formulations and different languages yet it will be misleading to say that *sphoṭa* is the bearer of meaning. It is rather the unit of linguistic potency which, when expressed is diversified into two elements, *dhvani* and *artha*. In one of its dimensions it is expressed as sound pattern and in another, it is the meaning-bearing unit. So *sphoṭa* should not be confused with the meaning-bearing unit. Rather, Bhartṛhari believes that *sphoṭa* along with expressing the meaning expresses itself. This may be evident from the following verse. He says, "Just as light/fire (*jyoti*) resides in the *araṇi* (churning) stick and being manifested becomes the cause for manifesting other objects; *śabda* resides likewise in the *mind* (*buddhi*, the inner faculty) and being manifested becomes separately the cause for manifesting itself as well as the meaning" (I.46). In the quoted passages we note that he uses the terms *śabda* and *sphoṭa* almost interchangeably. And both the terms seem to refer to a principle that includes both the sequential form of words and the meaning. This principle of unity itself is the *sphoṭa*. Moreover, this verse states very clearly that the locus of *śabda/sphoṭa* is *buddhi* or the inner faculty of cognition (*śabdo 'pi buddhisthaḥ śrutinām kāraṇam pṛthak*). In other words, if speech is taken to be meaningful stretch of sounds then *sphoṭa* (which exists in the mental level) is its cause. Of course, there is no unanimity of opinion among the scholars regarding the exact significance of the term *sphoṭa*. I have stated in the chapter on *sphoṭa* (Chapter 3) I would like to go along with B.K. Matilal in interpreting the term *sphoṭa* as signifying, "language-principle."[5] I also fully agree with B.K. Matilal when

5. B.K. Matilal, *The Word and the World*, p. 85.

   It appears from Bhartṛhari's exposition that *sphoṭa* stands for unitary sentence meaning (*vākya-sphoṭa*). Interestingly enough he uses the term with reference to words and phonemes (*pada-sphoṭa* and *varṇa-*

→

very insightfully he remarks that, "Language is not the vehicle of meaning or conveyor-belt of thought. Thought anchors language and language anchors thought. *Śabdanā*, languageing, is thinking; and thought "vibrates" through language. In this way of looking at things, there cannot be any essential difference between a linguistic unit and its meaning or the thought it conveys. *Sphoṭa* refers to this non-differentiated language-principle."[6] I intend to come back to discuss the deeper significance of this principle called *sphoṭa,* a little later. For the time being I would like to dwell a little longer on Bhartṛhari's conception of thought-language equation and explicate the issue from another angle.

We have noted that Bhartṛhari maintains a distinction between the "language in the level of thought" and "language in the level of speech"; between the "meaning to be expressed" and the "meaning actually expressed" through articulated stretch of sounds. But ultimately he seems to reject their autonomy. This may give rise to a paradoxical situation. But Bhartṛhari sees no paradox in his position. He may still hold that at a certain level there is an undeniable interdependence between language and thought. The implications of such a viewpoint will be clear if we examine Bhartṛhari's analysis of the processes of linguistic communication. Despite sounding repetitive we cannot but have to focus on his analysis of the process of linguistic communication from the speaker's angle. In this case, he identifies three discernible

---

→ *sphoṭa*, respectively). If we accept that Bhartṛhari conceives sentence as the ultimate point of unity and consequently, *sphoṭa* stands for sentence-meaning, then his monistic metaphysics would collapse. For, this would mean there could be innumerable number of unrelated *sphoṭas*. This inconsistency in his position can be solved if we take *sphoṭa* in the sense of "one and unitary" language-principle. He has already hinted that the power of expressibility, i.e. *śabda* or *sphoṭa* is in the inner faculty (*buddhi*) that is expressed through each meaningful utterance. So in all probability he used the term *sphoṭa* or *śabda* in an extended sense when he talked of *sphoṭa* in the context of words or sentences.

6. Matilal, *Word and World*, p. 85.

elements in an utterance, viz. the sound pattern/form of words (*vācaka*), the meaning expressed (*vācya*) and speaker's intention (*vivākṣa*). *Vācya* is the meaning to be expressed and *vācaka* is the meaning expressed through the stretch of sounds. In a broad sense, *vācya* stands for the meaning-content (*artha*) and *vācaka* for stretch of words. (*VP* I.50). For certain practical reasons, Bhartṛhari thinks, the distinction is to be maintained. If meaning would have been conceptually inseparable from words then the same meaning could not have been expressed in different forms of sentences: or we could not have translated the meaning of sentences from one language to another. But we must remember that the speaker's utterance is always presented sequentially, syllable by syllable. The moment one syllable is uttered it is replaced by another syllable. So how does the speaker manage to convey the meaning that has a unitary sense? Bhartṛhari's answer to the problem is interesting, yet profound. He would say that the level of utterance is just one part of the linguistic expressibility. So he introduces the notion of a three-tiered process of linguistic communicability. In this scheme the level of utterance is only the last stage of the process, which he calls the *vaikharī vāk* (elaborated speech). The level of utterance points to a deeper level of thought. It is the pre-verbal stage identified as the *madhyamā vāk*. "Mind is its only substratum"(*Vṛtti* under I.142). This pre-verbal stage is broadly comparable to the modern notion of an episodic but unexpressed pre-verbal thought. It is a thought with the same verbal content. In this stage the thought is already linked to an idea or object, but un-uttered. If we take thought to mean what the sentence purports to communicate then we can say that language presupposes thought and thought is operative through language. But uttered speech with discernible elements and the pre-verbal stage with the supposed distinction (though pre-verbal) between the word and the meaning refer to an ultimate stage where the distinction between *vācya* and *vācaka* is obliterated. It points to a level beyond *buddhi*. This stage is called the *paśyantī vāk,* a purely non-verbal stage of language. This is the stage in which the potentiality for the expressiveness is inherent, but not explicit. It is non-differentiated principle and is identical with the consciousness. This is also the stage of *sphoṭa*, the *language-principle,* from which meaning, as if, bursts forth (for, that is the etymological significance of the root *sphuṭ* from which the word *sphoṭa* is derived) along with the phonetic and syntactical elements. Though Bhartṛhari never explicitly associates *paśyantī vāk* with *sphoṭa* we can infer this from his commentary on the verse I.142. It is stated: "The seeing one (*paśyantī*) is that in which sequence is merged and though it is One the *power to produce sequence* has entered into it. It is *restless* (*calācala*) . . . the forms of the objects of knowledge has entered into it or merged into it." *Paśyantī,* described as *restless* points to a potency that has a tendency manifest itself in pre-verbal and verbal level. Understood in this sense we can be in a better position to understand Bhartṛhari's statement that the potency of language is like a peafowl's egg. All the colours of a full-grown peafowl are potentially there in the egg. These colours are manifested when the peafowl comes out of the egg. Similarly the *sphoṭa* or *śabda* is the potential stage in which the linguistic form, along with its power to mean is already there in all languageing beings (I.51). Elaborating the relationship between these three stages of the linguistic process Bhartṛhari says: "All the objects (meant) merge into the intellect (as potentialities) and intellect merges into sequenceless Word as potentiality (*Vṛtti* on I.118)." So there seems to be no incongruity in connecting the stage of *paśyantī* with *sphoṭa* or the principle of language.

But is it not a problematic stance adopted by Bhartṛhari? If languageing rests on unity then why does he maintain that a sort of duality exists at the initial stage of linguistic process between thought and language? It seems that Bhartṛhari assumes such a distinction as a convenient ploy, for otherwise languageing cannot be an act of communication. He says, "Just as the mind of the speaker first turns to the words, in the same way, the attention of the hearers also is directed towards them" (I.53). So he believes that even if the duality between thought and language is suppressed at the ultimate level, the residual force of the differentiation is not totally abandoned. So the moment a speaker desires to say something the duality is again operative. "It is this merging and emerging of word, which is looked upon as its activity" (*Vṛtti* under I.51). But, a relevant question may be raised at this point — if the element of differentiation is so important for communication what is the need for Bhartṛhari to conceive of a non-differentiated language principle, called *sphoṭa*? Why does he not follow the less complicated path of explaining the linguistic communication either in terms of duality, or else in terms either thought or language alone? In this context it may be of great interest to examine some of the modern Western theories of philosophy of language, especially, those theories that deal with the communicative dimension of language. Such an undertaking is likely to help us in assessing Bhartṛhari's philosophy of language, with reference to his theory of *sphoṭa*.

The Western Perspective

It is well known that the course of Western philosophy took, what is popularly known as, "the linguistic turn" in the first part of twentieth century. Since then prolific works have been produced on the concept of language. But it is neither necessary nor possible for me to scan the entire literature on Western philosophy of language. So I shall concentrate only on some important communicative theories of meaning and examine how such theories deal with the problem of language-thought equation. At the outset, I must make it clear that I do not intend to dwell on the points of similarity between the Western philosophers (such as, Derrida, Chomsky or Frege) and Bhartṛhari. I would rather concentrate on the points of difference for, this may be more helpful in explaining why Bhartṛhari needs to assume an initial distinction between thought and language and finally discard this initial dualism as far as communication of meaning is concerned. So I shall be taking up these two questions conjointly while discussing the relevant theories.

In the Western philosophy of language we primarily come across two divergent views regarding the relation between thought and language in the context of the expression of meaning.

On the one hand, there are philosophers like Wittgenstein,[7] Austin[8] and Searle,[9] who prefer to confine the problem of the communication of meaning within the limits language and its use, without treading the area of thought; on the other hand, there are intentionalists like Grice[10] and later-Searle,[11] who view language just as a medium of thought, thereby prioritizing language. There is also a middle line of thought represented by the Interpretationists like Davidson,[12] who seem to offer an equal status to both, thought and language. I shall discuss these three alternative positions in brief to examine the rationality of Bhartṛhari's position.

Wittgenstein and following him many others like Austin and Searle display a sort of apathy towards the possible role of thought in the analysis of language, often fearing that this would lead to a form of psychologism. Wittgenstein argues that we need not make a conceptual reference to mental states in explaining the nature and function of language. So we can clearly see that Wittgenstein would have reacted negatively to Bhartṛhari's way of looking at language-thought equation. He would have shared Bhartṛhari's position regarding the functional and the communicative role of language. But he would not at any cost buy the idea that there may be a complementary relation between thought and language. Wittgenstein (especially in his *Philosophical Investigations*) rather suggests that one should confine the analysis of the concepts of "language" and "meaning" within the limits of speech or verbal

---

7. L. Wittgenstein, *Philosophical Investigations*, G. Anscombe and R. Rhees, ed., with an English tr. G. Anscombe, Basil: Blackwell, 1953.
8. J.L. Austin, *How to do Things with Words*, Oxford University Press, 1962
9. J. Searle, *Speech Acts : An Essay in Philosophy of Language*, Cambridge University Press, 1969.
10. P. Grice, "Meaning," *Philosophical Review*, 1957, p. 66.
11. J. Searle, *Intentionality*, Cambridge University Press, 1983.
12. Donald Davidson, "Thought and Talk," in *Mind and Language*, ed. S.D. Guttenplan, Oxford: Clarendon Press, 1975.

utterance. He admits that we do talk of such mental concepts as "meaning," "belief," "understanding," "intention" in the context of linguistic expression, but they are nothing more than "grammatical fictions." He even goes to the extent of labelling such mentalistic hypothesis as a "general disease of thinking." Explaining his position on this issue Pitcher says:

> Once we have an overall view of variety of situations in which the terms "meaning" and "understanding" are used, and of various criteria of their use, there is nothing more to know about what meaning and understanding are. To know their meanings, Wittgenstein would say, is to know their use.[13]

So we note that Wittgenstein adopts a form of linguistic behaviourism as far as analysis of meaning is concerned. He outright discards the need for presuming an independent level of mental activity for understanding how we operate with meaningful expressions.

Austin and Searle, on the other hand, without sharing Wittgenstein's penchant for linguistic behaviourism, go along with him in claiming that the functioning of language can be well understood without bringing in the concept of thought. They come out with a theory of language that in spite of admitting the importance of the *intention* of the speaker to communicate does not hook up, in a way, the level of speech with that of the thought. Surprisingly enough, both Austin and Searle largely draw their inspiration from the communication-intention theory of Paul Grice that not only connects language with thought but also believes that language is thought-dependent. In all fairness to Paul Grice,[14] it must be admitted that it was he who provided a revolutionary turn to the philosophy of language by bringing to light the communicative intentional dimension of language as opposed to the purely semantic and formalistic interpretation of this concept.

13. George Pitcher, *The Philosophy of Wittgenstein*, Prentice Hall of India Pvt. Ltd., 1972, p. 275.
14. P. Grice, "Meaning."

I shall discuss his views on thought-language equation later. For the time being I shall focus on the speech-act theories of Austin[15] and Searle[16] who agree with Grice that language is an audience-directed activity, therefore communicative in nature, they also agree that the speaker may express his intention while communicating the literal meaning. But they prefer to explain the act of linguistic communication in terms of semantic and syntactic rules, thereby meticulously avoiding treading into the areas of "mind" and "thought" in their analysis of the linguistic communication. I have discussed in the previous chapter that Austin introduces the notion of "force," thereby bringing in a distinction between "meaning" and "force." However, in Austin's opinion the "force" or the intention of the speaker has nothing to do with the level of thought. For him, the "intended meaning" or "force" is ultimately dependent on linguistic and institutionalized conventions.

John Searle's account of speech acts, though an improved version of Austin's theory, toes the same line of thought as far as the speaker's intention and the hearer's understanding is concerned. Very much like Austin, he too, proposes to explicate the speaker's intention (force of an utterance) in terms of the constitutive rules (convention) of language. Therefore he talks of "force-indicating devices," such as performative verbs and sentential moods to explain the speaker's intention (force). So Wittgenstein, Austin and Searle, in a sense, prefer a form of reductionism, i.e. reducing thought to language, as they interpret the intention of the speaker as well as the understanding of the hearer either in terms of linguistic behaviour or else in terms of institutionalized and conventionalized linguistic rules. Besides, in case of these philosophers the question — how the meaning is conveyed from the speaker to the hearer — receives virtually no attention. Most probably it is taken for granted that knowing the conventions and syntax of a language is enough to guarantee the

15. J.L. Austin, *How to do Things with Words.*

16. J. Searle, *Speech-Acts.*

transference of meaning from the speaker to the hearer. Bhartṛhari would have outright rejected this type of reductionism. He definitely believes that language is an act, but as a communicative act it has to be connected to the level of thought at some level or the other. So thought, at no cost, can be reduced to language as long as we are talking of the speaker's intention to indulge in speech-act and the hearer's desire to understand the utterance.

Now, I intend to throw some light on the second viewpoint, which admits the importance and independence of thought as an element involved in linguistic communication. This theory, broadly known as Expressivism, is a popular view upheld by the philosophers of language and the philosophers of mind, as well. In this case, unlike the theories discussed above, primacy is attached to thought over language. According to this theory language is nothing more than expression of thought. So the primary function of language is to enable speakers to convey the content of their thought to the hearer. In other words, it is presumed that the speaker has a thought, with certain content and he chooses words in such a way that on the basis of these words the hearer is able to recognize that the speaker has a thought with such and such content. This doctrine is supposed to have its genesis in Frege's[17] famous theory of thought. According to him a sentence expresses a thought. He says: "I call a thought something for which the question of truth arises . . . thought, in itself is immaterial, clothes itself in the material garment of a sentence and thereby becomes comprehensible to us. We say a sentence expresses a thought."[18] Thus language, for him, is dependent on thought. As he points out: "when one apprehends or thinks a thought one does not create it. . . ."[19] Thus it stands as a *transcendental signified*, which remains constant, in spite of varied forms of utterance. However, we must not conflate Frege's theory with Expressivism. Thought,

17. G. Frege, "The Thought: A Logical Inquiry" in *Philosophical Logic*, ed. P.F. Strawson, Oxford University Press, 1977.

18. Ibid., p. 20.

19. Ibid., p. 30.

for Frege, has deeper nuances and in all cases does not mean the "content of thought," that the speaker intends to express. So it will be better if we concentrate on Grice's famous theory of thought-based semantics. As I have indicated earlier Grice can be said to be the first philosopher of language who explicitly focuses on the concepts like intention and belief in the analysis of communication of meaning. He attempts to explain what it is to mean something by an utterance in terms of speaker's communicative intention, i.e. the intention to induce certain belief in the hearer. In his famous paper entitled "Meaning" he specifies, "*A* meant something by *x*" is roughly equivalent to "*A* uttered *x* with the intention of inducing a belief by means of the recognition of this intention."[20] Such a concept of meaning implies that the speaker has an intention and he wants his intention to be understood by the hearer (audience) on the basis of his utterance. Grice wants to present a thought-based semantics of natural language in terms of thought via intention. So for him it is the thought-content that imposes meaning on language. But a theorist who explicates meaning in terms of communication of intention must realize the typical nuances of the language in use. For there may be cases where what is stated by an utterance is completely different from what is intended. Grice[21] in a later article admits the possibility of such linguistic anomalies that he prefers to call them as conversational implicature. In such cases, there is a big gap between what is stated and what is meant. Since for Grice and other communicative-intention theorists communication is a matter of encoding or signalling a thought-content, what matters is the utterance made by the speaker and his success in inducing certain belief in the hearer by recognition of the speaker's intention to communicate certain thought-content. But Bhartṛhari would like to solve the problem of conversational implicature by referring to both the speaker's and the hearer's power to be a part of the

20. "Meaning," p. 45.
21. P. Grice, "Utterer's Meaning and Intention," *Philosophical Review*, vol. 78, 1989.

communication process. As he points out, "Meaning in language is dependent on the usage and the speaker-hearer relationship, and the capacity of each one of them to express and comprehend what is going to be expressed and what has been expressed" (II.135). In case of Grice one might expect in his communicative intention theory an account of "what it is for an audience to understand by an utterance *x*," complementary to an account of "what it is for a speaker to mean by an utterance *x*." Unfortunately, in Grice's theory the hearer has no other clue than the speaker's use of words. But how can the hearer understand the speaker's intention unless something common is shared, both by the speaker and the hearer? The communication-intention theorists might say that communication is a kind of "co-ordination-game"[22] (Bach). But how such a game can be played without locating a basic co-ordination principle? If Grice's position is to be vindicated then it is necessary that the speaker and the hearer should *share an understanding of language*. Otherwise the meaning would remain uncommunicated. Thus, in case of Grice, the ideas of *thought content* and *shared understanding of language* by the speaker and the hearer are fundamental. But in that case he must explain what kind of thought-content is shared in communication. If it is inferrable from the choice of the words used by the speaker, then he has to face two kinds of problems. He has to explain how the speaker's intention is communicated; and he has to provide a solid foundation to his thesis that thought has a conceptual priority over language. He fails to offer solutions to both the problems. If we follow Grice then one has to ultimately *turn back to language to interpret thought-content*.

Now let me discuss in brief another important theory that tries to explain speech in terms of thought. Searle modifies his earlier position (undertaken in his speech-act theory) and in his book, *Intentionality*, presents a different kind of thought-based semantics. He successfully overcomes one of the important

---

22. Kent Bach, "Conversational Impliciture," *Mind and Language*, 9, 1994, pp. 124-62.

weaknesses in Grice's theory. He discounts Grice's claim that the speaker's intention in communication is always a case of inducing a belief in the hearer. Yet he goes along with Grice in admitting that meaning of an utterance is inherited from the content of intention. Searle explicates meaningful linguistic utterance in terms of the intentional states of the speaker's beliefs, desires and intentions. The basic features of his theory are (i) all our activities (including languaging) are governed by intentions, (ii) our assertions and beliefs are supposed to match the world, and so have a "mind to world direction of fit," and (iii) the world represented by a contentful mental act must be conditioned by criterion of satisfaction (broadly implying truth conditions). Applying these features to his theory of meaning we may say that the speaker, for example, in saying "it is raining" intends to say so, and has the utterance "It is raining" having the condition of satisfaction with "mind to world direction of fit" that "It is raining." In this case the meaning of utterance is determined by the content of intention with which an utterance is made provided it satisfies the relevant truth-conditions. So in case of both Grice and Searle it is the thought that anchors language, not vice versa. But one may very significantly ask — can such thought-contents exist independent of their linguistic expressions, if we are assuming that language is communicative? Besides, both Grice and Searle interpret thought-content in terms of episodic thoughts, not thought in general. So we are bound to fall back on linguistic utterances to interpret such episodic intention of the speaker. In that case, can we still maintain that thought is independent of language? For language is an important source of the acquisition of new beliefs and concepts. In this context, Peter Carruthers (1996) raises a very important question, i.e. "how are we to explain our ability to entertain unlimitedly many *new* thought-contents . . . except *generatively*, in terms of the construction of new linguistic means for the expression of those thoughts, by putting together old parts in new ways?"[23] Therefore, we may safely claim that

23. P. Carruthers, *Language, Thought and Consciousness*, Cambridge University Press, 1996, p. 85.

unless the Bhartṛharian position is admitted, that is, unless we presuppose that thought anchors language and language anchors thought, the theory of thought-based semantics remains inexplicable. This problem raised by Carruthers is a central problem that any philosopher of language must address to. Unfortunately, most of the Western philosophers of language seem to be obsessed with the language of assertion and truth-conditionality (in Searle's case, "condition of satisfaction"). This does not allow them to give sufficient attention to this problem. But in case of Bhartṛhari this problem seems to have an easy solution. In his *Vākyapadīya* he discusses in detail multiple kinds of activities a man can perform with language, including metaphorical, elliptical, satirical and even ornamental expressions. This, to some extent, is clear from the following explanatory note on verse I.13. He says: "On language depends maybe the speaker's intended meaning, the possibility of applying words to things, the ability to combine words into sentences, the connecting of objects with actions, identification of a thing as to be accomplished, or the projection of the content of an awareness as an external object." So he must have sought an answer to the question — how does our language function in limitless ways? And his answer would be that the power to use language in limitless ways is rooted in the dispositional linguistic ability that is present within each conscious human being. And *sphoṭa* is the basic ground of this linguistic ability itself.

So far I have given a brief outline of two radically opposite theories about the relation between the language and the thought as far as linguistic communication is concerned. Now I shall make an attempt to examine the plausibility of a theory that may look apparently closer to Bhartṛhari's position. Donald Davidson in his paper entitled, "Thought and Talk" (1975) conceives these two concepts as interdependent. He says, ". . . the parallel between the structure of thoughts and structure of sentences provides no argument for the primacy of the either, and only a presumption in favour of their interdependence."[24] From this basic premise he

24. Donald Davidson, "Thought and Talk," in *Mind and Language*, ed. S.D. Guttenplan, p. 10.

goes on to conclude that, "a creature must be a member of the speech community if it is to have a concept of belief. And given the dependence of other attitudes on belief, we must say more generally that a creature that can interpret speech can have the concept of thought." So far Davidson's position seems very akin to Bhartṛhari's initial position regarding the relation between thought and language. But the primary purpose of Davidson here is to offer a theory of Interpretation based on the modified version of Tarski's theory of truth. So he makes it clear that, "We usually think that having a language consists largely in being able to speak, but in what follows speaking will play an indirect part, what is essential to my argument is the idea of an interpreter, someone who understands the utterance of another."[25] This notion of an interpreter does not seem to differ very much from Bhartṛhari's notion of a hearer. But the points of similarities end once we try to know the very basis of interpretability. According to Davidson the method of interpretation "puts the interpreter in general agreement with the speaker, according to the method the speaker holds a sentence to be true under specified conditions, and these conditions obtain, in the opinion of the interpreter, just when the speaker holds sentence to be true."[26] So Davidson is ultimately assuming that the condition of sentences being held true is the determinant factor for referring to the thought. So Davidson describes thought as interlocking system of beliefs that can be held true. But Bhartṛhari looks at the problem of language-thought equation primarily from the standpoint of communicability of meaning. He does not need to bring in the concept of "belief" to work as a counterpart of **assertions being held true**, simply for the reason that truth is not the connecting link between meaning and an utterance. Rather the spoken words and its meaning refer to a state which serves as the preliminary stage of the expressiveness of meaning, for there is no verbalisability without cognisability. Interestingly enough, Davidson in the concluding

25. Donald Davidson, "Thought and Talk," in *Mind and Language*, ed. S.D. Guttenplan, p. 9.

26. Ibid., p. 21.

part of his paper comes to the conclusion that we can only meaningfully talk of "belief" from the role of belief in interpretation of language. Therefore, "the notion of true belief depends on the notion of a true utterance, this in turn there cannot be without a shared language." So from the notion of interpretation he comes to the notion of truth to return back again to interpretation in terms of "shared language." The speaker and the hearer communicate because they are the interpreters of "truth"; and this is made possible on the basis of a shared language. Though he does not specify what does he exactly mean by this term, yet it is obvious that he prioritizes speech over thought. It is obvious that he does not intend to go beyond the level of speech, but carefully avoids falling into the trap of linguistic behaviourism of Wittgenseinean kind.

From our discussion on three important strands of philosophy, viz. speech-act theories, thought-based semantics and interpretationalism it becomes clear that some of the important issues regarding communication of meaning between the speaker and the hearer remains unattended. Much is taken for granted. Though these theories accept that linguistic communication is inter-subjective in nature, the fundamental question that needs to be answered, i.e. how does the speaker convey the meaning to the hearer — seems to take a backseat. Should we say that meaning is an entity that can be transported in the manner we load the contents of one car into another car. Had it been so the following problems would not have bothered the philosophers of language:

1 The speaker has to express his thought through temporal and instantly destroyed sound utterances having sequence and multiplicity. The hearer, too, receives them in their multiplicity and sequentiality. But the "sense" communicated is unitary in nature. How does the hearer grasp the unity and sequenceless whole, called meaning?

2 Why in certain cases does the hearer fail to get the meaning even if he had listened carefully to each word uttered by the speaker? Again, in certain cases the hearer can grasp

the meaning even if the speaker has not completed his utterance. How this is possible?

3 The speaker's utterance not only conveys the literary meaning, but also the "implied" and "implicit" meaning (which in modern philosophical parlance is called "implicature" and "impliciture," respectively). How does the hearer grasp them from the stated meaning?

These are the questions that Bhartṛhari does not want to leave unattended. Here, the notion of *sphoṭa* comes in handy. Bhartṛhari would say, because both the speaker and the hearer share the common *sphoṭa,* meaning is communicated. *Sphoṭa* is connected with inherent linguistic potency (*śabda bīja* or *śabda bhāvanā)* present within all conscious human beings. Therefore human beings have a natural linguistic competence. When the speaker intends to say something, he grasps the unit of meaning first, and then expresses it in a sequential form. The hearer, on the other hand, catches the audible and sequential forms of words first and these words evoke his linguistic potency, and this gives him the competence to understand what the speaker intends to say. If the speaker's utterance fails to arouse the linguistic potency there is a gap in communication. On the other hand, if the hearer is able to grasp the sense conveyed by the speaker then an incomplete sentence is enough for the purpose. In this case he need not listen to the whole series of words to assess the meaning. Nor does he require to mentally compute the uttered words to gather the unitary sense conveyed. To the question — how the same sentence can be used to communicate, besides the literal meaning, implied, implicit and even metaphorical meaning — Bhartṛhari's answer is remarkably clear. He says that we are guided by the "power" of words. The speaker takes the help of this power when he intends to speak depending on the choice of the right word. When the hearer follows the fixed power of words to convey a meaning through reasoning based on meaning, context, indication, interconnection etc. people look upon the capacity of the words as the reasoning of the hearer (*Vṛtti* under I.137). The ability to express meaning and apprehend the meaning is potent in the *sphoṭa*, which also refers to human linguistic potency (*śabda bhāvanā*).

The explanation of linguistic communication in terms of *sphoṭa* or *śabda* may not sound very appealing to the Western mind, but their solution to the issue has not been very satisfying either. In the context of communication of intention, Grice does talk of a "shared understanding of the language." But ultimately, such understanding is grounded on linguistic convention. But linguistic convention alone is not sufficient to explain the complexities associated with communication of meaning. Similarly, Davidson[27] tries to locate the basis of inter-subjectivity in "shared language," but this phenomenon, though not implying linguistic convention, is finally set to rest on systems of beliefs and truth-conditions which indirectly means that he does not want to go beyond the language of assertion, and thereby neglects the multiplicities of dimensions of the phenomenon called language. What is more worrying is that these theories of linguistic communication pay scanty attention to the unlimited creative power of thought and the generative power of language.

Thought and Language: The Conceptual Perspective

Now I shall try shift the focus of my discussion to another dimension of thought-language equation. It is not directly connected with communicative meaning. The issue is confined to the conceptual level. We know that language and thought are two important aspects of human existence. So the question that is likely to puzzle the philosophers is about the conceptual priority of one over the other. It is usually believed that it is a one-way relationship. Thought is conceptually prior to language since language serves as the conveyor belt of thought. Dismissing this popular stand Bhartṛhari claims that it is thought which presupposes language. Naturally, he does not have many sympathizers in Indian classical as well as modern Western philosophical traditions. Of course, in contemporary academic

27. Donald Davidson, "Thought and Talk," in *Mind and Language*, ed. S.D. Guttenplan, p. 10.

circles the issue has generated much debate in the field of philosophy of mind and introspective psychology. Philosophers like W. Sellars,[28] Jerry Fodor,[29] and Peter Curruthers[30] support a thesis which may give credence to Bhartṛhari's stand on the issue. However these philosophers mostly look at the problem from the standpoint of philosophy of mind and introspective psychology. But Bhartṛhari explicates the issue absolutely from a different angle. Language is his apparatus as well as the goal of his philosophical investigation. Specifying his approach he states very clearly that as a *śabda-pramāṇaka* (which approximately can be translated as "analyst of language") his primary concern is language, not the nature of things. So he announces, "What the word presents is the only reality for us" (*Mahābhāṣya Dīpikā*). Accordingly, he formulates a unique metaphysics, in which the highest status is accorded to *śabda* or Word-principle. *Śabda*, for him, is the ultimate reality (*śabda-tattva-Brahman*). Therefore, he has no problem in explicating thought as well as the objective world, in terms of the *śabda-tattva*. As far as his metaphysical stance is concerned he is an unflinching monist. So *unity* is the key principle in his philosophy. Applying this to the level of language-in-use he conceives meaning as a unity of three distinct elements, i.e. thought, language, and the object meant. His commitment to monism would not allow him to retain the distinction between thought and language. Therefore, he believes that human consciousness is impregnated with the Word-principle. In *Vākyapadīya* he declares: "It is the speech which prompts all mankind into activity. Without this power man is nothing more than a log of wood or a piece of stone" (I.127). To understand Bhartṛhari's position on conceptual priority of language over thought we must refer to the following verses of his treatise.

---

28. W. Sellars, *Science, Perception and Reality*, Kegan Paul, 1963.

29. J. Fodor, "Propositional Attitudes," in his *Re-Presentation*, Harvester, 1981.

30. P. Carruthers, *Language, Thought and Consciousness*.

> There can be no awareness in this world without being intertwined with language. All cognitive awareness appears as if it is interpenetrated with language. — *VP* I.123

In this verse Bhartṛhari uses the word awareness in a distinctively different sense. We as conscious beings are aware of the innumerable factual and mental events and objects surrounding us. The general impression is that we are aware of them because of the perceptual process. But Bhartṛhari argues that our awareness is not a matter of accumulating contents through the perceptual process, because even our simple perceptions involve cognizing through names and forms. That is the reason why he claims that there cannot be any cognitive awareness without being intertwined with words.

The next verse throws some further light on the nature being aware of objects and events. Herein it is stated:

> If the language-impregnated nature of awareness went away from it, then a cognition would not manifest (any object), for that (language-impregnated nature) is the distinguishing nature of our awareness. — I.124

In this verse he uses two terms, *prakāśa* and *pratyavamarśa*, to explicate the process of human consciousness. However Bhartṛhari does not offer us the detailed implications of these terms in his *Vṛtti*. So we have to take help of a later grammarian, Utpala, for the interpretation of these terms. Utpala says that the very nature of illumination (*prakāśa*) is *vimarśa*, i.e. discrimination; otherwise illumination would be inert and passive like material object, such as a mirror or a crystal. To express it in simpler terms the word-potentness of thought functions in two ways, it reveals the content of thought along with discriminating it from other thought-contents. Matilal, while anaysing the import of this pair of concepts says, "illumination means removal of darkness but simple removal of darkness does not reveal the object unless one is able to distinguish the outline of the object from its immediate surroundings or environment."[31] Therefore, Bhartṛhari and other grammarians believe that even in case of bare awareness, these twin principles of concept formation (awareness), i.e. subsuming an object/event experienced under a name and distinguishing it from other similar experiences of objects/events, is very much operative. Without such *vāgrūpatā* (word-loadedness), which Bhartṛhari identifies with *pratyavamarśa,* i.e. "determination by word" (which the later grammarians call as *vimarśa*) an awareness is no awareness. So he says, "What is called awareness (*saṁjñā*) is having the form of speech or word (*vāgrūpatā*). Consciousness in all beings never goes beyond it, that is, it is never different from the fact of having the form of the word."[32] In direct contrast to the views of some of the traditional Indian theories like Nyāya and Mīṁāmsā, Bhartṛhari holds that there cannot be any pre-linguistic bare awareness (*nirvikalpa jñāna*). In Indian epistemological tradition it is commonly accepted that language has a minimum role to play as far as cognition is concerned. This belief is very articulately presented in the *Nyāya-Sūtra* of Vātsyāyana, where he defines perception (*pratyakṣa*) as being characterized by non-verbalisability (*avyapadeśya*). He distinguishes between the cognition of those who have the linguistic ability and who lack it. Later commentators include the mute and the infant in the latter category. As far as awareness is concerned Vātsyāyana finds no difference between the two categories. It is obvious that Bhartṛhari was very much aware of this problem. In his commentary on I.125, he says, "Speech (*vāk*) indwells or inheres in all cases of awareness just as illumination does in fire and consciousness in the mind (*antaryāmin*). The subtle nature of *vāk* (speech) [i.e. *sūkṣmo vāgdharma*] penetrates and permeates even such states as lack of ostensible mental activity (*asañcetitāvasthā*)."[33] Even the awareness of a child is word-potent. Bhartṛhari emphatically states, "All

---

31. Jonardon Ganeri (ed.), *Collected Essays of Bimal Krishna Matilal,* Oxford University Press (Indian Edition), 2002, p. 135.

32. Ibid.

33. Tr. by Matilal, *The World and the World,* pp. 134-35.

knowledge of what is to be done in this world depends upon the word. Even the child, with residual traces from previous birth has such knowledge" (I.121). Though a child lacks the capability of forming definite concepts, its raw awareness is subsumable under the vague concepts like "this" or "that." He points out, "The residual trace of speech has no beginning and it exists in everyone as a seed in the mind. It is not possible that it should be the result of the effort of any person. Movements of the articulatory organs by a child are not due to instruction by others but are known through intuition. Who, indeed, can make or make known these human properties as other than residual traces of the word?" (*Vṛtti* on I.122).[34] In other words, he wants to drive home the point that the **linguistic potency is innate and universal** in each-conscious being. Unless a child has the latent capacity of languageing in him he cannot make an effort to reproduce language through his own effort. Thus language is not acquired through external influences, but it is the inherent constituent of our awareness, about which we gradually become conscious when the learning process starts. We only become aware of the word-potentness of thought when the words are expressed in a sequential and articulate manner to express our thought. In fact, for Bhartṛhari, the word-potentness is the very basis of distinction between the sentient (*sasaṁjñā*) and insentient being (*visaṁjñā*). But, from this it does not follow that thought is a form of "inner speech," as conceived by Sellars; nor does the theory say that being conscious means being constantly in the process of using words. There is definitely a distinction between verbalization and verbalisability. All our thought and awareness **need not be wordy**, but they have the **potentiality to be expressed through words**. To put it in different words "whatever is thinkable is sayable." At the same time Bhartṛhari is not reducing thought into words. He is interested in justifying the conceptual dependence of human consciousness on the principle of language.

34. Tr. by K.A.S. Iyer, *Vākyapadīya*, I.

Bhartṛhari's explication of the conceptual relation between thought and language may appear unusual. It may sound sometimes like a mystical rhapsody. But given his metaphysical position no other conclusion could have been possible. However, recent studies in philosophical and introspective psychology[35] (refer *Language, Thought and Consciousness* by Peter Carruthers) can be taken as an ample evidence for the fact that, even after a considerable lapse of 1500 years, Bhartṛhari's philosophy can withstand the test of time.

35. For instance, Jerry Fodor explicates the linguistic potency in terms of *Mentalese*. He argues the sentences that human beings use in communication belong to an innate, universal, language of thought. This he calls as *Mentalese*. This linguistic potency consists of an innate lexicon, or vocabulary, and an innate set of combinatorial rules for the production of completed sentences, held in common by all human beings.

7

The Word and the World

Semantics and Ontology

IN the previous chapter I have hinted at Bhartrhari's triadic analysis of language. This involves an explication of twofold relationship, i.e. the relation between word and thought, and the relation between word and the world (referent). I have already dwelt on Bhartrhari's conception of word-thought relationship. Now I will like to take up for discussion the word-referent relationship. This issue is more complicated in nature, for most often this epistemic issue tends to turn into an ontological one. We generally believe that words mean the things. In other words, we use language to describe the existent reality. So meaning has commonly been conceived as a function of "naming." It is a sort of naming the referent or the object-meant. But this is not the end of what we conceive regarding word-world relationship. Discussions on the nature of the relationship often boils down to the question on "what there is?" In fact, it sometimes appears that there is a two-way relationship between semantics and ontology. For often the philosophers tend to believe that the problem of explaining the nature of the world can be better solved by probing into the nature of "what do we do with words?" As Quine puts it, "It is no wonder, then, that ontological controversy should end into controversy over language."[1] Therefore, we note that there is a subtle connection between the theory of meaning and the theory of existence, even though theoretically they belong to two separate

1. W.V.O. Quine, *From a Logical Point of View*, Harvard University Press, 1953, p. 16.

areas of study. The semantical analysis of language is supposed to be confined to the explication of relation between the word and referent or facts. One can confine oneself within the strict boundaries of such an analysis if he is involved in the semantics of *formal* language. But when it is about the natural language, even the most rigorous form of semantics implicitly suggests some ontological commitments. And most often it over-reaches its boundary to trespass into the area of ontology. This tendency is natural. The philosopher's conception of the world and its status often determines how the word should relate itself to the world of objects and events. While discussing Bhartṛhari's world-view in Chapter 2, I have explicitly stated about his phenomenalistic stand. His world-view, naturally, influences his notion of semantics.

Bhartṛhari maintains that there is a close relationship between the word and what is meant by the word. It was already been noted earlier (in Chapter 4) that he describes the relationship in terms of *saṁjñā* and *saṁjñin*. In most of the standard books on Bhartṛhari, these two terms are translated as "name" and the "named." But I feel the translation of *saṁjñā* as "name," may present certain difficulties, especially, for those who are acquainted with the Western theories of meaning. *Saṁjñā* in a broad sense also implies a concept or an idea that we form about the use of a term. *Saṁjñā* stands for the definition of a word. It will be convenient for us, in the present context, to use the term in the above sense. This will help us to present Bhartṛhari's views in clearer terms.

The definition of meaning as a function of "naming" implies that words stand for "names." The term "name" often holds the philosophers captive of a sort of picture-thinking (to use Wittgenstein's phrase). The use of the term "name" suggests the picture of a corresponding object "named." There are some words which have their objective counterpart in the world. But the word "pegasus" does not correspond to an existing entity in space and time. Still the picture of "name and the named" leads some philosophers to conceive of a "mental entity" none the less existent, i.e. existent in a different sense. Russell exploded the myth by very rightly pointing out that the so-called singular descriptions using names can be used without supposing that there might be such entities. But Russell's theory is more about the definite descriptions than about names. Rather Frege is more explicit when he shows that there cannot be one-to-one relationship between the word (name) and the referent (named). "Morning star" and "evening star" are two different word-compounds implying two different meanings yet having one referent. In this case one referent is described in two ways. From this it becomes clear that the use of the word "name" has duped the philosophers in the past. So it is better for us to avoid the term "name" in explaining Bhartṛhari's word-referent relationship. He never has conceived words in that sense, because he clearly states with examples (as cited earlier) that there are many words without any objective referent.

In case of Bhartṛhari *saṁjñā* and *saṁjñin* relationship can be best described as a relationship between definition and definiendum. In fact, Bhartṛhari would say, we use words to describe or to express. But what we describe or express need not be about objects. We have some sort of compulsion of thinking about the objects as the things-meant if we take words to be the ultimate unit of meaning. Bhartṛhari has no such compulsion, for he attributes primacy to sentence-meaning, not to word-meaning. Besides, he believes that primary meaning of any referential word is the universal, not particular. And lastly, according to him both the *saṁjñā* and *saṁjñin* are linguistic in nature. The object referred to is not originally extra-linguistic. The last two ideas cited above will become clear as we proceed with Bhartṛhari's theory of word-world relationship.

Some time back I had hinted at the relation between semantics and ontology. I had also pointed out that the ontological scheme of a philosopher has its bearing on his conception of word-world relationship. Let us therefore examine Bhartṛhari's ontological status. In Indian context we may broadly pinpoint three types of rival ontologies. They are — Realism, Atomism and Holism.

Nyāya-Vaiśeṣika offers a realistic world-view according to which the world is populated by real particulars, universals and relations. So when we talk of a "table" it refers to an existing table out there in the space and time. Buddhists, especially Diṅnāga envisages the world to be populated by momentary particulars (*svalakṣaṇas*). They are not nameable. Our words which describe objects are not adequate enough to catch within its net the true nature of the momentary and structureless particulars. So concepts and words are linguistic constructs (*vikalpa*). The third type of ontology is offered by Bhartṛhari. It is Holistic. According to him, the reality is an undifferentiated and unanalysable whole. But in our thought and language, we are in the habit of cutting bits and pieces out of this whole reality and assigning them a "metaphorical existence." The real word is beyond our grasp. Our words (also word-impregnated concepts) are mental constructs (*kalpanā*) or linguistic constructs (*vikalpa*). In other words, our language does not and cannot refer to the objects or real referents. The last two views about the world (objects) and the language are radically different from the Nyāya-Vaiśeṣika Realism. The notion of the word/ language in relation to the world is developed in different ways by Diṅnāga and Bhartṛhari. Yet it is interesting to note that they share a certain degree of common semantical notion. In view of such similarities I intend to make a comparative analysis of Bhartṛhari's and Diṅnāga's views on the topic. It may help us in revealing an interesting aspect of philosophy of language as a whole. It is interesting, because here is the case of two philosophers whose rival ontological views lead them to a common converging point in semantics.

It is well known that Diṅnāga quotes some crucial passages from Bhartṛhari's *Vākyapadīya* in his treatise *Pramāṇasamuccaya*[2] to vindicate his own views. On the basis of this evidence it can be claimed that there are subtle shades of similarity between *sphoṭa* theory of meaning, and the *apoha* theory of meaning propagated

2. K. Potter, *Encyclopaedia of Indian Philosophies*, vol. V, p. 28. Diṅnāga quotes *Vāk*, III.14.8, II.158, II.155.

by Diṅnāga. Yet the moment we try to analyse their respective philosophies we become aware of the vast range of differences between them. They adopt divergent approaches in their handling of metaphysical and epistemological issues. For Bhartṛhari *śabda* is a primary form of *pramāṇa*, whereas for Diṅnāga *śabda* does not have even an independent status as a *pramāṇa*. This makes our task of tracing similarities more interesting. To do full justice to the task in hand, I need to dwell briefly on the metaphysical and epistemological background of both these philosophers. We must start by highlighting the points of difference till we reach the point of convergence.

I need not discuss much about Bhartṛhari's position. We have discussed them earlier. But while summing up his position it can be said that he is a Monist in his metaphysical stance and his world-view is Holistic. And in his epistemology he offers primacy to *śabda*. In other words, it is a form of Pan-verbalism, which explains all forms of knowledge and cognition in terms of "word-loadedness." In Bhartṛhari's conceptual scheme "unity" is the key-word. It alone is primary and real.

The Buddhist (Diṅnāga's) Viewpoint

Diṅnāga, on the other hand, in true Buddhist tradition, denies the status of unity, whole and eternity. His metaphysical position is pluralistic and atomistic. But his pluralism is logical in nature. He conceives the ultimate Reality as unique particulars, which are known as *svalakṣaṇa*s. They are no ordinary particulars, i.e. objects or things, but a series of fleeting moments and point-instants. They are devoid of any characterization, nor are they locatable in space and time. Yet these *svalakṣaṇa*s or "the essence of their own being," are independent of our mind. They are cognizable because they are perceivable. Diṅnāga describes *svalakṣaṇa* in the following manner: "The perception of sense-perception is *rūpa* (i.e. that belongs to the sensory faculty) which is cognizable simply as it is and which is **inexpressible**" (*Pramāṇasamuccaya*, Ch.I., Verse 5, ed). In other words, they are simple, unanalysable units perceivable but not conceivable. This sort of atomistic stand by

Diṅnāga stems from Buddha's famous pronouncement : "One sees blue, but one does not see 'It is blue'." The moment one says "It is blue" he objectivises the fleeting moments. Objects occupy space and time and they have some amount of stability and continuity in existence. But *svalakṣaṇa*s cannot be understood with reference to space, time and stability. They are existent not in ordinary sense but in a logical sense. The moment we try to talk about them we objectivise them by attaching names and concepts to them. So the ideas of objects and things occur when the pure percepts are confused with the mental categories and concepts. Concepts are the products of mind. So any kind of conceptualization involves projection through imagination (*kalpanā*) and mental construction (*vikalpa*). Concepts present a unified picture of what is particular. Therefore *svalakṣaṇa*s (the ultimately Real) is inconceivable and unutterable.

This sort of metaphysical atomism has its ramifications in his theory of epistemology. Unlike Bhartṛhari, he believes that there can be concept-free cognition and awareness. Diṅnāga specifies that there are two sources of knowledge, i.e. percept and concept. Percept is the direct source of knowledge, whereas concept is indirect. Epistemologically, percept and sense-awareness precede concepts. The former is the means of cognizing the unconditioned and ultimate Reality, i.e. *svalakṣaṇa*s, whereas the latter leads to the knowledge of the conditioned Reality. However, when we take recourse to expressing our awareness and experience through language, we have no way but to take help from the faculty of concepts. All linguistic expressions are done through the mode of conceptualization, and these in turn, are a form of universalization. So the unique and particularized reality cannot be grasped by the concepts in its true nature.

So far we have been concentrating on the contrasting characteristics of Bhartṛhari's and Diṅnāga's metaphysical and epistemological background. Let us now have a look at their semantic position. The central issue of semantics is — how to relate the word with the world. It is a common belief that language has, primarily, a referring role, i.e. words must denote the things and events of the world. This belief arises because we want to bridge the epistemic gulf between the subject and object of knowledge, between the knower and the known. So it is taken for granted that the knower is the possessor of language and concepts; and concepts must refer to objects. The issue is crystallized in the form "what does the word refer to?" The obvious answer is — "Object." When one says "cow" it refers to the object cow. But how do we know that the object is a cow? To call some object a "cow" one must classify the object as belonging to the class "cow," for the same word can be used to refer to similar objects as cows. However, classification is a form of universalization. Universalization in turn leads to concept formation. So the referring role of words requires conceptualization and universalization. On this issue few philosopers would disagree. So the problem acquires a new form, i.e. do we conceptualize and classify on the basis of real universal qualities present in the objects of a class? To put it more articulately — are the universals mind-dependent or object-dependent? The Realists like Nyāya-Vaiśeṣikas will say that universals are real and object-dependent. For them, universal is as real as the particular. The particular, qualified by the universal, constitutes the true denotation of a word. They define the universal (*jāti*) as that which exists in the different particulars of the same species. This makes the application of the same name to different particulars of the same class possible. But Diṅnāga and Bhartṛhari take the opposite stand. According to them universal is a mental category. We see the objects as qualified by universal qualities because our mind projects them in that way. The philosophical position of these two thinkers is a radical departure from the prevalent Realism of their time. This Mentalistic and Nominalistic stand, at the outset may appear to be implausible and unsound. But they both offer sufficient logical justification for this novel way of interpreting the concept of universal.

Bhartṛhari and Diṅnāga on Word-World Relation

We have noted earlier that Diṅnāga's and Bhartṛhari's ontological positions are widely divergent. Bhartṛhari's Pan-linguism and Holism is in direct contrast with Diṅnāga's Linguistic Phenomenalism; again the former's monism is contrary to the latter's atomism and pluralism. Yet in the matters of semantics they agree on some crucially important points. They are: (1) no application of word is possible without universalization, (2) the thing-meant or object-denoted cannot be known directly through words, (3) universals are mind-dependent, and (4) universalization and conceptualization necessarily involve differentiation and negation. Let us now examine how both these thinkers expound their views in this area of study.

Bhartṛhari's entire attitude towards the word-object relationship is guided by Patañjali's crucial remark: "We are the linguist analysts, for us what word says is our guide." Bhartṛhari further elaborates this as "what is the use of our reflecting on the nature of things? The object is for us what the word presents." One may note the direct influence of this attitude when he comes down to the analysis of relationship between the form of the word (*grāhya*) and what a word conveys or denotes (*grāhaka*); and the relationship between the name or words (*saṁjñā*) and named (*saṁjñin*). He specifically points out that we cannot refer to the objects directly without referring to the form of the word. Unless and until the form of the word is understood meaning remains uncommunicated. So words primarily refer to the *vācya* or the form of the word. From this it follows that *grāhya* and *grāhaka*, and *saṁjñā* and *saṁjñin* are identical. At the level of utterance when we make differentiation, we can at best directly refer to the level of **words** not the **world**. He admits that words are, of course, used to denote objects or facts. But in all such cases, the object-meant is grasped by the hearer's awareness and then it is transferred to the objects-meant. According to Bhartṛhari, every word is a concept and hence is universal. So each word at the outset refers to the universal of the word and then it is superimposed (*adhyāropakalpanā*) on the universal of the thing-meant (*VP*, III.1.6). The meaning of a word cannot be an object or substance-meant, but a mental construct (*vikalpa*) produced in us of the object (*VP*, III.1.9). So the object-as-such is never captured by the words. This is because an object can be described in innumerable ways: for example, a man may be referred to as "father," "farmer," etc. The concept referring to the object represents how and under what guise it is captured by our mind. So he calls these referential words as *vikalpa*. This is determinate in nature. They are word-generated. Yet such word-generated concepts are not private and subjective. They are shared by all conscious beings, because that is how language works.

Now the question arises that even if these referent or objects are word-generated, what should be their true nature? Does the word refer (even indirectly) to the objective universals? In other words can there be objective universals corresponding to the mental category of universals? The Realists like Nyāya may argue that even if all universals are not object-dependent, at least, some are. They are out there in the world, and because particulars share a specific universal essence they are cognized as belonging to that class. For example, a particular object is called a "cow" because the universal essence of "cowhood" is really present in the object. Bhartṛhari, however, would not agree with such a conception of universal. He brings out to our notice certain subtle nuances of the concept of universal, neglected by the Realists. The Realists explain "universal" in terms of object-universal (*artha-jāti*). Bhartṛhari on the other hand shows that the concept of object-universal is not fully explicable without reference to the word-universal (*śabda-jāti*). If the basis of the use of the word "cow" is "cowhood," Bhartṛhari argues, then what is the basis of the term "cowhood" itself? If we follow the Realist's line of thought then we will be compelled to accept that there is another thing-universal for the term "cowhood" and so on *ad infinitum*. Therefore, the Realists, like Nyāya, do not admit that there can be a universal in universal. But paradox cannot be ignored so easily. Here Bhartṛhari comes forward with the solution with the introduction of the concept of word-universal (*śabda-jāti*). He argues that "not only could the 'basis' or 'ground' for using a name be a universal, but also uniform basis of application of names to varying things deserve a uniform 'basis' or 'ground' of application and usage."[3] He also offers two very crucial arguments in support of his thesis of word-universal. First, if varying particulars are themselves made the basis for using a class name on the ground that they share a common-essence, then the problem of innumerability (*ananta*) would arise. Learning a name like "cow" and what it means will be difficult, for there are innumerable number of cows (including past, present and future cows). How can one know what the universal "cowhood" refers to without knowing all particulars and the essence they share? So it is safer to start with word-universal and once we know what the word "cowhood" as a term means then one can apply the term to innumerable cases on the basis of the word-universal. Secondly, if we believe that universals are present in the object we may face the problem of variability (*vyabhicāra*). The particulars in connection with which we learn a name and the vast cases to which the term is applied, may vary. So Bhartṛhari puts forward the thesis that words, first of all, mean the word-universal and thereafter superimposes (*śabdādhyāropa*) them on thing-universal. The identification or rather the confusion between *śabda-jāti*/word-universal and *artha-jāti*/thing-universal can be compared to the case of a crystal reflecting the redness of a flower placed near it. In such a case one may say that the crystal is red though it is due to the false identification of the reflection of redness with the actual colour of the crystal.

From the above explanation it should not be concluded that Bhartṛhari is a hard-core Nominalist, who interprets the objective world as a mental projection or *kalpanā*. His position is more Phenomenalistic than Nominalistic. He only says that the real nature of thing-as-such cannot be shown by our words. The things/objects that we refer to by the use of words are determined by how we define the word-universal. They are limited by mind-

3. B.K. Matilal, *The Word and the World*, p. 85.

dependent attributes and qualities. The real-existence understood through words is determinate (*savikalpaka*). The real-existence as such is beyond verbal penetration. He calls this sort of existence *mukhya sattā*, which is unutterable and indeterminate (*nirvikalpaka*). The existence that is presented through language has a secondary status. This is called *upacāra sattā*, which can be translated as "metaphorical" existence. In a metaphor we superimpose the qualities of one object on another: for example, "This boy is a lion." We understand the meaning of the statement by attributing the characteristics of lion such as bravery and ferociousness, to the boy. In Reality a boy cannot be a lion. Similarly the reality as-such, according to Bhartṛhari, is not expressible in language. The elements of uttered speech, i.e. the differentiation between word, referent and meaning is not there at the level of ultimate Reality, but is superimposed on it when we describe it through language.

This leads us to realize that, according to Bhartṛhari, conceptualization is a way of determination and limitation (*upādhi*). It necessarily involves the process of differentiation (*bhedya*). So he makes it clear that, "A universal property is that property common to all members of a class which distinguishes a particular member of that class from non-members. Or some say, the general feature (*ākṛti*) is that which is spoken of as common, and again it is spoken of as a particular substance (*dravya*) to indicate differentiation. But differentiation and identity require limitation by something (other than the things differentiated or identified)."[4] In other words, he implicitly states that each word implies the negation of its contrary. It involves the process of assertion and negation. Bhartṛhari's way of interpreting word-universal and word-object relationship seems to have strong influence on Diṅnāga. Bhartṛhari was the elder contemporary of Diṅnāga. His indebtedness can be noted in his work, *Pramāṇasamuccaya* (*vṛttis* on *Apohapariccheda*). Especially *Jātisamuddeśa* of *Vākyapadīya* III plays a very important role in the formation of his theory of *apoha*. He quotes Bhartṛhari to support the argument that a universal word

4. B.K. Matilal, *The Word and the World*, p. 37.

(*jāti-śabda*) can be directly applied to universals; and to support the argument that a universal word may never be applied directly to the another universal.[5] Though some authentic books on Diṅnāga like *Buddhist Logic* by Stcherbatsky do not mention anything about this, some later writers like K. Kunjunni Raja, B.K. Matilal, Massaki Hattori give sufficient hints about the strange similarity of views between Bhartṛhari and Diṅnāga in the matters of language analysis. Here I shall discuss in brief Diṅnāga's views on universal and word-object relationship to expound the subtle points of similarity.

Diṅnāga maintains that words cannot directly refer to objects. What we call objects are the products of conceptualization. For word is the source of concept and concept is the source of word (*vikalpa yonaya śabdaḥ vikalpa śabda yonayaḥ*).[6] Conceptualization, on the other hand, is not possible without the use of universals. The so-called objects or things-meant are unreal in nature. For Reality is plurality of moments or point-instants (*svalakṣaṇa*s). They can be perceived but not conceived. They are indeterminate (*nirvikalpaka*). Diṅnāga calls them things-as-such (or rather moments-as-such). And they alone are ultimately Real Beings (*paramārtha sat*). What we project as objects and referents are empirically real (*saṁvṛtti sat*). The "given" or the "reality" which are referred to through our language are concept-dependent. One may note here the similarity of distinction between Bhartṛhari's *mukhya sattā* and *upacāra sattā* and Diṅnāga's *paramārtha sat* and *saṁvṛtti sat*. Both maintain that the world-as-such or Reality-as-such is **unutterable**. What is utterable is the phenomenal reality. The only metaphysical difference being, that for Bhartṛhari the ultimate Reality is **one Brahman**, and for Diṅnāga this is the **plurality** of *svalakṣaṇa*s. But this opposite metaphysical stance does not affect their semantical position. Both are phenomenalists in

5. *Vākyapadīya*, III.I.14-24. As summarised by A. Aklujkar in *Encyclopaedia of Indian Philosophies*, vol. V, Delhi: Motilal Banarsidass, 1990, p. 154.

6. F.Th. Stcherbatsky, *Buddhist Logic*, I, New York: Dover Publications, 1962, p. 459.

this respect. Diṅnāga's Phenomenalistic position does not allow him to accept universal as real and object-dependent. He argues out how a common essence can be shared by a particular object, because particular objects themselves are mentally constructed out of dissimilar unique particulars (*svalakṣaṇas*). So the concept of a real universal (*jāti/sāmānya*) is replaced by the concept of names and mental constructs (*śabda-vikalpa*). The universals are mere names (*saṁjñā-mātram*); they are mere concepts without the external reality serving as their basis (*vastuśūnya vikalpa*). So Diṅnāga holds that universality is purely mental in nature which is converted into external objects through words. "And such are the habits of thought of common humanity that they believe this projection to represent a real universal."[7] "This projection-dispersion of things entirely residing in the intellect, as if they were external, is settled by the cognizer, according to his manner of thinking, as a universal."[8] So names do not represent a real-universal. The theory that names represent the real universal is rejected on the ground of "infinity and discrepancy" (*ānantyād vyabhicarāc ca*).[9] These two arguments are almost similar to Bhartṛhari's arguments, discussed in this chapter earlier. B.K. Matilal points out that Bhartṛhari's arguments are "fully absorbed by Diṅnāga who propounded his theory of *apoha* or "exclusion" as word-meanings rejecting the reality of thing-universals or phenomenal universals."[10] The concept of *vikalpa* or the mental construct refers to the *śabda-jāti* through which he explains the concept of names and classes. He explains the term *vikalpa* as *dvāvidhi*, i.e. the bifurcation of consciousness into subject and object (*grāhya-grāhakatva vikalpa*).[11] One may, again, note convergence of views of both Diṅnāga and Bhartṛhari. Bhartṛhari also shows the

7. F.Th. Stcherbatsky, *Buddhist Logic*, I, New York: Dover Publications, 1962, p. 465.

8. Ibid., p. 465 f.

9. Ibid., p. 461 f.

10. Matilal, *The Word and the World*, p. 37.

11. *na jāti-śabda bhedānām vācaka ānantyād* । — *Buddhist Logic*, I, 461.

bifurcation between the word and the object-denoted as mental and word-generated. Like Bhartṛhari, Diṅnāga too believes that not only universals but other categories like particulars, substance, etc. are the products of linguistic usage and hence conceptual constructs.[12]

Diṅnāga's conception of universal and concepts ultimately lead us to his famous theory of *apoha*. The theory implies that "to mean is to exclude." Whenever we use words to mean anything we use the category of universal on the basis of certain functional property. To define the boundary of what it includes one must know what it excludes. Universalization means negation of counter-positive. Whenever we mean anything by "cow" we also mean that it excludes from its meaning all "non-cows." Differentiation is the means to unity. In case of universalization we bring dissimilar objects under one unitary class on the basis of differentiating and excluding the functional properties other than the property which serves as the basis of unification. It is unfortunate that some of his contemporaries branded it as a theory of negative judgement. But it is sheer misrepresentation of a logically sound theory. As Jinendrabuddhi in his commentary on Diṅnāga's *Pramāṇasamuccaya* points out, "our opponents are ignorant of the real essence of the Negative Meaning of words. They impute us (a theory which we never professed)."[13]

Understanding of words and concepts through the logic of exclusion can be possible if one adopts a Linguistic Phenomenalism. Both Bhartṛhari and Diṅnāga believe that the explication of the concept of meaning is not possible without applying the notions of determination through exclusion. It is not possible to adopt such a theory without accepting the concept of word-universal. The word-universals alone can be negated and excluded not the thing-universal. For this will lead to self-contradiction, as an existent thing cannot be both positive and negative in nature.

---

12. Diṅnāga understands by the term *vikalpa — nāma, jāti, guṇa, kriyā, dravya kalpanā, pramāṇa samuccaya,* 1.3. Refer *Buddhist Logic,* II.20.

13. *Buddhist Logic,* I.471.

Linguistic Phenomenalism: An Assessment

From our discussions above it becomes largely clear that, both Diṅnāga and Bhartṛhari share a common platform regarding word-object relationship. Both adopt a sort of Linguistic Phenomenalism in the matters of semantics. Now let us assess the logical plausibility of such an unusual approach to the issue. At first sight, it may appear that they are making the semantic analysis unnecessarily cumbersome and complicated. It also seems to militate against the common sensical and general understanding of the problem of semantics. But a little probe will show that the Linguistic Phenomenalism of Bhartṛhari and Diṅnāga are better equipped to solve certain ticklish issues associated with word-object relationship.

We use language to communicate our thought. But we should note that language is not always used to refer to and designate objects of the world. Linguistic usage has multiple dimensions. It can be used to mean matters concerning morality, emotions, aesthetics, religion, etc. And in all cases there are no corresponding objects out in the world. Bhartṛhari very rightly cites the example of words like "wheel of fire," "sky flower" etc. Nowhere in the empirical world such objects exist. This peculiarity of language has forced the later Nyāya to make a distinction between real universal (*jāti*) and nominal universal (*upādhi*). But the problem does not end there. Two more important difficulties are pointed out by Bhartṛhari. First, most of our linguistic expressions are judgemental in nature. So the subject or the substance is related to quality, action, number, etc. If we follow the Realistic logic then they are real and object-dependent. In a judgement the subject and predicate are to be related, for example, "The table is red." Here the concept "table" and "red" are said to have a relation. The relation, according to the Realists, is a real and objective category. Bhartṛhari points out that to explain the relationship between the subject and predicate one has to presume a further relationship between the concept of "relationship" and the actual relationship, and so on *ad infinitum*. Bhartṛhari and Diṅnāga get out of this "paradox" by understanding empirical facts in terms of conceptual constructs and *śabda-jāti*. Secondly, if language is judgemental then most of the sentences either assert or negate facts. If one follows the Realistic logic then it would be difficult to explain the negative propositions, such as "the tree does not exist." According to the Realists the term "tree" denotes a real object tree. So the moment "tree" is uttered it is implied that tree is existent. But how can we say "tree does not exist," for by saying "does not exist" in the predicate we are negating a primary being denoted by the term "tree"? How can an object exist and not exist at the same time? This will be a contradiction. Similarly, in case of an assertion, such as "the tree exists," the predicate "exists" is redundant because the term "tree" itself implies an existing tree. So the statement becomes tautological.[14] These arguments of Bhartṛhari are repeated by the Buddhists.[15] Such logically ticklish issues can be resolved if one agrees with Bhartṛhari and Diṅnāga that words do not refer directly to the objects and relations, but to the words and conceptual constructs (*vikalpa*s).

The problem of conceiving language in primarily a referential role has always created metaphysical tangles for the philosophers in the East as well as in the West. Plato conceived words as universals, but believed that universals are real. The world being unreal the real universals "subsist" in the mystical "other world." Aristotle demystified it, but still believed that universals are real and objective. The tradition was followed by Mill and Meinong. However, the problem takes a new turn in the recent century. The referential model in essence is retained, but instead of believing that words denote objects it is stated that the propositions or statements refer not to the objects but to states-of-affairs or to events. Early Wittgenstein, Frege and Russell contributed to this

14. *Vākyapadīya*, III, Pt. I.14-15. See K.A.S. Iyer, *Bhartṛhari*, Poona: Deccan College, 1969, p. 209.

15. *Nyāya-Varttikā Tātparyaṭīkā* of Vācaspati Miśra, p. 486. See K.K. Raja, *Indian Theories of Meaning*, Adyar, The Adyar Library and Research Centre, 1963, p. 82.

Referential theory of meaning. This has resulted in attaching primacy to assertions and negations in the scheme of linguistic expressions. It is only after later Wittgenstein pointed out that language is not primarily referential in nature that philosophers started becoming aware of the multiple dimensions of meaning-analysis. Yet one cannot say that philosophers of our time have totally got rid of the "dogma of reference." It seems that Bhartṛhari and Diṅnāga could avoid the dogma and the problems associated with it because of their Linguistic Phenomenalism. One can say that they are not bewitched by the designative role of language because Bhartṛhari is primarily a *śabda-pramāṇaka,* i.e. linguistic analyst and Diṅnāga is primarily a logician. And, as is well known, neither the language analyst nor the logician have anything to do with the existence and non-existence of empirical facts. Therefore, both aim at defining "semantic" categories, such as universal and substance, whereas the Realists like Vaiśeṣika and Nyāya take resort to "ontology" in their analysis of language.[16]

16. B.K. Matilal, *Logic, Language and Reality,* Delhi: Motilal Banarsidass, 1985, p. 389.

8

Word-Meaning and Sentence-Meaning

Sentence-Holism versus Word-Atomism

ONE of the noteworthy features of Bhartṛhari's philosophy of language is his theory of *akhaṇḍa pakṣa*. This theory stands for sentence-holism of a unique kind. According to it the sentence is the primary and indivisible unit of meaning. In the Part II of *Vākyapadīya*, he devotes full attention to the problem of sentence and sentence-meaning. He advances as many as eight main views regarding the nature of sentence-meaning. These theories offer us a glimpse of the complex nature of the problem. Bhartṛhari, in his inimitable style solves the problem, even at the cost of going against the prevalent and popular theories of his time. His concept of *akhaṇḍa pakṣa* is a logical corollary of his communicative notion of language and meaning.

Bhartṛhari, himself, notes that basically there are two approaches to the problem of sentence and sentence-meaning. The first one is the indivisibility thesis (*akhaṇḍa pakṣa*) and the second one is the divisibility thesis (*khaṇḍa pakṣa*). Following Matilal we can also call the former, "sentence-holism" and the latter "atomism." The Mīmāṁsakas advocated the latter view and Bhartṛhari advocated the former view. As most of the Indian philosophical systems, more or less, admit the communicative role of language, they raise the significant question — "how does the hearer cognize the whole "sense" that a sentence conveys?" According to Bhartṛhari sentence is an indivisible whole and sentence-meaning is grasped as a whole. No doubt, we use several words in a sentence. But the words and word-meanings have no independent status in the communication of meaning through sentences. We can, of course, abstract words from a sentence, analyse them and examine them. But such abstractions are necessary for the study of linguistics and grammar. Isolated words and meanings are useful for such studies (*śāstra vyavahāra*).[1] But they are not fit for worldly transactions or communication (*loka vyavahāra*).[2] A sentence is not a compound-whole of words. Similarly sentence-meaning cannot be grasped by a computation word-meaning individually considered. The atomistic or *khaṇḍa pakṣa* theorists, on the other hand, argue that word-meanings are not totally subservient to sentence-meaning. They have a sort of independence. The Mīmāṁsā theory of *khaṇḍa pakṣa* has been interpreted in two ways by its two sub-schools. However, both the schools agree that a sentence is a composite entity constituted of words. These constitutive elements (words) are connected to make the "whole" of the sentence. But regarding the question, how these constitutive elements are connected to produce the sentence-meaning, there is a difference of opinion. It is not a question of how the speaker connects them, but of how the hearers grasps the whole meaning from the separate units of word-meanings. Does he cognize the word-meanings separately and later on grasps them as conveying an unitary sense? The Bhaṭṭa school of Mīmāṁsā says that the hearer understands the individual word-meanings first, and then joins them together to get the complete sentence-meaning. They are like separate railway coaches joined by couplings. But Prabhākara says that the hearer cognizes the whole sentence by hearing simply the word-meanings in the context of the whole sentence. The first theory is called *abhihitānvayavāda* and the latter theory *anvitābhidhānavāda*.

According to the first theory, propagated by Bhaṭṭa, the hearer while listening to an utterance concentrates on individual word-meanings. But Prabhākara believes that the hearer grasps the whole meaning directly and deciphers the word-meaning in the context

1. K.A.S. Iyer, *Bhartṛhari*, p. 183.
2. Ibid.

of a sentence. By implication it follows that for Bhaṭṭa sentence-meaning cannot mean anything more than the summing up of the word-meanings. On the other hand, for Prabhākara the sentence-meaning may be something more than the joining together of word-meanings. For him word-meanings, though independent, are not context-free. We also learn the meaning of a word only with reference to the sentence in which it occurs. Prabhākara's view may seem closer to Bhartṛhari's theory of *akhaṇḍa pakṣa*, but it is not so. The question for Bhartṛhari is not simply the question of how we learn language or what is the actual process of hearer's understanding of the sentence-whole. His theory goes deeper than this. He considers the whole issue from the standpoint of his general philosophy of language.

Bhartṛhari's Argument for Sentence-Holism

At this stage a crucial question can be raised. I have claimed that most of the schools of Indian philosophy envisage language as communicative and most of them put emphasis on hearer's meaning. Then why does Bhartṛhari adopt a totally different stand regarding the problem of sentence-meaning? He could have accepted anyone of these *khaṇḍa pakṣa* theories, which were more popular. There are, of course, sufficient reasons for Bhartṛhari to go against the current. Bhartṛhari himself offers a series of arguments in support of his unique stand. Before I examine these arguments, I will like to indicate some important facts which led Bhartṛhari to adopt sentence-holism. Bhartṛhari's explication of the communicative process of linguistic expression is radically different from other theories prevalent in Indian philosophical systems. For Bhartṛhari *vāk* is not just "uttered and articulated speech." It is a multi-layered phenomenon, and uttered speech (*vaikharī*) is the final stage of the externalization of the linguistic process. Before the speaker expresses himself audibly through uttered speech, he has to think of the appropriate words, and the meanings they are supposed to convey. Otherwise his utterances will be chaotic and in some cases mechanical. So *vaikharī* (uttered) *vāk* presupposes a mental and pre-utterance level, i.e. *madhyamā vāk*. This, in turn, further points to a level of unity. It is the level of unitary linguistic potentiality in which the series of words and their meanings are not discernible. This is the level of *paśyantī vāk*. The potent stage of verbalisability is thus manifested in the form of particularized thought and intention. This, in turn, is externalized in the form of particular utterances. This way of explicating the speaker's way of communicating meaning implies that the uttered level along with its particularities and differentiations actually reflect the unity of thought and meaning. Whenever the speaker says something he expresses a "sense" or a "thought." This sense or thought is one and unitary. For example, *S* intends to express that he is hungry, so he would utter "I am hungry." Here the sentence contains three words, yet the "intention" or what the speaker means, is unitary in nature. So for communicative purposes the unitariness of sentence-meaning has to be assumed by the speaker. Though he has to express what he intends to say through a series of words, yet the "sense" expressed has a unity. Therefore, there is no implausibility in Bhartṛhari's claim that sentence and sentence-meaning are primary and an undifferentiated whole.

Again, if we look at the problem from the hearer's angle we are likely to understand the soundness of Bhartṛhari's claim. Hearer's understanding (*śābdabodha*) implies the grasping of a "structured thought." It is another way of saying that what he understands is the unitary sense expressed by the speaker. It is not a fragmented or piece by piece understanding. It cannot be denied that the hearer listens to the speaker's utterance in a sequential order, i.e. syllable by syllable. But he understands the unitary meaning by his inherent linguistic disposition (*pratibhā*). It is the power of understanding the meaning as a unitary whole. The hearer does not go on computing isolated words spoken by the utterer to understand the import of what is conveyed to him. In short, communication implies transference of a "sense," "idea" or "thought." And this can be possible if sentences, not the words, are taken to be the primary units of meaning.

We have examined the logical grounds of *akhaṇḍa pakṣa* theory. Now let us see how Bhartṛhari defends his theory against his opponents. Bhartṛhari argues that if for the hearer's understanding, the sentential form of presentation is required, then why should we put unnecessary emphasis on the word-meanings. Most often word-meanings do not retain their individuality when fitted into a sentence. For example, the sentence *vṛkṣo-nāsti* (the tree, there is not) has two individual word-meanings. The meaning of the word "tree" implies an existent object. But when we utter the second word *nāsti* (is not there), the first individual word implying "existence" is cancelled by the second word. In such a case self-contradiction results, if the word-meanings are said to be independent, and a sentence is conceived as a conjunction of individual word-meanings. (*Vāk*. II.241). Therefore, sentence-meaning is something more than concatenation of word-meanings, for there is a certain completeness and unitariness about sentence-meaning. Though sentence-meaning is presented through individual words, they do not have any autonomy in the matters of communication of meaning. Bhartṛhari says: "just as the senses which have each their essential field of operation, cannot perform the function without the body, in the same way individual words though expressive of their own meaning, have no meaning at all if they are isolated from the sentence." (*Vāk*. II.419, 420).

However, it may be argued (as Bhartṛhari himself points out)[3] that sometimes the hearer may understand the whole sentence excepting just one word. In such cases the understanding of meaning of that particular word is helpful in making the cognition of the sentence complete. This proves that word-meanings are not totally statusless. For example, a man living in a city may not understand the import of the sentence, "bring a cuckoo from the forest," for he does not know what a "cuckoo" means. In such a case it may be claimed that clarification of the meaning of one word "cuckoo" would make the understanding of the sentence

3. The objection is raised by Bhartṛhari in *VP*, II.74 and answered in *VP*, II.94.

complete. Therefore, sentence-meaning is not self-complete, it is rather the word-meanings, which independently contribute to the completeness of sentence-meaning. But Bhartṛhari rejects this claim. According to him such confusions may arise due to the similarity of grammatical forms among some sentences. The sentence "bring a cuckoo from the forest" has a structural similarity with the sentence "bring firewood from the forest." This sort of similarity misleads us into thinking that the man who does not understand the word "cuckoo" has actually grasped the rest of the meaning, "bring a ' . . . ' from the forest." But Bhartṛhari argues that the commonness of grammatical form does not imply that the sentences have certain commonness of meaning. The import of the first sentence is totally different from the second one. There is nothing as the "so-called" common-part. It is wrong on our part to conceive that the two sentences have similarity of meaning-components excepting one replaceable word ("cuckoo" in place of "firewood"). They are two independent sentences having two different sorts of implication. One does not bring a cuckoo in the same way as one brings the firewood.

> Just as one indivisible cognition appears to resemble another indivisible cognition in one part and to differ in another part, in the same way, even though the two sentences are indivisible and differ from each other completely, one perceives resemblane and difference between them in parts. The point may be illustrated by taking two pictures, the colour of one is green-blue while that of the other is green-yellow. The two would resemble each other partly and differ from each other partly. But in reality, they are two partless wholes. Similarly, two sentences which appear to resemble each other in having common words are really indivisible wholes.[4]

We may try to provide some more clear-cut examples to prove Bhartṛhari's point. "The coin is real" and "the time is real" — these two sentences have similar structure. But in the first case

4. Iyer, *Bhartṛhari*, p. 195. Refer *VP*, II.93-94.

"real" means "not a counterfeit" and in latter case the term "real" means something quite different. On the basis of the structural and grammatical similarity if one tries to interpret both the sentences as having similar import, then he is definitely misguided. It is the sentence-context and situation-context which determines the meanings of abstracted words.

Regarding the misconception that the knowledge of constitutent word-meaning is a surer path of the knowledge of the sentence-meaning, John Brough offers a very fitting example. By this he tries to prove Bhartṛhari's point. He states:

> We are apt to say from time to time, when struggling with a difficult passage in a foreign text, that we know all the words, but the meaning of the sentence escapes us. This however is a delusion. In such circumstances we are presumably attributing to one or more words a "meaning" which has not been extracted from this particular context, and the obvious comment is that we do not know all the words, since our knowledge does not include the manner of their occurrence in the context in question. In practice, of course, a more general, if vague, or of a meaning extracted from **similar** contexts frequently gives us sufficient clue; but this leads us in the first place to an understanding of the meaning of the sentence as a whole, and only afterwards, by an analysis of this understanding, to the attribution of meaning to the individual words.[5]

From the question of ambiguity of one word in a sentence, let us now move to the problem of "one-word" sentences. We often notice that sometimes the hearer can grasp the whole meaning, even if the speaker utters a single word or a phrase. A panic-stricken single word "fire" can convey to the hearer that there is fire somewhere in the house. If the sentence-meaning is a conjunction of several word-meanings then such "one-word" sentences are impossible. Here, by one-word sentence-meaning, we mean the completeness of what is to be conveyed or

5. John Brough, "Some Theories of Meaning," in *A Reader on the Sanskrit Grammarians*, p. 419.

understood is achieved through the utterance of one word. Some schools of Indian philosophy believe that such completeness of meaning is possible because the hearer mentally supplies the words expressive of it. For example, when the hearer listens the single word "fire," he mentally completes the sentence by inserting the words "The house is on —." Bhartṛhari does not subscribe to this view. The word actually uttered cannot bring the words unuttered to the mind. Rather when a single word is uttered, be it a noun or verb, it conveys the total meaning to the hearer without intervention of mental ordering of missing words. In such cases fitting in of the missing words do not supply the meaning. It is the context which is of more help in the grasping of the whole meaning.[6] Completeness of meaning is the test of a sentence. Therefore a single word can afford to have the significance of a sentence-meaning.

Bhartṛhari further clarifies this conception of "completeness." Incompleteness is more in the saying of a thing, rather than in the thing itself. There can be many instances when the word-meanings literally mean something, but imply something else. I have already discussed about Bhartṛhari's distinction between literal meaning, and implied or intended meaning. I need not repeat those examples. Let us take an example from our day-to-day experience. We often come across sentences which literally means praising somebody. But such sentences contain an element of sarcasm. When a boss reproaches his insincere employee by saying "Ah, here comes the most sincere worker," it implies that he hints at his employee's insincerity. If the employee does not understand this intended sense, then the boss has failed to communicate his intention. This distinction between the literal meaning and intended meaning of a sentence very clearly proves that isolated word-meanings cannot be taken as the basis of sentence-meaning.[7]

---

6. Iyer, *Bhartṛhari*, p. 198. Refer *VP*, II.336 and Puṇyarāja's commentary on the verse.

7. *stutinindā pradhāneṣu vākyeṣvartho na tādṛśaḥ* ।
padānāṁ pravibhāgena yādṛsaḥ parikalpyate ॥ *Vāk.*, II.247.
See Pillai for trans.

It is the sentence-meaning and the sentences, which are the primary units of linguistic communication.

These are some of the grounds on which Bhartṛhari rejects the primacy of word-meaning. What Bhartṛhari tries to establish is that sentences and sentence-meanings are indivisible and primary units, and they alone are real (*satya*). The individual words and their meanings have neither definiteness nor reality. In case of communication through language the speaker and the hearer have to operate with this factor of **unity**, which is achievable by sentence only. By saying that word-meanings are non-real, Bhartṛhari does not exactly denigrate the role of words. Bhartṛhari as a grammarian, cannot afford to indulge in such a contradiction. He talks of reality of sentence-meaning in the context of linguistic communication. We neither express ourselves nor understand what is spoken to us through a series of meaning-units. "After a sentence has been understood we may look back at it, analyse it into words and maintain that we discern words in it. But if we do so during the course of the utterance itself, we are apt to lose the meaning of the sentence."[8] In essence, Bhartṛhari intends to make a distinction between language-in-use and "language" as a subject-matter of the study of grammar and linguistics. As Brough very rightly points out:

> Bhartṛhari's view is simply that words and 'word-meanings' belong to the latter sphere. They constitute apparatus (not necessarily adequate) for the description of language events, but (roughly speaking) do not themselves 'exist' in the events described.[9]

Bhartṛhari's theory of *akhaṇḍa pakṣa* has no parallel in Indian philosophy of language. As a result, we note that the concept of sentence-meaning has been analysed and explained in a totally different way by other philosophers of language. The *padavādin*s

8. Brough, "Some Indian Theories of Meaning," p. 417.
9. Ibid.

or the "atomists," do not want to do away with the autonomy of words and word-meanings. So their main concern is to analyse the basic conditions of sentence-meaning. These conditions are presumed to give a completeness and unity to sentence-meaning. The three main conditions incorporated are *ākāṅkṣā, yogyatā,* and *sannidhi*. The *ākāṅkṣā* stands for syntactical completeness, whereas, *yogyatā* and *sannidhi* stand for semantical competence and phonetic contiguity. But Bhartṛhari has no need for assuming such conditions as he considers sentence-meaning as a self-complete and non-divisible unit. The later Nyāya adds *tātparya* as the fourth condition. But *tātparya* refers more to the extra-linguistic contextual elements than to the proper linguistic elements. This condition is specifically meant for deciphering the contextual meaning with reference to the sentence as a whole. But it is never treated as a factor contributing to the completeness of sentence-meaning.

With this divergent attitude to the concept of sentence-meaning, it is natural for us to expect arguments and counter-arguments in support of each theory. Any book on Indian theories of language and meaning can provide us with a detailed account of such debates.[10] Especially, the opponents' argument figures most prominently, because *khaṇḍa pakṣa* or atomism of word-meaning theory was the most popular and well acknowledged theory of that time. Therefore, I will like to shift to a brief discussion on the modern way of handling the debate over the issue.

Two Opposing Modern Views on the Problem

The twentieth-century theories of language and meaning initially were dominated by the Referential model. As a result the word meaning was considered to be primary. The Referential theory demands that words be directly connected with referents. So it is believed that a satisfactory theory of meaning must provide an account of how the meaning of a sentence depends upon the

10. B.K. Matilal, *The Word and the World*, Chapter X, for a critical exposition of *khaṇḍa pakṣa* theories.

meaning of words. The popularity of the theory gets its support from one of the most perplexing features of linguistic usage, i.e. how do we manage to express unlimited number of sentences out of the limited vocabulary? The problem is sought to be resolved by assuming that our knowledge of word-meanings allows us to formulate varied sorts of sentences with the help of such word materials. Therefore without the knowledge of word-meanings, sentence-meanings are not decipherable. Some modern thinkers on Indian philosophy also present similar arguments in support of word-meaning primacy. But this view is not without flaws. Bhartṛhari's answer to such an argument would be that this perplexing feature of language does not necessarily imply the primacy of word-meaning. The isolated word-meanings do not lead us to the grasping as well as interpretation of sentence-meaning unless and until we know how the words are used in the particular context. The sum of word-meanings is not equivalent to a sentence-meaning. We can use the words in innumerable ways, not because we know the meanings of each word in the vocabulary, but because we have an inherent linguistic latency (*śabda-bhāvanā*) to use language in innumerable ways. By that he does not mean that knowledge of word-meanings is of no help in linguistic expressibility. There are sciences like grammar and lexicography which concentrate on words and word-meanings, and also on the valid rules of the ordering of the words in linguistic expression. What Bhartṛhari would like to vindicate is that in our analysis of communicative process, we have to assume that sentence-meaning is presented as a one and whole. And it is also understood by the hearer as one and whole. Donald Davidson in his famous paper "Truth and Meaning," seems to echo a similar argument. He says, "knowledge of the structural characteristics that make for meaningfulness in a sentence, plus knowledge of the meanings of the ultimate parts, does not add up to the knowledge of what a sentence means." But the reasons for his supporting the above view is in no way the same as that of Bhartṛhari's. Davidson is in search of a holistic theory of sentence-meaning in terms of semantical theory of truth.[11] We shall come to Davidson's theory a little later. Full credit must be given to Frege who made a clear distinction between "sense" and "referent." According to him the sentences express a "thought" and the meanings of sentences are dependent on the "sense" they represent. So he said that "only in the context of a sentence does a word have meaning." It was later Wittgenstein, who presented this thesis in another way by saying that words have meanings in the context of their *use* in language. Thereby he wanted to move away from the idea that our talk of the meaning of words must always be hooked to a referent. The "Use theory" of meaning, is largely responsible in creating an awareness about the primacy of sentence and sentence-meaning. But his theory, in no way can be compared to Bhartṛhari's sentence-holism. For Bhartṛhari sentence is an undifferentiated whole. But Wittgenstein envisages that words get their significance only in the context of their use in a sentence. The autonomy of word-meaning in a sentence-context is not totally denied. So Wittgenstein's theory is rather akin to *anvitābhidhānavāda* of Prabhākara. Both the theories are, very broadly speaking, sentence-contextual in nature. The concept of sentence-contextuality is almost unanimously accepted by subsequent philosophers. The central issue of sentence-context principle is, how do the words contribute to the meaning of a sentence? Regarding this issue modern philosophers of language have broadly taken two different stands. Davidson and others analyse the problem from the standpoint of semantics, whereas Grice and his followers put emphasis on pragmatics of meaning.

To offer an account of how sentence acquires its meaning, another crucial question is brought in, i.e. what is the general character of those rules which in some sense must be mastered by anyone who speaks and understands a given sentence? Donald Davidson offers an answer to the question which rests on the notion of truth-conditions. According to him an adequate account of meaning-rules for a language L, will show how the meanings

11. Donald Davidson, *Truth and Meaning*, Synthese XVII, (1967).

of a sentence depend on meanings of words in L. Therefore a theory of meaning in any L, can be adequate if it contains a recursive definition of truth-in-L. In other words, in any language L, meaning of each element consists in what these elements (words or syntactical parts) contribute to truth-conditions of a sentence that contain it. According to him the relation between the definition of truth and the concept of meaning is as follows: "the definition works by giving the necessary and sufficient conditions for the truth of every sentence, and to give truth-condition is a way of giving the meaning of a sentence. To know the semantic concept of truth for a language is to know what it is for a sentence — any sentence — to be true, and this amounts, in one good sense we can give to the phrase, to understanding the language."[12] He adopts Tarski's notion of semantic truth to give a general picture of understanding meaning in any language. However, in the same paper he admits the inadequacy of the theory in handling many types of sentences which are not convertible into truth-condition principles. Those who believe in the supremacy of semantic notion of meaning, more or less, agree with Davidson, but they suggest some modifications here or there. I do not want to go into details of Davidson's very valuable paper, as our concern is limited to the question of sentence-meaning.

Grice and his followers on the other hand move in another direction. They are hard-core Communication-intention theorists, and believe that we do not need any general semantic rules for the communication of meaning. They locate all facts about the communicative intentions and beliefs of language users, and regularities concerning them, in pragmatics, not in semantics. What a sentence means is always relative to language. And language is an abstractly defined function. So all the dimensions of language cannot be caught within the framework of semantical definitions. Grice would contest Davidson's way of defining meaning by pointing out that he ignores the fact that most of our linguistic

12. Ibid., p. 310 — Davidson's theory is a complex one, I have provided a very sketchy version of it, keeping in view our central issue, i.e. the notion of sentence-meaning.

behaviour is conversational. No conversational behaviour would happily respond to such generalizations. So the contention of Grice and Schiffer is as follows: the speaker's meaning can be identified with what he is intending, in a certain way, to activate in his hearer a certain belief or action. The communicative meaning does not presuppose anything conventional or linguistic. Hence, **linguistic** meaning can be explained in terms of conventions over such intentions. The subsequent notions of referring and illocutionary forces are similarly non-conventional in their definition. Some philosophers view Grice's notion of speaker's "intention" and "intended meaning" as psychological. In case of lingustic or literal meaning he accepts the importance of convention. Therefore, it is presumed that he connects the semantics and the psychological elements of communication with the aid of practice and convention.[13]

I have given a brief outline of two opposing views regarding the nature of sentence-meaning. It can be summed up further as follows: one group of philosophers conceives sentence-meaning in terms of truth-conditions contributed by each element in a sentence; the other group does not bother about syntactical or linguistic elements nor about their truth-conditions. For them the communication of intended meaning of the speaker by an utterance, is all that matters. The debate that ensues from these two diverse outlook is still alive and hot.[14]

I do not want to fit in any of the above theory in Bhartṛhari's model. Bhartṛhari, no doubt, understands meaning in terms of communication. But he does not identify meaning with the speaker's intention or the hearer's understanding. In such an

---

13. Grice, "Meaning," in *Philosophical Review,* LXVI (1957), and "Utterer's Meaning, Sentence-Meaning and word-Meaning," in *Foundations of Language,* IV (1968). Also see Stephen R. Schiffer, *Meaning,* Oxford: Clarendon Press, 1972.

14. *Truth and Meaning: Essays on Semantics,* ed. G. Evans and J. McDowell, Oxford: Clarendon Press, 1976. Please see the "Introduction" and "Two Theories of Meaning" by Brian Loar.

ancient theory it is futile to seek for the distinctive elements of semantical and psychological notions of language. Nor can we discern very clearly the elements of pragmatics and semantics in his theory of meaning. The problem of "truth" does not figure at all in his theory of meaning, because he considers the "referents" as belonging to the realm of "linguistic constructs." He is not also very much bothered about the varied uses of language, as all of them are parts of the meaning communicated. At trans-verbal level he considers the linguistic potency to be one whole, and each sentence represents a part of that whole.

9

The Knowable and the Sayable

Bhartṛhari on What Can be Said

A SURVEY of Bhartṛhari's philosophy of language makes it clear that there is no end to what we can do with words (if not words then, at least, word-potency). We think with words, conceive with words, carry on all sorts of conscious activities with words, including the act of communication. There is no limit to linguistic proliferation. Whatever is knowable is sayable and vice versa. But is this sort of Pan-verbalism tenable as a theory? Can we talk of any concept, including the concept of word or language without drawing its limits? Does the concept of word or language defy all possibility of a structural boundary? Bhartṛhari should have some answer for such vital questions about word itself. Here, in concluding my discussion on Bhartṛhari, I try to seek answers to such questions, which no philosoper of language can avoid.

To get the answer we must first of all be aware of the subtle distinction between the analysis of language-in-use (the act of language) and the notion of language as a concept. In other words it is a distinction between what can be said **about** language and what can be said **in** language. I feel Bhartṛhari implicitly maintains this distinction in his philosophy of language. He mostly concentrates on the notion of language-in-use or what can be said **in** language. But while doing so he leads us very carefully to the structural bounds of language. At both the levels he maintains a Holistic stand.

When Bhartṛhari analyses the nature of language as a communicative act he leaves no aspect of it untouched. It is an accepted fact that we communicate with language. But it is not a simple matter of verbalization. To talk we must think, we must experience, and we must discriminate. When somebody talks without thinking we call it an incoherent talk. Similarly when we listen to a tape-recorded talk we do not say the tape-recorder is talking. We say somebody's talk has been recorded. When we say a computer out of nowhere produces a sentence, we do not mean that the computer is writing. We say that a computer is programmed to produce such and such set of languages. In short, a thinking being can verbalise or at least has the potentcy for verbalization. A machine cannot think so it cannot talk in the sense man can talk in infinite number of ways with a limited vocabulary at his disposal. That is why Bhartṛhari includes in his analysis of language-in-use the concepts of "thought," "cognition" and "ideas." In such cases he is not indulging in a psychological analysis of the processes of awareness and thought. Rather he says that our explication of the verbal level of language remains incomplete without bringing in the concepts of "thought," "awareness" and "cognition." We cannot understand how we do things with words just by keeping ourselves within the narrow confines of actual linguistic utterance. To do so is to indulge in a form of linguistic behaviourism. Even later Wittgenstein who disposes of such mental concepts as "understanding" and "thinking" as misnomer has admitted this, for he says : "If a lion could talk we could not understand him." (*PI*, p. 223)

Why does he say so? Simply because the lion does not intend to communicate, nor is he aware of what he is saying. Lion's talking is not an expression of his thought and experience. Therefore according to Wittgenstein, ". . . speaking is a part of activity or a form of life." The "form of life," Wittgenstein often talks of in his *Philosophical Investigations*, will turn into a routine running of the machine, if it does not include man's experience, thought and consciousness. We always express a chunk of our experience, knowledge, emotion, etc. through verbal expressions. This is why Bhartṛhari does not hesitate to talk of connecting language-in-use with the mental level. Of course, his time and cultural background did not allow him to be a captive of the craze for specialization. There is no watertight distinction between the philosophy of mind and the philosophy of language, between psychology and epistemology, in Bhartṛhari's philosophy. Therefore, with equal ease, he points out that not only language needs thought, but thought needs language. He very rightly points out that thought in any form, be it cognition or awareness, needs conceptualization. And conceptualization, in turn, needs word-loadedness. Conceptualization implies discrimination and assimilation, and this is done through words. He offers a comprehensive account of knower, known and knowledge; and consciousness, referent and linguistic usage. For, all of them are bound by word-interpenetrability. As long as we are thinking and talking about phenomenal world or the experiences of our life there is no epistemic gap between the thought, language and referent. Understood in this sense, Bhartṛhari's position can be summed up as, whatever is **knowable** is **sayable**, and whatever is **sayable** is **knowable**.

Coming down to the level of utterances Bhartṛhari seems to exhibit the same trend of Holism and comprehensiveness of attitude. For him language is not primarily meant for reporting facts or states-of-affair. Indian thought, as such, shows no partiality towards assertions and factual statements. Excepting Nyāya, which adheres to a Realistic world-view, for other systems there is no clear-cut epistemic gulf between independent objective reality and consciousness. Especially in case of *śabda* as a method of knowledge, it has always been insisted that such knowledge acquired through language is not primarily about facts. It is conceived as a method of acquiring knowledge about non-factual things like morality, injunctions or philosophical speculations. The question of factual knowledge is left to the methods of *pratyakṣa* (perception), *anumāna* (inference), etc. In case of *śabda-pramāṇa* "truth" is not the central point, rather "validity" occupies the key position. So "truth" is not exclusively the defining characteristic of *pramā*, whereas in Western epistemology knowledge means "truth." It is a contradiction in terms to say, "I know but it is false." For Bhartṛhari, who primarily conceives *śabda* as the only basis of his philosophical analysis does not leave any scope for interpreting language exclusively in terms of factual knowledge. Language as an element of expressiveness is connected with multifarious dimensions of awareness and cognition, including the cognition of facts. We can linguistically express our thoughts about facts, as much as about religion, poetic emotions, *dharma* (moral principles including injunctions), metaphysical predilections, about the rules of grammar and many more things. Bhartṛhari never seems to bother about this element of multiple uses of language. He seems to take this important feature of language for granted. But in connection with explanation about some philosophical misconceptions about language he cites examples to show the difference of form. For example, to show that words and sentences need not primarily refer to existing facts he offers the example of *gandharva nagara* (celestial city), which may be used in fiction, poetry or in story-telling. Again he very meticulously shows that we can talk of time, space, existence, substance, in general sense as concepts, as well as in specific sense, when used in particular contexts. There are plenty of evidences where he analyses particular forms of sentential use to show the differences in their contextual meanings. But nowhere does he make any conscious effort to show that they are different "language-games" (to borrow Wittgenstein's phrase). As such in Indian philosophy of language, the plurality of linguistic structure has never been seriously challenged. Instead Indian philosophers, including Bhartṛhari, have been more bothered about the layers of meaning. So a rich and powerful discussion on the types of communicated meaning, such as primary meaning (*abhidhā*), metaphorical meaning (*lakṣaṇā*), suggestive meaning (*vyañjanā*), etc. are carried on by most of the schools of Indian philosophy. But the issue of deciphering the meaning of different forms of language is left to the hearer's mastery of language. "It is evening now" and "time is eternal" — these are two sentences of different forms about one concept, i.e. time. But Bhartṛhari would see no scope for confusion here. He would take it for granted that the speaker as well as the hearer (and for that matter anybody who has mastered a language) can know that the first sentence is about a particular time and the second is about "time" as a general concept. In case of the first sentence the hearer may respond by looking at the sky, or hurrying back home. But in the latter case he is given a choice either to accept the conceptual scheme about time or reject it. Here there is no scope for linguistic misunderstanding or confusing the rules of one language-game with another. This easy acceptance of pluralistic language-view may be due to the fact that Bhartṛhari does not have a model-oriented theory of meaning. According to him "meaning" means what is communicated by the speaker to the hearer. In this regard Bhartṛhari's attitude is clearly antagonistic to what Carnap has to say about the scope of meaningfulness.

> Many linguistic utterances are analogous to laughing in that they have only expressive function, no representative function. Examples of this are cries like "oh," "ah," on a higher level lyrical verses . . . have only an expressive function. Metaphysical propositions are neither true nor false, because they assert nothing — But they are like, laughing, lyrics and music, expressive.[1]

Carnap in one sweep not only denigrates metaphysics to the level of laughing but also bundles up poetry, aesthetics, values, and morality into meaningless emotive outbursts. To be meaningful is to assert and such assertions either have to be true or false. A straightforward version of this attitude can be noticed in Wittgenstein's remarks. He advises:

> To say nothing except what can be said, i.e. propositions of natural science. — *Tractatus*, 6. 53

And,

> A proposition shows how things stand if it is true."
> — 4.022

---

1. Carnap, *Philosophy and Logical Syntax*, London: R.K.P., 1935, p. 28.

Some Modern Views on the Problem

Both these versions of Referential model draw their line of **sayability** and **knowability** within the bounds of what fits into the mould of truth-conditionality. A sentence is meaningful if, and only if, the speaker has the knowledge of the conditions under which it would be either true or false. One cannot fit in the sentences on religion, morality, poetics, political ideologies, grammatical rules and many more significant linguistic expressions within its scope. The modern philosophy of language and meaning is the typical product of a period which marked the triumph of natural science and death of metaphysics. So the fascination for natural sciences, along with its emphasis on truth and neatness of structure continued to guide the development of subsequent philosophy of language. One comes across the strong fascination for "truth-conditions," and "assertions" in subsequent theories of meaning. The central core of most of the philosophy of language is a theory of truth, and sometimes at the periphery lies a theory of "force." The types of "force" that Austin and Searle enlists are more about various modes of assertions (either in the form of imperative, interrogative, promise statements, etc.), than modes of experience. By experience, I mean all sorts of it, which are co-extensive with life. Sometimes, these philosophers talk of Holism.[2] But it is not a Holism of Bhartṛhari's type. It is a limited sense of Holism, with reference to a particular theory of truth or a particular form of language. In this connection I deem it fit to quote some Indologists who are very frank about this mono-model adopted by modern philosophers of language. John Brough, the famous scholar on Bhartṛhari and Indian philosophy of grammar, puts it more explicitly:

> Most philosophic discussions of meaning confine themselves to a relatively small portion of language behaviour, namely, statements which describe or report a state of affairs — the propositions of the natural sciences, or, more generally, such

2. Davidson, *Truth and Meaning.*

> statements as are traditionally handled by logic. This part of language possesses enormous importance and prestige, and is also the least difficult to deal with in a more or less clear fashion. But its treatment frequently suffers from a forgetfulness of the fact that propositions (or the formulae of symbolic logic) are none the less language; and I would suggest that a wider linguistic understanding is most desirable . . . logic, mathematics, linguistics, science in general, all convey their messages in language, and this language, however technical, **cannot be understood** save in a manner which is fundamentally similar to the understanding of everyday language. As the ancient Indian might say, the utterances of the costermonger, the language of the great poet, and the formulae of the atomic physicist are all in some sense manifestations of the same divine *vāk*.[3]

Harold Coward, another important scholar on Bhartṛhari is more cautious in his remarks. He says:

> While not all may agree with Indian approach in general or with Bhartṛhari in particular, it is a view of language which makes sense of poetry, revealed scripture, science, the mystical chanting of *mantra*s, and in addition, strongly resonates with our ordinary everyday experience of coffee-cup chat.[4]

Many Indologists like J.G. Arapura,[5] Frits Staal[6] and others are also very vociferous in their criticism of a form of reductionism adopted by modern philosophers which reduces language analysis into the model of scientific and factual referents. They admit the

---

3. John Brough, "Some Indian Theories of Meaning," in *A Reader on the Sanskrit Grammarians*, p. 423.
4. Harold G. Coward, *The Sphoṭa Theory of Language*, Delhi: Motilal Banarsidass.
5. J.G. Arapura, "Some Perspectives on Indian Philosophy of Language," In *Revelation in Indian Thought*, ed. Coward and Sivaraman, Dharma Publishing, 1977.
6. Frits Staal, "The Concept of Metalanguage and its Indian Background," in *Journal of Indian Philosophy*, III (1975), p. 319.

importance of the Holistic approach of Indian philosophy of language.

I referred to these views not to prove that all that the modern philosophers of language present, are of no value. I simply argue in favour of a comprehensive and holistic account of the language — a language that we use in our life. Without this, the philosophy of language would be alienated from the level of practice. The concept of "language" is dynamic and a "living" concept and it should not be robbed of its life by lifting it to the thin air of models and forms. As Wittgenstein who suggested a monomodel of language earlier, himself realizes:

> Man possesses the ability to construct a language capable of expressing every sense, without having any idea how each word has meaning or what meaning is . . .
>
> Everyday language is a part of human organism and is no less complicated than it. — *Tractatus*, 4.002

Later on a grand attempt was made by Wittgenstein first, in his *Philosophical Investigations*, and then in subsequent works, especially *Culture and Value* to breathe life into the philosophical study of language. Grice and his followers also contributed their mite to keep language within the bounds of its naturalness. I must refer here to Wittgenstein's contribution in a little detail to show that the obsession with factual language is not the whole of the story. In *Philosophical Investigations* Wittgenstein makes efforts to reveal the close relation between life and language. Language is presented here as a part of life. But to a large extent it turns out to be a negative way of analysis. He treats philosophers and their ontological commitments as muddled and confused in nature. But he is more forthright in his books, *Culture and Value* and *Philosophical Remarks*, etc. In these books we note that there is a conscious opposition to the intellectualists' categorization of language and reality. He attempts to check the tendency to theorize or rationally build up theoretical superstructures. And by doing so he openly accepts the validity and significance of our linguistic expressions about values, aesthetics, religion, even mystical experiences. Grice, on the other hand believes that language is a matter of conversations and primarily a matter of communication of intention. They point towards a more comprehensive and holistic treatment of natural language. In future newer and better models of comprehensive and holistic theories of language are likely to emerge. I shall like to conclude this part of my discussion by quoting a very significant remark made by Strawson. He says:

> Nevertheless the actual use of linguistic expressions remains his (Philosopher's) sole and essential point of contact with the reality which he wishes to understand, conceptual reality: for this is the only point from which the actual mode of operation of concepts can be observed. If he severs this vital connection, all his ingenuity and imagination will not save him from lapses into the arid and absurd.[7]

Bhartṛhari on the Limiting Concepts of Knowability and Sayability

In the last section, I have deviated from the central theme of our discussion about the idea of **knowable** and **sayable**. But I feel such a deviation was necessary to prove that the limits of the knowability and sayability must not be bound by an artificial superstructure, however neat it may be. We have examined Bhartṛhari's views on what we can say **in** language; now let us dwell briefly on what his views are regarding what we can say **about** language. He explains the concept of linguistic communication with the help of two fundamental presuppositions. They are: (1) there is an inherent fitness in words to express meaning (*yogyatā*), and (2) there is an inherent ability to understand the meaning expressed through language (*pratibhā*). In a sense, both these concepts represent two dimensions of communication; the speaker's ability to convey meaning or thought and the hearer's ability to grasp the meaning. In case of both the

7. P.F. Strawson, "Analysis, Science and Metaphysics," in *The Linguistic Turn*, ed. R. Rorty, Chicago: Chicago University Press, 1967, p. 320.

concepts Bhartṛhari admits their ineffability. They can be presumed but they cannot be explained and defined. In other words they are neither **knowable** nor **sayable**.

(A) YOGYATĀ

Yogyatā is one of the basic presuppositions **about** the nature of language. Language implies the use of words with certain grammatical form and syntactical structure. But words are not themselves language. It is **language** because it expresses meaning. So words are endowed with the capacity to express meaning, and there is an inherent fitness in the words to express the meaning. This is called *yogyatā*. Therefore according to Bhartṛhari there is an internal and eternal relation between word and meaning. The relation between word and meaning is indicated by the use of genitive case ("*Y* is the meaning of *X*"). Though the relationship is the basis of communicative language, yet there is no expression to designate this relation as a **relation**. Therefore Bhartṛhari uses analogies like illumination and illuminator (*prakāśa* and *prakāśatva*), etc. to explain the nature of this relation.[8] The nature of "**Relation**," regarding relationship between word and meaning is not directly expressible. While stating this unique theory Bhartṛhari expects objections from his opponents. The opponents may raise a valid objection. If "Relation" is inexpressible then one cannot even use the word "inexpressible," because in saying so he has expressed something. Here Bhartṛhari's answer is very insightful and it directly hints at the paradoxes of linguistic presuppositions. He says, in stating "all that I am saying is false" (*sarvaṁ mithyā brabhimi*) "one does not intend to include that very sentence in the scope of its meaning, for then, as what one is saying would be implicitly false, the intended meaning would not be conveyed. Generally, what is expressive cannot at the same time be what it expresses,

8. *Vākyapadīya*, III.3.3. — B.K. Matilal renders the translation of the verse in the following manner: "This is the signifier (*vācaka*) of that, and that is the signified (*vācya*) of this. The that-ness (*tattva*) of the connection between the word and what it means is thus understood from the genetive ending. Hence its own nature (that-ness) is designated.

and if something *X* is conveyed by *Y* then *Y* cannot itself be expressed by something other than *Y*."[9] The argument reminds us of its Western counterpart, i.e. the "paradox of the liar."

This interesting critique of the notion of signification relation between word and meaning has been discussed by H. Herzberger and R. Herzberger in detail,[10] They call it "Bhartṛhari's paradox." This Paradox is based on the general notion of the axiom about "relation," i.e. non-relation can be its relata. The paradox that Bhartṛhari presents can be justified on another ground also "An item is usually signified by a signifier, "linguistic expression," on the basis of some property or aspect belonging to the signified object, but since characters or aspects of the signification relation (or relation in general) are completely exhausted by its two relata, it is completely colourless — in fact too colourless to be significant at all."[11]

> But there is no (proper) designator of the (said) relation that speaks of (or designates) it on the basis of its own feature (*dharma*). (For) due to its being totally undermined by others (its two relata), its own feature is not designated.
>
> — Verse III.3.4[12]

Bhartṛhari argues that since the speaker utters the designator (words) in order to convey the designated (the meaning), each utterance implicitly suggests that "this (word) **is** that (the meaning expressed)." So the relation is implicitly **shown**, but it cannot be **said**.

(B) PRATIBHĀ

The other fundamental concept **about** linguistic communication is *pratibhā*, the intuitive flash of understanding through which the

9. *Vākyapadīya*, III.3.3-28 — translation taken from *Encyclopaedia of Indian Philosophies, VP*, 158.
10. H. Herzberger, and R. Herzberger, "Bhartṛhari's Paradox," in *Journal of Indian Philosophy*, no. 9, 1981, pp. 3-32.
11. B.K. Matilal, *The Word and the World*, p. 130.
12. Tr. B.K. Matilal, *Word and World*, p. 130.

hearer grasps the meaning of expressed words. Of course, the term *pratibhā* has been used by Bhartṛhari with wider implications. I shall here focus only on the concpet of *pratibhā* in relation to linguistic understanding. For him this intuitive capacity is different from the perceptual and inferential ways of knowing. This is the means of understanding of the undifferentiated meaning of a sentence as a whole. But it implies something more than this. It is a knowledge of the meaning communicated, in which the sentence expressed through the sequential presentation of words, and the meaning implied, are merged into one. So sometimes it is identified with *śabda bhāvanā* (linguistic latency). This unified principle is presupposed to explain the hearer's understanding, for, while understanding a sentence the hearer does not distinguish words from meanings. However, this principle of understanding, as such, is not definable. Bhartṛhari says, "This (*pratibhā*) cannot in any way be explained to others in terms such as "it is this"; its existence is ratified only in the individual's experience of it, and the experiencer himself cannot describe it" (*VP* II.146).[13] This again shows that the structural concepts of language cannot be described in language. It is not **sayable**. And on the basis of Bhartṛhari's identification between the **knowable** and **sayable**, we can say that *pratibhā* is not also **knowable**. The limits of knowability and sayability gradually point to further limits which reflects Bhartṛhari's metaphysical position. Ultimately he shows that no language can say anything about the Reality, be it the linguistic reality or be it the reality of the phenomenal world. Our sentences are nothing more than the fragments and bits of meaning-whole. The principle of language as such, is not **sayable**, for whatever is sayable is only a part of the whole, that our mind selects for practical and worldly transactions. Similarly what the world **is** cannot be expressed, because we can at best explain a particular dimension of the objective world that we intend to know and talk about. We presuppose that the world **is** there, and the language **is** there, but these presuppositions themselves are not

13. Tr. John Brough, "Indian Theories," p. 420.

sayable. Whatever is **sayable** is finite and differentiated manifestation of the one *śabda-tattva*.

Wittgenstein on the Limits of Sayability

But one last question remains: if all sorts of linguistic expressions are not real from the ultimate point of view, then why does Bhartṛhari labour to produce such a big treatise on the nature of language? Does he conceive the entire programme of philosophical analysis the way Wittgenstein understands it in *Tractatus*? Wittgenstein at the end of his book declares:

> My propositions serve as elucidation in the following way: anyone who understands me eventually recognizes them as non-sensical, when he has used them as steps to climb up beyond them. (He must, so to speak, throw away the ladder after he has climbed up it.) He must transcend these propositions, then he will see the world alright. — *Tractatus*, 6.54

But Bhartṛhari's programme as well as goal is totally different from Wittgenstein's *Tractatus*. Bhartṛhari would say that we need to know about the nature and functioning of language in order to transcend it to attain the knowledge of the ultimate Reality, i.e. *śabda-Brahman*. He undertakes the programme of philosophical analysis of language to prove that everything is phenomenal, and is explainable only in terms of the principle of language. So the entire knowledge about the language-in-use can be thrown like a step once we have climbed it and achieved the knowledge of the *Brahman*. But, for Wittgenstein the programme is meant for saving the philosophers from indulging in nonsense. We cannot and should not talk of things that are not factual in nature. Our statements about ethics, aesthetics, religion and metaphysics as well as the very nature of language lie beyond the scope of the **sayability**, for they do not talk of the world.

Appendix 1

Eternality of Word-Meaning Relation vis-à-vis Contextuality

> Have you ever noticed this — that people never answer what you say? They answer what you mean — or what they think you mean. Suppose one lady says to another in a country house "Is anybody staying with you?" the lady does not answer "Yes, the butler, the three footmen, the parlour-maid, and so on," though the parlour-maid may be in the room, or the butler behind her chair. She says: "There is nobody staying with us," meaning nobody of the sort you mean. But suppose a doctor enquiring into an epidemic asks, "who is staying in the house?" Then the lady will remember the butler, the parlour-maid and the rest. All language is used like that; you never get a question answered literally, even you get it answered truly."
>
> — G.K. Chesterton, *The Invisible Man*

USING language is largely a matter of convention. So when somebody asks — "How do you know, a particular word or string of words convey a particular meaning?" — the obvious answer is, "It is through convention." Convention not only enables a language system to be stable through the determination of word-meaning relationship, but also allows it to function inter-subjectively. So one is likely to feel uncomfortable with the philosophical position which claims to dismiss the conventional origin of language, and instead upholds the view that the relation between the word and the meaning is eternal. Two of our ancient Indian traditions — the Mīmāṁsā and Vyākaraṇa school of Bhartṛhari vigorously defend this theory. What makes their position paradoxical is their avowed objective in doing philosophical analysis of language. Mīmāṁsā aims to provide hermeneutics of Vedic injunctions, and Bhartṛhari's objective is to unfold the semantics of natural language. These objectives remain unfulfilled without admitting that there cannot be one-to-one relation between word and meaning since flexibility in our operation with language constitutes the very basis of our linguistic usage. Thus the eternality theory, propagated by these schools, seem to contradict their respective avowed objectives. As both, the Mīmāṁsā and Bhartṛhari's theory of language need detailed examination, and unfortunately the scope of my paper is limited, I shall concentrate on Bhartṛhari's position with occasional reference to the Mīmāṁsā position.

Any language is supposed to have the following characteristics:

1. It must consist of certain articulate phonetic pattern.
2. It must have a definite form and syntax.
3. The use of sound patterns and syntax is acquired through certain process of learning.
4. The system must be the result of certain convention, i.e. agreement amongst a group of people. This is something which is shared by the members of each linguistic community.

Neither Bhartṛhari, nor the Mīmāṁsakas would contest the first three presuppositions. But they would partially dismiss the idea that language (which consists in using words to express meaning) is the product of a convention. They would concede that we acquire the mastery of a particular language by following the convention. But the relation between word and meaning is not the product of a convention. It is *eternal* and *natural.* In defending their theses they (especially, Mīmāṁsakas) cross swords with the Naiyāyikas, who argue for the conventional origin of word-meaning relationship.

Patañjali, the grammarian philosopher, says that the relation between word and meaning is eternal.[1] He raises the question of relationship in order to introduce Kātyāyana's *vārttika,* which states

1. Patañjali, *Mahābhāṣya.*

that it is of the nature of *siddha*[2] (*siddhe śabdārtha saṁbandhe*). Patañjali interprets the term *siddha* as *nitya,* i.e. eternal. Following him Bhartṛhari also states that the relation between word and meaning is *nitya.* But Jaiminī in his *Mīmāṁsā-Sūtra* (1.2.5) uses the term *autpattika* for this relationship. Most often the term is translated as "eternal," but following Matilal[3] I would like to use the words "non-derived" or "non-created" to understand *autpattika,* because it seems closer to the spirit of the theory further developed by Śabara and Kumārila Bhaṭṭa. Śabara says *autpattika* means "not created by human convention." In this respect, Bhartṛhari and Mīmāṁsakas agree that human beings cannot create the relation between words and meaning. The words have certain inherent power *śakti* (according to Mīmāṁsakas) and natural fitness, *yogyatā* (according to Bhartṛhari) to express meaning, like the sense-organs, which have the potency to perceive whatever comes within their purview.[4] In similar vein, both the schools argue that there was no first stage when verbal usage did not exist nor a future stage when it would not exist.[5] Thus word-meaning relation continues to be there and its origin cannot be traced. Bhartṛhari as well as Śabara show the paradox involved in accepting the conventional origin of language.[6] If the word-meaning relationship is fixed by convention, then it must be the result of a mutual agreement amongst a group of people. But without a shared language no communication, hence no convention is possible. To set-up a convention some form of language is necessary, which itself must be the product of a convention. Again that convention would need use of some language formed on the basis of a third convention, and so on *ad infinitum.* Thus to get rid of this paradox the older Nyāya school, which believed in the

---

2. Kātyāyana's *Vārttika.*
3. B.K. Matital, *The Word and the World,* New Delhi: Oxford University, Press, 1990, p. 27.
4. Bhartṛhari, *Vākyapadīya,* III.29.
5. *VP,* I.28.
6. *VP,* III.38.

convention is set-up by the will of God. The power of the words to express meaning, i.e. *śakti* has been defined by some Naiyāyikas as "convention made by the will of God that such and such a meaning should be derived from such and such a word."[7] But Mīmāṁsā challenges this presupposition by arguing that the relationship is not traceable either to human or to divine agent. Thus far there seems to be some agreement between Bhartṛhari and Mīmāṁsakas. But if one follows the arguments and counter-arguments of Nyāya versus Mīmāṁsā debate on the issue one is convinced about their eagerness to pinpoint the stabilizing factor of language. If Nyāya locates this in the will of God, then Mīmāṁsā locates it in the inherent power of the words to express meaning. But for both of them, word and meaning are two distinct phenomena, which need a ground for stability.

But certain relevant issues are raised by Naiyāyikas which need to be attended by both Bhartṛhari and Mīmāṁsakas. It is asked — if the relation between word and meaning is eternal then how the same word can signify different objects and different words signify the same object? We can extend the scope of the question a little further and ask — how can the eternalists explain the presence of not only synonyms, but also the phenomenon of extended meaning, metaphorical meaning and implied meaning, in natural language. The success of eternalist view will largely depend on how they sort out the issue.

In the context of the issue raised we have to look deep into the eternalist position. Following the clue offered by Bhartṛhari, we may say that the theory could be presented from two angles.[8] The relation between the word and the meaning can be stated in two ways — either as, "This (expressive power/meaning) belongs to that," or else as, "It (word) is that (the expressive power/meaning)." The former way of looking at the relationship is based on the principle of distinction, whereas the latter is formed on the basis of identity. Bhartṛhari admits that the former is helpful for

7. Anāmbhaṭṭa, *Tarkasaṁgraha.*

8. *VP*, I.59. 1.1.ff.

the grammarians and lexicographers, as both these sciences deal with isolated and abstracted words to explicate the rules of their use; and deciphering their phonetic origin and syntactical pattern. This method also suits the Mīmāṁsakas, who believe in the priority of word-meaning over sentence-meaning. According to them the sentence-meaning is more or less a concatenation of meanings expressed by the words. As opposed to this Bhartṛhari believes that word-meaning, as such, has no reality.[9] They function only in the context of a sentence. This theory, otherwise known as *akhaṇḍa pakṣa* theory, finds its strengh from the communicative and intentional nature of language. The most important factor in linguistic communication is the "sense" conveyed by the speaker to the hearer. So it is the sentence which alone can convey a sense. Thus he assigns preference to the expression of the word-meaning relation in the form – "It is that." Elaborating the nature of the relationship he says:

> Where there is an idea of mutual appurtenance, the relation between word and meaning in the form "It is this" is, since meaning cannot be assigned (by grammar), eternal, self-existing and not something not known before and made known for the first time.[10]

In this version of Bhartṛhari's eternality theory the emphasis is on the phrase, "mutual appurtenance," which can only be expressed in the form "It is this." So it is obvious that for him, the word and the meaning are identical. For the Mīmāṁsakas, on the other hand, word and meaning are two distinct linguistic phenomena connected by a bond. It is a relation between the object of cognition and the causal factor of cognition (*pratyaya-pratyāyaka*). For Bhartṛhari, word-meaning relation though non-created, is not a connection between two distinct phenomena. Rather it is an identity expressed in terms of two distinct concepts.

Let us discuss in little detail how Bhartṛhari explicated the nature of the relationship. In section III of *Vākyapadīya*, *kāṇḍa* III,

9. *VP*, II.419-20.

10. *VP*, *Vṛtti* on I.23.

Bhartṛhari discusses the concept of *sambandha* (relationship) with reference to words and meaning. Here he makes it clear that in any case of linguistic utterance, three elements are discernible. They are — (i) the form of the word, (ii) the meaning and, (iii) the speaker's intention.[11] The relation between the first two is called *vācya-vācaka bhāva*. The form of the word as the conveyor of meaning or expression itself, is called *vācaka*. That which is conveyed or expressed is called *vācya*. When the speaker intends to say something he has to use the appropriate words so that the speaker rightly conveys the meaning to be communicated. Thus, in any case of linguistic communication, both the *vācya* and *vācaka* are involved. In the pre-verbal stage they are identical and indistinguishable. They emanate from our linguistic disposition. But when the language is manifested in the form of utterance, both the elements are distinguishable. In a very broad sense, these two elements can be called *dhvani* and *śabda*. To explain Bhartṛhari's contention, let me quote some relevant verses from *Vākyapadīya*.

> In the words which are expressive, the learned discern two elements: one is the cause of the real word, while the other is used to convey the meaning.[12]

The commentary explicates the verse in the following way:

> In the sequenceless nature of speech (*vāk*) both the power, the power to be articulated or the expressive power (*śruti-śakti*) and the power of being expressed (*artha-śakti*) are merged.[13]

Again he says:

> As the light has two powers, that of being revealed and that of being the revealer, similarly all the words have two distinct powers.[14]

---

11. *VP*, III.3.1.
12. *VP*, I.44.
13. Ibid., *Vṛtti*.
14. *VP*, I.55.

> Just as the fire which is within the churning sticks is the cause of the fire (which is kindled), similarly, the word which is in the mind (of the speaker) becomes the cause of the different expressive words.[15]

The quoted verses and the commentaries make the relation of identity indicated by the form — "It is this" — fully explicit. *Vācya* and *vāckaka, śruti-śakti* and *artha-śakti,* are not two distinct phenomena, but two facets of the same linguistic principle, called, *sphoṭa*.

Bhartr̥hari's theory of *sphoṭa* is a complex as well as controversial concept. I am not in a position to go into its details within the limited scope of the paper. So I shall discuss *sphoṭa* only in the context of word-meaning relationship. *Sphoṭa* is derived from the root *sphuṭ,* which can be translated as "bursting forth." Following Nāgeśa Bhaṭṭa,[16] another grammarian philosopher, we may say *sphoṭa* is that from which meaning bursts forth and also that principle which is expressible through utterance. It is the indivisible unit of meaning, which is connected with verbal dispositional ability of the speaker as well as the hearer. For the sake of communication between the language users, the *sphoṭa* is manifested in the form of uttered words, which along with manifesting itself, manifests the meaning. Thus *śabda* (in this case, word) and *artha* (meaning/thought/object-meant) are identical. It remains latent as *śabda bhāvanā* (linguistic potency) both in the speaker and the hearer. This potency includes linguistic disposition and all varieties of differentiation of linguistic items. Thus by *sphoṭa* (in this context) we may mean the "sense" of an expression, which when manifested by an utterance, can be meaningfully expressed by a speaker, and when heard, can be grasped by the hearer. In this sense, words and meanings are not created, because it is nobody's decision (either human or divine) to use words to communicate the sense. Thus Bhartr̥hari's version of eternality thesis is different from that of the Mīmāṁsakas.

15. Nāgeśa Bhaṭṭa, *Sphoṭa Vāda*, Madras: Adyar Library, 1946, p. 5.

16. *Mahābhāṣya Dīpikā,* Pt. I, p. 28.

It is interesting to note Bhartṛhari's analysis of the term eternality. In his commentary on Patañjali's *Mahābhāṣya,* he introduces a distinction between two types of eternality[17] — *kūṭaṣtha nityatā* and *pravāha nityatā.* When some principle is understood as unchangeable and absolute, it is called *kūṭaṣtha nityatā.* Word-meaning relation is not eternal in this sense. But there can be another type of eternality which means continuity amidst variation. It is a stream-like continuity, known as *pravāha nityatā.* In case of Bhartṛhari's explication of word-meaning relationship, we note that, according to him both words and meanings are purely linguistic elements. Words are not primarily meant to denote objects, not the objects themselves. If that would have been the case, then with the destruction of the objects, words would have been rendered meaningless. But this is not the case. Rather, we can talk meaningfully about things which are non-existent, e.g. "rabbit's horn," "wheel of fire." Thus the use of words brings to our mind the concept meant. This inherent relation continues to be there despite variation in expression and of the speaker. This continuity of relation is called *pravāha nityatā* by Bhartṛhari. Thus for Bhartṛhari, not only the word-meaning relation is eternal but even the words and meanings themselves are eternal. Once we connect his eternality theory to the concept of *sphoṭa,* we have no difficulty in understanding why Bhartṛhari holds such a position. His eternality thesis, understood in the sense of *pravāha nityatā,* along with his theory of sentence-holism, (i.e. sentence alone is adequate enough to communicate a complete sense) allows him to highlight the flexibility of the natural language. His eternality thesis is not aimed at showing the rigidity of the linguistic structure. He leaves this job to grammar and convention, as is evident from his following remark:

> The grammatical treatises are composed from time-to-time by spiritual elite in deference to differing capacity of individuals by taking into consideration the changed capacities of expression as far as merit and demerit is concerned.[18]

17. *VP,* I.135-37.

18. *VP,* I.13 *Vṛtti.*

In another context he makes it clear that language can be of two types — produced and eternal. Produced word is needed in verbal usage, but eternal word is the source of all linguistic activity. Here, the eternal word obviously refers to *sphoṭa* and *śabda bhāvanā.* Thus eternality, understood in the sense of continuity of linguistic usage and inherent nature of language to be expresser and expressed, does not contradict Bhartṛhari's eagerness to show that extra-linguistic factors like speaker's intention and contextual factors like place, time, situation, accent, etc. can determine the functioning of the natural language.

I have already pointed out that according to Bhartṛhari three elements are involved in any act of linguistic utterance – (i) form of words (*vācaka*), (ii) meaning (*vācya*), and (iii) intention of speaker (*vaktā abhiprāya*). We have so far been discussing the relation between the word/form of the word and meaning. Now let us see what role Bhartṛhari assigns to the intention of the speaker. He identifies the relation between the first two elements (*vācya* and *vācaka*) and intention of the speaker as *kārya-kāraṇa bhāva.* It is a sort of cause-effect relationship. Only when a speaker intends to communicate he uses the expressive words. So intention of the speaker is the cause of the utterance. On the other hand, it is the utterance which arouses in the hearer the need to understand what the speaker intends to say. Thus there is a relation of cause and effect between the intention of the speaker and the language expressed for communication of meaning. In his analysis of *artha pravṛtti* (the principle of the use of meaning) he also highlights the importance of the intention of the speaker. He explains, "The basis for the expression of a meaning is that what the speaker intends to communicate, not whether the object-meant has external existence as an object or not."[19] Thus we find that Bhartṛhari does not hesitate to show that there can be a real distinction between "what is said" and "what is meant." Depending on what the speaker intends to communicate "sometimes what the words say

19. *VP*, I.136. *Vṛtti.*

is not meant" (1.136). He illustrates the point with several examples. Here I cite a few of them.

(A) "He should release the speech after seeing the star" — Here "seeing of the star" is meant to convey a particular time, when stars are usually visible.[20]

(B) "Let the curds be protected from the crows" — Here by the statement the speaker intends to convey that the curd should be protected from all sorts of damage, thus by "crow" he means any animal.[21]

(C) Sometimes a statement of praise may mean blame or vice versa. Puṇyarāja, while commenting on this *kārikā* offers the example of a verse which literally means "king's glory has illuminated everything," but the verse contains four objects which remain dark even after illumination.[22]

(D) In case of elliptical/one-worded sentence like "door," the hearer understands that he is commanded to do something with the door. If it is winter, the intended meaning is "close the door," and if it is summer, the intended meaning is "open the door."[23]

Besides, it is the speaker who decides how to present the facts. So Bhartr̥hari says:

> With whatever use a meaning/object-meant is sought to be conveyed by the speaker, the meaning is established like (in that context), because meaning has several capacities.[24]

If intention of the speaker plays a key role in the communication of meaning; and if there is the possibility of a gap between what is "meant" and what is "said," then hearer must be well-equipped to understand "what is meant." Without some such conditions of

20. *VP*, I.136. *Vr̥tti.*
21. *VP*, II.427.
22. *VP*, II.333.
23. *VP*, II.430.
24. *VP*, II.314.

deciphering what actually is intended by the speaker language cannot serve as an adequate means of communication. The problem may become more acute if we realize that no developed language system consists of a catalogue of one-to-one relation between words and meaning. The presence of synonyms, homonyms, metaphors and ambiguous words, not only makes a language system rich, but also allows it to function in an effective manner with limited vocabularies at its disposal. Bhartṛhari pays a good deal of attention to such issues. So he spells out the contextual factors, which help the hearer to understand the meaning intended. He says:

> The meanings of words are determined according to sentence, situation, purpose, propriety, place and time, and not according to mere eternal form.[25]

This list of six contextual conditions, according to some interpreters, were originally given by Śaṅkuka in his *Bṛhaddevatā*. Bhartṛhari however gives another extended list of twelve conditions which cover a wide range of contexts.[26] They are — association, dissociation, companionship, opposition, purpose, situation, indication, proximity of another word, capacity, propriety, place, time, person/gender, and accent. The list is neither exhaustive nor mutually exclusive. But it is obvious that he takes grammatical, syntactual and situational factors into account. Some of them are relevant only for Sanskrit. But if we go by the spirit of what Bhartṛhari has to say, then he makes it amply clear that no language can function as a communicative tool unless the intention of the speaker (*vivakṣā*), and the contextual factors (*prakaraṇa*) are taken as an integral part of the analysis of word-meaning relationship. Thus he reconciles the two basic needs of linguistic act — stability and flexibility. The stability is provided by convention, but it is a convention which admits the importance of the intention of the speaker and contextual factors. Convention

25. *VP*, II.317.

26. *VP*, II.430.

and intention to communicate are not opposed to each other, but there is a constant interplay between them. Thus, there seems to be no oddity when Bhartṛhari says:

> With whatever use (in view), a meaning is sought to be conveyed by the speaker, the meaning is established like that (in that context), because meaning has several capacities. — II.430[27]

The problem of determination of meaning in terms of contextual factors was sorted out by later Naiyāyikas, through the concept of *tātparya*. Some of them even maintanin that ordinary sentences like, "bring the pot" can be understood depending on what the speaker intends to mean by a "pot."[28] But in this case, the intended meaning will not be taken as the primary meaning but the secondary meaning or *lakṣaṇā*. In order to sort out the ambiguities and incongruities in sentential forms, Nyāya, Mīmāṁsā and Vedānta Schools admit a distinction between the denoted meaning (*abhidhā*) and indicated meaning (*lakṣaṇā*). But Bhartṛhari does not have any need to accept the distinction, because the "sense" to be communicated can only be manifested by a sentence, not words.

The problem Mīmāṁsā theory faces to accommodate eternality thesis with the contextuality of word-meaning is of different nature. Its unwillingness to accept the speaker's intention, as well as extra-linguistic factors emanate from their eagerness to prove the infallibility of vedic injunction. They do admit the importance of contexts — but they are limited to Vedic passages alone.

Before I wind up the discussion I want to attend to one last question — If meaning is determinable in terms of intention of the speaker and varieties of contextual factors, does it not lead to Humpty-Dumpty-ish form of linguistic behaviour? How do we know, how and when a word is used, with what meaning? Bhartṛhari's probable answer to this question would be —

---

27. Jhalakekare, *Nyāyakoṣa*, p. 327.
28. *VP*, I.137, *Vṛtti*.

> Human reasoning is the power of words. . . . It is the word which is the instructor. Speakers follow the power of words and act when urged by a desire to speak based on the availability of the right word. When the hearer follows the fixed power of words to understand a meaning through reasoning based on meaning, context, indication, interconnection, etc. people look upon the capacity of the words as the reasoning of the hearer.[29]

29. *VP*,

Appendix 2

Vākyārtha and Ākāṅkṣā

THE issues of *vākyārtha* constitute an important segment of the Indian philosophy of language. We all know that a sentence, i.e. *vākya* is constituted of words. In fact, it is a string of words arranged in a particular syntactic order. But how these individual components generate a unified meaning? This question has bothered the traditional schools like Mīmāṁsā and Nyāya, as well as the grammarian philosophers like Bhartṛhari. According to Nyāya and Mīmāṁsā, it is *ākāṅkṣā* or mutual in a sentence. This view is challenged by Bhartṛhari, who holds that sentence itself is the primary unit of meaning; therefore *ākāṅkṣā* as a condition of sentence-meaning is redundunt. Bhartṛhari's claim is unconventional and needs further analysis. This paper aims to examine Bhartṛhari's stand regarding the issues.

It was Mīmāṁsā (that analysed Vedic injunctions) which took up the concept of sentence/sentence-meaning for its analysis of *Yajurveda*, written in the prose form. Hence we come across the first precise definition of a sentence in *Mīmāṁsā-Sūtra* of Jaiminī. It states that "a group of words serving a single purpose (*artha*) forms a sentence when on analysis words are found to have mutual expectancy (*ākāṅkṣā*)" (2.I.46). In this famous definition of a sentence we note two basic components. (1) Taken as a whole it must express a single purpose or meaning (*arthaikatva*). (2) When it is examined part by part the constituents of a sentence possess the quality of mutual expectancy or interdependence. Most of the philosophical schools accept this definition with certain variations in the implications of the term *ākāṅkṣā*.

Pānini, the first Indian grammarian to offer a systematic account of the rules of language, did talk of *vākya* in a vague way. But later interpreters felt that his definition of a compound word in terms of *sāmarthya* (competence) (2.1.1) could have an extended use in case of sentences too. Kātyāyana assumes that *sāmarthya* could stand for semantic connection by syntactic elements. He deciphered two elements in the concept of *sāmarthya*: (1) *ekārthībhāva*, unity of purpose or meaning, and (2) *vyāpekṣa*, mutual interconnectedness of words. This is similar to the Mīmāṁsā concepts of *arthaikatva* and *ākāṅkṣā*. However, Patañjali rejected such an iterpretation and felt that both the elements were exclusive in nature. So, for him, unity of purpose or meaning is the only criterion of a sentence. According to him, the acceptance of *vyāpekṣa* would lead to a theory wherein words would be supposed to retain their individual meaning in a sentence. Bhartṛhari seems to develop Patañjali's notion of *ekārthībhāva* to its logical conclusion in the form of the theory known as *akhaṇḍa pakṣa* (indivisibility of sentence/sentence-meaning). He defines sentence as *eko na avayavośabdaḥ*, i.e. sentence is one without parts.

Bhartṛhari's indivisibility theory of sentence stands opposed to the *khaṇḍa pakṣa* (divisibility) theory of Mīmāṁsā, Nyāya and Vedānta. According to these schools, though the sentence expresses an unitary meaning yet the word-meanings that constitute it do not lose their autonomy. Words, in order to be concatenated to form a sentence, and for understanding of the unity of meaning by the hearer, need to fulfil three basic conditions — (1) *ākāṅkṣā* (for the time being let us translate it as syntactical order), (2) *yogyatā* (semantic competence), and (3) *asatti* (phonetic contiguity). Out of these three, *ākāṅkṣā* is regarded as essential for the formation of sentence/sentence-meaning. Bhartṛhari, in the second part of his treatise *Vākyapadīya*, deals at length with the notion of sentence-meaning. He gives as many as eight definitions of a sentence. Though he is not explicit, it is evident that his *pūrva pakṣa* is Mīmāṁsā.

To understand Bhartṛhari's position on sentence-meaning we have to presume at the outset that he was interested in providing the semantics of natural language. While dealing with sentence meaning he focuses his entire attention on language-in-use. According to him language-in-use is an act by which the speaker communicates his intention to the hearer; and also in the process "secures an uptake" from the hearer. What the speaker intends to express is an idea or "sense." This can only be communicated by a sentence, so according to Bhartṛhari, words taken individually are unfit for communication. Unless we take sentences as the minimum unit of meaning communication of sense is not possible. The sentence, "I am hungry," expresses one sense. Taken separately some of the words may not have any importance in the expression of the sense. "Just as the senses which have each their own essential nature and their own field of operation cannot perform their function without the body, in the same way, the individual words, though expressive of their own meaning, have no meaning at all if they are isolated from the sentence" (2.419-20). Bhartṛhari makes it clear that, "the meaning in the nature of an interconnection is grasped when things are connected together. (When the word meanings are in isolation) the essence (of the sentence-meaning) does not become clear because it is seen to be different from the word-meanings"(2.421). We should not confuse the theory of *akhaṇḍa pakṣa* with sentence-contextualism. According to sentence-contextualism, which was adapted by Prabhākara, a word gets its meaning only in the context of a sentence. But Bhartṛhari's theory can be classed as a form of sentence-holism. According to him words that constitute a sentence lose their individual meanings since they form a part of a unitary sense. Taken in this sense there can be even one-worded sentences which in spite of having no syntactical order can express a complete sense.

So far there seems to be no opposition between Bhartṛhari and the protagnoists of *khaṇḍa pakṣa* theory. In Indian tradition the communicative role of language is emphasized and hence words taken individually are not taken to be adequate to express a thought. The unity of sentence meaning is sought through the syntactic order (*ākāṅkṣā)* and semantic competence (*yogyatā*) of words to mutually fulfil the expectations they raise. What makes Bhartṛhari's stand different is his emphasis on the primacy of the unity aspect over the analytic aspect of language. Therefore, mutual interdependence of words or syntactic order is not an essential part of sentence-meaning. What can be the reasons for taking such an unusual stand? It can be justified by looking at some of the peculiar features of ordinary language. Bhartṛhari, being involved in unravelling the syntax and semantics of language-in-use, cannot afford to close his eyes to these peculiarities of natural language. Some of these features are very clearly stated in his treatise.

(1) Each individual word stands for a universal. It becomes particularized when stated in a sentential form. For example, "white" and "cow" have class connotation, but when used in a sentence "this cow is white," the nature of meaning of individual words changes from universal to particular and becomes object-specific. Moreover our eyes have the potency for seeing. But unless they are directed towards an object the actual vision of the object is not possible. Similarly, a word and what it signifies can have many dimensions. The word "cow" can be used to refer to its colour, shape, etc. So, it is the speaker who chooses the exact way that he is going to present his idea of the cow. Hence, the automomy of word-meaning is bound to be lost when the word becomes a part of the sentence.

(2) Contextual factors play a vital role in the process of our linguistic communication. There are many words in our ordinary language which have more than one meaning. And again, there can be many words standing for one meaning. In such cases, context, place, time, propriety, etc. help to determine the significance of a sentence. Bhartṛhari is one of the earliest thinkers to offer a precise list of such extra-linguistic factors. Of course, later Nyāya accepts *tātparya* or contextual meaning as one of the conditions of deciphering sentence-meaning. But the entire force of what the speaker intends to mean will be lost if the sentence is taken to be a concatenation of words in a particular syntactical order. Here, more than the syntax, the force of what is meant becomes predominant. Such sentences

become effective if understood in a certain context only. Besides, there may be a big gap between what is *said* and what is *meant*. For instance, when a traveller tells his companion, "one has to go, look at the sun," though the sentence asks one to look at the sun it really indicates that it is already late (2.310). Similarly, there may be many cases where what is said and what is meant can have opposite implications. An ironic sentence of praise may mean an offence to the hearer (2.247). Again as words are gradually grasped in a particular syntactic order, one understands the meaning in a particular way. But when the whole sentence is heard, the same meaning appears to be quite different. For instance, the sentence *vṛkṣo-nāsti* (the tree, there is not) has two individual word meanings. "Tree" implies an existence. But "there is not" cancels out the first individual word, and finally implies the absence of the tree.

(3) From the similarity of grammatical and syntactical structure between two sentences it does not follow that they have similarity of meaning. For instance, "bring a cuckoo from the forest," has structural similarity with the sentence, "bring firewood from the forest." This sort of similarity misleads us into thinking that a man who does not understand the word "cuckoo" has actually grasped the rest of the meaning. But Bhartṛhari argues that commonness of grammatical form does not imply that the sentences have commonness of meaning. There is nothing like a so-called "common part" between sentences. They are two independent sentences having two different sorts of implications. One does not bring the cuckoo from the forest in the same way as one brings the firewood. So, syntactical similarity can create confusions in our understanding of meaning.

It is obvious from the above example that the nature of ordinary language is full of varieties and complications. It is very difficult to put this vast variety in the straightjacket of a well defined syntactical and semantic rule. But Bhartṛhari would not deny the fact that the sentences which are supposed to imply an unitary meaning are uttered in a sequence — syllable-by-syllable, word-by-word. The hearer also receives this string of words in a sequence. So there must be some formal structure to give unity to a sequence of words. After all, any and every series of words does not compose a sentence. Bhartṛhari does not deny the importance of a syntactical order. But this order is not wholly guided by the rules of strict grammar. For him, the most essential feature of a sentence-meaning is implying an act. We not only "do something in saying something" but also "do something by saying something" (as Austin would put it). Bhartṛhari says, "no word-meaning whether true or false is understood in a communication except as connected with some action" (2.424). Again, "it is the action which is first analysed from the meaning of a sentence because it is the main thing. The accessories are employed for the sake of the action to be accomplished" (2.427). But, for that, we need not present in our utterance the entire set of verbs, nouns, etc. always. Even a single word like "door" can communicate to the hearer the complete meaning, "shut the door." It is the context which determines what is to be accomplished. Mīmāṁsā would say that in cases of such one-worded sentences the hearer mentally supplies the word "shut" before the word "door" and only then understands the meaning by inference *śrutyarthāpatti*. But Bhartṛhari does not accept this mental completion of the syntactical order of a sentence. According to him the hearer does not compile the meaning of individual words first and then understands. Understanding (*pratibhā*) occurs in a flash or instantaneously. Therefore, he states that how the process and action should be presented has no fixed order. It is the speaker who thinks of something as the process and something else as the accessory. And it is he who thinks of the relation between the two (2.2.429). What ultimately matters in a sentence-meaning is the completeness of the sense expressed. There need not be a complete parity between the manner of the use of words in a sentence and the meaning it conveys. Thus in the two sentences, "recite while moving about" and "move about while reciting," there is a similarity of meaning in spite of the difference of structure.

So, according to Bhartṛhari, what ultimately matters in the communication of meaning through a sentence is completeness of sense. If there is any incompleteness of understanding it is not because of meaning but expression at a verbal level. When someone says, "Devadatta cooks," the sentence is complete, though how and what he cooks is not mentioned. But if one says, "Devadatta cooks his," one at once feels that the sentence is incomplete. Here, Bhartṛhari intends to make it clear that completeness in a sentence is always logical, not psychological. Each sentence may arouse in the listener hundreds of expectancies. There is no limit to it. So, if *ākāṅkṣā* is taken in the psychological sense even a whole passage cannot satisfy the expectancy of a listener. But at the same time, the completeness of syntactical order is not wholly dependent on the formal structure of the sentence only. "Where there is a bare statement of fact and its implications are understood from its expressive power (*śruteḥ*) without the use of words to express them, then the sentence is complete" (2.446). Explaining this aphorism further, Bhartṛhari says, "the incompleteness must come from the words themselves. Otherwise the sentences must be considered complete, even if the listener understands more than what the words actually say. The words used do not require other words for yielding a complete meaning" — that is the mark of completeness. So, Bhartṛhari ultimately comes to the conclusion that "where the mode of performance of the action (denoted by the sentence) is desired to be known because of its very nature (*sāmarthyāt*), that sentence containing no verbal incompleteness is said to be complete in meaning" (2.445). So, we find that in Bhartṛhari's opinion *ākāṅkṣā* is necessary for converying the meaning. But it should not mean a strict syntactic order. What is of primary importance is the understanding of the complete sense by the hearer. In other words, it is *nirākāṅkṣā* (completeness) than this *sākāṅkṣā* (with mutual expectancy of words) which is the essential condition of communication. The sentence is one and self-sufficient, but for analytical and practical purposes, it is explained in terms of individual words which appear to figure in sentences and which require one another.

Thus, Bhartṛhari's theory of sentence-meaning is entirely focused on the nature of language-in-use and his primary concern is with the pragmatics of language. He does not deny the role of grammar in verbal communication, but the grammar is flexible enough to adjust to the needs of communication. As a grammarian he is interested in language as an object of analysis but as a philosopher his emphasis is on the communication-intention aspect of language.

Glossary of Sanskrit Terms

Adhyāsa	superimposition.
Āgama	scriptural truth or verbal means of knowledge.
Ahaṁkāra	ego.
Akhaṇḍa pakṣa	the theory that believes that sentence is the primary unit of meaning.
Anumāna	inference.
Artha	word-meaning as distinct from the word-sound.
Ātman	self.
Avidyā	the obscuring veil of human ignorance that, when removed, reveals knowledge of reality.
Bhāṣya	commentary.
Brahman	the Absolute, the Reality.
Buddhi	the intellect or the level of consciousness characterized by intelligent discrimination.
Darśana	philosophical point of view or philosophical system.
Dhvani	the uttered syllables of a word.
Jñāna	knowledge or cognition.
Kalpanā	mental constructs.
Kāraṇa	cause.
Kārya	effect.

Krama	sequence.
Madyamā Vāk	language as thought that has not yet been uttered.
Mahāvākyas	the great criterion sentences of the Upanisaḍs, e.g. "That thou art."
Manas	the mental organ that collects and co-ordinates information.
Māyā	the illusion of the manifoldness of the world which is really the unitary Absolute or *Brahman*.
Mokṣa	liberation or release from the suffering and bondage of this world leading to identification with the Absolute.
Nāda	physical sound.
Paśyantī Vāk	the level of intuitive understanding of the sentence-meaning as whole non-verbal level of language.
Pramā	true cognition or knowledge.
Pramāṇa	valid methods of knowledge.
Pratibhā	the capacity to directly grasp the real meaning.
Pratyakṣa	perception.
Pratyaya	concept or idea.
Śabda	language as a general concept or the linguistic principle.
Śabda-Brahman	language or linguistic principle as the ultimate Reality or the intertwined unity of word and consciousness that is the one and ultimate Reality according to Bhartṛhari.
Śabda-Pramāṇa	the verbal method of knowledge.

Śabda-Tattva	the word principle.
Śabda Bhāvanā	the linguistic potency inherent within conscious being.
Saṅskāra	a memory trace that has the dynamic quality of expressing itself.
Saṁketa	convention of language or linguistic convention.
Saṁjñā	definition, named.
Saṁjñin	definiendum, name.
Śāstra	authoritative teaching or analytical discourse about a particular branch of knowledge.
Sattā	existence.
Sphoṭa	meaning whole or linguistic potency that eternally exists within consciousness and which can be manifested by spoken words.
Śruti	primary scripture such as the Vedas, the Brāhmaṇas and the Upanisaḍs.
Satkāryavāda	the theory that effect is pre-existent in cause.
Tātparya	contextual meaning.
Upacāra Sattā	metaphorical existence.
Vācya	signified, the meaning-content.
Vācaka	signifier, the words that express the meaning.
Vaikharī Vāk	the level of uttered speech.
Vāk	language that is thought of as having various levels of manifestation, from the level of spoken word to the level of intuitive understanding of meaning.
Vākya	sentence.

Varṇa	letter sounds.
Vikalpa	linguistic construct.
Vṛtti	a commentary.
Vyākaraṇa	grammar, the grammar school — one of the traditional schools of Indian philosophy dealing with language and the linguistics.
Vyāvahārika	worldly usages or worldly affairs.
Yogyatā	logical compatibility. In the context of word-meaning relation it means the inherent capacity of words to express meanings.

Select Bibliography

Arapura, J.G., "Some Perspectives on Indian Philosophy of Language," in *Revelation in Indian Thought*, ed. H.G. Coward and Sivaraman, Dharma Publishing, 1977.

Austin, J., *How to do Things with Words*, London: Oxford University Press, 1962.

Ayer, A.J., *Language Truth and Logic*, New York: Dover Press, 1946.

Bhartṛhari, *Vākyapadīya* I, ed. and tr. K.A. Subramania Iyer, Poona: Deccan College, 1966.

———, *Vākyapadīya* II, K.A.S. Iyer, Delhi: Motilal Banarsidass, 1971.

———, *Vākyapadīya*, Part III, K.A.S. Iyer Canto. II, 1974.

———, *Vākyapadīya*, Canto I and II, K.R. Pillai, Delhi: Motilal Banarsidass.

———, *Vākyapadīya*, S.N. Shukla (with commentary), Chowkhamba Sanskrit Series, 1961.

Bhattacharya, B.P., *A Study in Language and Meaning*, Calcutta: Progressive Publishers, 1962.

Bhattacharya, J.V., *Nyāya-Mañjarī of Jayanta Bhaṭṭa*, Delhi: Motilal Banarsidass, 1965.

Bradley, F.H., *Principles of Logic*, Pts. I and II, London: Oxford University Press, 1922.

Brough, J., "Some Indian Theories of Meaning" and "Theories of General Linguistics of the Sanskrit Grammarians," in *A Reader on the Sanskrit Grammarians*, Delhi: Motilal Banarsidass, 1972.

Cardona, G., *Pāṇini : A Survey of Research*, The Hague: Mouten and Co., 1976.

Carnap, R., *Philosophy and Logical Syntax*, London: Routledge and Kegan Paul, 1935.

Chakravarti, *Linguistic Speculation of Hindus*, Calcutta: Calcutta University Press, 1983.

Coward, H.G., *Sphoṭa Theory of Language*, Delhi: Motilal Banarsidass, 1980.

Coward and K.K. Raja (eds.), *The Encyclopaedia of Indian Philosophies*, vol. V, (The Philosophy of Grammarians), Motilal Banarsidass, 1990.

Cultural Heritage of India, vol. I., Calcutta: The Ramakrishna Mission, 1982.

Davidson, D., "Thought and Talk," in *Mind and Language*, ed. S.D. Guttenplan, Oxford: Clarendon Press, 1975.

———, "Truth and Meaning," *Synthese* XVIII, 1967.

Datta, D.M., *Six Ways of Knowing*, Calcutta: Calcutta University Press, 1972.

Daya Krishna, *Indian Philosophy : A Counter Perspective*, Delhi: Oxford University Press, 1991.

De, S.K., *Studies in the History of Indian Poetries*, London: Luzac and Co., 1925.

Evans, G. and Mc-Dowell, J., *Truth and Meaning : Essays on Semantics*, Oxford: Clarendon Press, 1976.

Frege, G., "The Thought — A Logical Inquiry," in P.F. Strawson's *Philosophical Logic*, Oxford: Oxford University Press, 1977, pp. 17-38.

Grice, H.P., "Meaning," in *Philosophical Review*, LXVI, 1957.

———, "Utterer's Meaning, Sentence Meaning and Word Meaning," In *Foundations of Language*, IV (1968).

Herzberger, H. and Herzberger, R., "Bhartṛhari's Paradox," in *Journal of Indian Philosophy*, 67, 1970, pp. 145-67.

Iyer, K.A. Subramania, *Bhartṛhari*, Poona: Deccan College, 1969.

———, *Vākyapadīya — Some Problems*, Poona: Bhandarkar Oriental Research Institute, 1982.

Joshi, S.D., *The Sphoṭanirṇaya of Kauṇḍa Bhaṭṭa*, Poona, 1976.

Keith, A.B., *A History of Sanskrit Literature*, Oxford: Oxford University Press, 1928.

Kunjunni Raja, K., *Indian Theories of Meaning*, Madras: Adyar Library, 1969.

Lewis, David., "Languages and Language," in *Language, Mind and Knowledge*, ed. K. Gunderson, Minneapolis: University of Minnesota Press, 1975.

Locke, John, *Essays Concerning Human Understanding*, Book III, 1894.

Matilal, B.K., *Perception*, Delhi: Oxford University Press, 1986.

———, *The Word and the World*, Delhi: Oxford University Press, 1990.

———, *Language, Logic and Reality*, Delhi: Motilal Banarsidass, 1985.

McGinn, Collin, *The Character of Mind*, Oxford: Oxford University Press, 1982.

Misra, G., *Language, Reality and Analysis*, New York: E.J. Brill, 1991.

———, *Advaita Philosophy: Its Method, Scope and Limits*, Bhubaneswar, 1976.

Murti, T.R.V., *Studies in Indian Thought*, Delhi: Motilal Banarsidass, 1983.

Pāṇini, *Aṣṭādhyāyī and Padamañjarī of Haradatta*, ed. D.D. Sastri and K.P. Shukla, Bharati Series, Varanasi, 1965-67.

Patañjali, *Vyākaraṇa Mahābhāṣya, Bombay Sanskrit Series*, ed. F. Kielhorn, 1892.

Pandeya, R.C., *The Problem of Meaning in Indian Philosophy*, Delhi: Motilal Banarsidass, 1963.

Passmore, J., *Recent Philosophers : A Supplement to Hundred Years of Philosophy*, London: Duckworth, 1985.

Patnaik, Tandra, "Language, Thought and Communication — An Appraisal of Bhartṛhari's Theory of Language," in *Indian Philosophical Quarterly*, vol. XV, no. 3, July 1988.

———, "Some Reflections on Bhartṛhari's Notion of Sentence-Meaning," in *Visva Bharati Journal of Philosophy*, vol. XXIV, no. 2, vol. XXV Feb.-August, 1988, Published in 1989.

———, "A Note on Bhartṛhari's Theory of Sphoṭa," in *Prajñā*, Utkal Journal of Philosophy, vol. XI, March 1990.

———, "Intention and Convention in Communication — "Re-understanding Bhartṛhari," in *Indian Philosophical Quarterly*, vol. XIX, no. 4, October 1992.

———, "The Word and the World — Bhartṛhari and Diṅnāga," in *Visva Bharati Journal of Philosophy*, XXVIII, no.2, Feb. 1992.

———, "The Problem of Intention in Bhartṛhari's Philosophy of Language," in *Prajñā*, vol. XII, March 1990.

Pitcher, G., *The Philosophy of Wittgenstein*, Prentice Hall, 1964.

Quine, W.V., *Word and Object*, Cambridge, Mass.: Technology Press, 1960.

———, *From a Logical Point of View*, Harvard University Press, 1953.

Radhakrishnan, S., *Indian Philosophy*, vols. I and II, London: George Allen and Unwin, 1962.

Ryle, G., *Collected Papers* II, London: Hutchinson and Co. Ltd., 1973.

Śaṅkara, *Brahma-Sūtra-Bhāṣya*.

Sastri, G., *A Study in Dialectics of Sphoṭa*, Delhi: Motilal Banarsidass, 1980.

———, *The Philosophy of Word and Meaning*, Calcutta: Sanskrit College, 1959.

Searle, J., *Speech Acts — An Essay in Philosophy of Language*, Cambridge: Cambridge University Press, 1969.

Sellars, W., "Conceptual Change," in *Conceptual Change*, ed. D. Pearce and P. Maynard, Dordrecht, 1973.

Stace, W.T., *A Critical History of Greek Philosophy*, Macmillan, 1982.

Stall, F., "Sanskrit Philosophy of Language," in *Current Trends in Linguistics*, vol. V, ed. T.A. Sebeok et al.. The Hague, 1969, pp. 46-94.

———, "The Concept of Meta-Language and Its Background," in *Journal of Indian Philosophy*, III, 1975.

———, *A Reader on the Sanskrit Grammarians*, Delhi: Motilal Banarsidass, 1972.

Stcherbatsky, F. Th., *Buddhist Logic*, New York: Dover Publications, 1962.

Strawson, P.F., *Logico-Linguistic Papers*, London: Methuen and Co., 1974.

———, *Analysis and Metaphysics*, Oxford: Oxford University Press, 1992.

Tarski, A., "The Semantical Conception of Truth," in *Philosophy and Phenomenological Research*, 1944.

Wittgenstein, L., *Tractatus Logico-Philosophicus*, Routledge and Kegan and Paul, 1974.

———, *Philosophical Investigations*, London: Basil and Blackwell, 1978.

———, *Blue and Brown Book*, London: Basil and Blackwell, 1958.

———, *Culture and Value*, Oxford: Basil and Blackwell, 1980.

Index